R. E. Peach

Historic Houses in Bath

R. E. Peach

Historic Houses in Bath

ISBN/EAN: 9783337152352

Printed in Europe, USA, Canada, Australia, Japan

Cover: Foto ©ninafisch / pixelio.de

More available books at **www.hansebooks.com**

HISTORIC HOUSES IN BATH,

And their Associations.

DEDICATED, WITH GREAT RESPECT, BY PERMISSION,
TO
THE RIGHT HONOURABLE LADY LLANOVER.

BY

R. E. PEACH.

LONDON: SIMPKIN, MARSHALL, & Co., STATIONERS' HALL COURT.
BATH: R. E. PEACH, 8, BRIDGE STREET.

1883.

PREFACE.

IN presenting this small work to the public, we entreat their kind and indulgent forbearance. We are conscious of its many defects, and we feel, after all, that we may have only been the humble pioneers of some more able worker in the field of local Biography, Bibliography, and History. The chief difficulty we have had to contend with has been to condense the ample—too ample—materials which we found existing, into the space at our command, so as to render them interesting and of value to the general reader. Another difficulty, however, was to deal with the local stories and traditions which abound in such endless profusion in relation to the past. Fact and tradition have become so intermingled that the effort to separate them gave us no small trouble, the result being in many instances that the tradition was worthless and the fact useless. The gossip, the scandal, and the follies of a past age are not worth reviving; but there is a good deal, besides what is to be found in books and the ordinary records, which, although possibly beneath the notice of the dignified historian, is not without its intrinsic value in the annals of a city like Bath. What the Romans left us we have long known; and recently have been brought to light once more the evidences of their ingenuity, skill, and wondrous power, in adapting Nature's bounteous healing springs to the luxuries, as well as to the ills, of a people whose epoch closed sixteen centuries ago.[1] These researches to the comparatively few are all important; modern art—or

---

[1] No new discovery has been made, as many suppose, with regard to these Roman Baths. In 1754-5, excavations were made, laying bare what we now see, and what was known (imperfectly, no doubt) to exist centuries before. It is due to Major Davis, F.S.A., that the present operations have been undertaken with a more definite object, and are likely to be attended by a permanent and practical result.
It is certain that much of what the Romans left, much that they either discovered, or on which they brought to bear their superior intelligence and power of development, has been altogether lost, though much perhaps may gradually be re-discovered. An instance is worth quoting. Lady Verney says: "Royal is a watering-place which has lately sprung into favour; it has hardly yet indeed attained its majority. Five and twenty years ago a cure remarked that in winter the snow often melted at a particular spot; a hole was dug, and the hot water bubbled up from the old volcanic

relics of the last century which only speak of the taste and grandeur of that period— to them is of mere passing interest; but to the many it possesses a charm and interest which requires little or no special knowledge to understand and appreciate. It is easier to call up visions of those whose names we bear, whose wit, whose wisdom, whose benevolence, perchance, reflected honour upon the family, than of sturdy Roman, Saxon, or Dane, whose exploits adorn the pages of Palgrave, Kemble, or Freeman. If Mrs. Riddell had written the following passage with direct and special reference to Bath, she could scarcely have succeeded better in describing the earlier built but now neglected mansions of the last century:—" So " the neighbourhood, ... notwithstanding the depth of the valley in " which it is now reposing, stood, in the days that are gone, on the very summit " of the hill of fashion; and there still remain a few of the ancient houses, that " speak, with their wide staircases and massive balustrades, and spacious chambers " and strange carved chimney-pieces, voicelessly yet eloquently, of the wealth and " magnificence that once abode in them." Gallaway's Buildings, once the abodes of the lively Mrs. Thrale, of the brilliant Mrs. Delany, and of the amiable Miss Burney, and a few houses scattered about the same locality, fully answer to this description. When we contemplate the substantial character as well as the elegance of these houses, we think they justify the belief that in all the characteristics of substantial advantages in a dwelling they will bear comparison with the best nineteenth century houses of the same class. They are dingy and dirty now, because they have been hidden by modern gim-crack buildings which, not having answered even the purpose for which they were intended, have met a worse fate than their older neighbours, which are stately even in their neglect and obscurity.

If we go back a century earlier, it is clear that the wealthy valetudinarians who sought the Baths for health, or who came for recreation and change of scene, endured no great hardships in the parlours and dining-rooms of those quaint old houses, whose fronts and windows protruded far into the narrow streets, ill paved and ill-lighted as they were. In the days of PRYNNE and HENRY CHAPMAN (1660), the public health and sanitary precautions gave little trouble to the governing body of the city; and yet, notwithstanding the fact that the city was immured within the city walls, and thereby excluded from a free current of air, we do not

" communication in the heart of the earth, which once raised the line of sugar-loaf hills, the now
" extinct craters of the Puy-de-Dôme and its neighbours, and poured forth the streams of lava which
" still can be distinctly traced along their sides. The waters were known to the Romans, who, with the
" wonderful instinct which detected everything of value or interest in a new province, had made their
" stone piscina, and used the spring for their warm baths, traces of which were disinterred when the
" [illegible] was [illegible] covered." Contemporary Review, December, 1882.

find any record of those terrible visitations of disease to which most cities at that time were often subjected. A century earlier still we know that Queen Elizabeth emphatically declared, in the very sweetest part of the city, that her Royal nose was offended by a stink; and although "Her Highness" distinctly expressed her good pleasure that the cause of the said "stink" must be removed, and means and money were provided for that purpose, the cause and the "stink" remained. It may be worth mentioning that the extent and boundaries of the city in 1572 are supposed to be delineated in the Map, called Jones's Map, because it is sometimes found done up with that old writer's book, "The Bathes of Bathes Ayde," but it is an error made by nearly every writer on Bath. That book was published without a Map, and there is no Map entitled to be called Jones's Map at all. The late lamented Dr. Wilbraham Falconer was, previous to his death, engaged upon an enquiry into the genuineness of the so-called "Jones's Map," and he was fully convinced that this Map was published at a later period than Jones's work. This conclusion of Dr. Falconer is partly established by the fact that a gentleman of this city has, amongst many other curious maps and prints, a tracing or drawing of a Map, quite unique, in the Sloane Collection of the British Museum.[1] Now, on comparing this Map of 1572 with the so-called Map of Jones of the same ostensible date, the latter is found to contain a much larger area than the former, and this naturally determines the fact that Bath was smaller in Elizabeth's reign, and during her visit, than it has been commonly supposed to be. At this period it is probable—almost certain, indeed—that Bath had to a great extent regained some of that former eminence from which it had declined. Many historians and antiquaries are of opinion that, after the devastating fires and massacres from which Bath suffered after the Norman Conquest, there was a second "Period of Desolation." This seems to receive some confirmation from the words of an early chronicler, which are given in "Malvern Chase; an episode of the Wars of Roses and Battle of Tewkesbury," 1472 :— "We rode to the VILLAGE OF BATH, famous for its hot springs and Roman "ruins, and from thence I sent scouts to the important city of Bristol, where they

---

[1] "*The coloured sketch-book of Geo. Smith, dated* 1572, *in the Sloane Collection of the British* "*Museum, and numbered* 2596. *It consists of coloured Maps he made of Exeter, Bristol, Oxford,* "*York, and Bath; and three Views of London, and one of Stonehenge. The Bath Map faces directly* "*south. The difference between this and Jones's map consists in this having a complete row of houses* "*on each side of Broad Street, continuing up from the church of St. Michael's (extra muros). It has* "*four small towers on the east Town wall, three on the south east, and three on the south west, and the* "*wall is equally fortified and complete all round the city, these towers and wall not appearing in Jones's* "*map. There is also a church, which Jones does not give, in Claverton Street, just as the road turns*

"learned that the Lancastrian army was embarrassed by the presence of Queen "Margaret, her son, Prince Edward, and daughter-in-law, the Princess Anne; "also that they had been well received by the Bristol citizens, who furnished them "with food, men, and money."

This inversion of chronological order exhibits more clearly the contrasts of the periods referred to. In the earliest it is clear that, although the walls were intact, there was no garrison, and the city offered no strategic point of resistance or attack to the contending forces. Municipal government had either ceased altogether, or had become powerless, if not useless. Trade, which once had been so flourishing, had declined, and all public spirit appears to have been crushed out of the citizens. In the following century, when Leland visited the city (1542), there would seem from his account to have been no municipal archives, and little tradition to guide him in his description of the city. His account of the walls, given entirely from his own observations, is curious, and shows great acuteness and intelligence. It is remarkable, moreover, that his description, when compared with the Map of Smith (1572), confirms the statement made by later writers as to the renovation of the walls and rebuilding of the towers, not long before Queen Elizabeth's visit in 1574. Leland says—"In the walles at this tyme be no Tourres, saving over the Toune Gate." There was also, he says, "a peace (of the wall) lakking about Gascoyn's-Tower." In Smith's map the towers are depicted, and the walls are without a rift of any kind. There had evidently been a revival of the trade in this century, though Leland says— "Syns the death of Style, Kent, and Chapman, the clothe trayde hath summewhat "decayed." The trade, however, rapidly revived, and with it the municipal spirit, for it is clear that, at the time of Queen Elizabeth's visit, the Baths and public institutions, which had fallen into neglect, if not decay, were objects of which the citizens were proud. And, no doubt, the visit of the Queen gave so much encouragement to the city, that it led to the obtaining of that Charter under which its LIBERTIES were enlarged, and its civic institutions consolidated and improved. The vicissitudes of later and troublous times are too well known. Bath shared, with the rest of the nation, the shocks and turmoil of civil war; but with the return of more settled government, the city sunk for a time into ignoble contentment and lethargy. The walls remained, though they afforded neither protection nor utility. It was *pardonable that the citizens should cling to them with affection.* They could not bring their minds to destroy the historical symbols of an earlier age and ruder times. And when the WAVE of civilization and advancement came with such irresistible force in the following century, it swept away the whole structure, leaving scarcely a " rack " behind." It seems, indeed, a matter much to be deplored, that some vestiges of these walls were not preserved in localities where, by their preservation, no inconveniences would have been experienced, and which would not have retarded for one moment the progress of modern enterprise.

We have exceeded the limits we proposed to ourselves, though leaving much to be done. We hope, however, that whilst completing the work so far as it goes, we shall be able, at no distant day, to bring out a SUPPLEMENTAL SERIES to comprehend the subjects we are obliged to omit from the present.

R. E. PEACH.

July, 1883.

NOTICE.

We respectfully inform our readers that in consequence of our great desire to include as much as possible in the body of the Work, we have been obliged to omit an Index; but, as we have already stated, it is our intention to publish either a SUPPLEMENT *to or a Second Series of the present Volume, with which a Copy of the Index will be issued gratis to the Subscribers of the present Series.*

Introductory Chapter.

"They are the abstract, and brief chronicles of the time."

THE object of this little work is to supply what cannot readily be obtained in the ordinary way from Guide-Books and Local Histories. To the general reader who is interested in Bath and its past associations with eminent personages, who have made it their home by adoption, or who were native-born citizens, this compendious sketch may afford information or amusement, and perchance both.

It is, perhaps, worth explaining that, from a variety of circumstances, absolute accuracy is difficult of attainment, even in cases coming within comparatively recent times. Localities which were the fashionable quarters and promenades of the last century, are such no longer. Many of the houses once so elegant and commodious, are either partly removed or are so transformed, that they can no longer be recognized. The portions still remaining are disfigured with mean modern additions or frontages, to adapt them for trading purposes.

Again : it happens, from the exigencies of changes in localities or other vicissitudes, that many houses occupied by "worthies" of a past age have disappeared altogether, and only the sites can be traced on the old maps.

Of the City Gates scarcely a trace remains, but the historic interest of these buildings survives; and we propose in the course of these pages to give them their due share of honour.

Bath, in common with many other old cities of greater or less historical importance, has suffered severely during the close of the last and the beginning of the present century, from the ruthless hand of the destroyer, or the pestilential spirit of utility, which has been too apt to consider rather what *goods* were to be found in pulling down fine houses, or in hiding them by hideous parasitical surroundings, than the *good* to be perpetuated in preserving them. To illustrate our meaning, let us mention Ralph Allen's town-house —one of the elder Wood's masterpieces—a fine example of classic architecture. A stranger might look in vain for it amidst the incongruous and mean structures that hide it from observation; and many people who have lived years in Bath may have never seen or even heard of its existence, although what remains of it stands in the very heart, and close to the most frequented thoroughfare, of the city. Standing at the north-western end of the North Parade, facing Hampton Down and Sham Castle (built by Allen himself), it must have presented a most beautiful object before it was sacrificed to meet a mean spirit of doubtful utilitarianism. It is incomprehensible that, as soon as the breath was out of the body of this genial and generous-hearted man, who had done so much for Bath, and had encouraged by his munificent patronage the genius of Wood, the city should have permitted almost the first and most useful effort of that genius to be utterly obscured by such unsightly buildings as those by which it is surrounded. It has been used as a printing office, and at the present time it is let out in "flats" to working men.

The imperious demands of modern progress doubtless sometimes render it necessary to sacrifice buildings which from association, if not from any intrinsic architectural importance, are replete with historic interest and touching memories of the past. One such instance may be especially mentioned here—namely, Bell-Tree House, which stood upon a portion of the site now occupied by the Royal United Hospital in Beau Street, then called Bell-Tree Lane.* This house, which is depicted on the maps from 1735 to 1785, was formerly the Rectory-House of St. James's parish before the benefice merged in that of St. Peter and St. Paul † during the reign of Elizabeth. This house reverted to the Corporation, and became the Roman-Catholic Mission-House from 1718 to the close, almost, of the century.

For many of the interesting facts given in the body of the work relating to this Mission, we are indebted to Mrs. Jervis, of 28, Holland Park, London,

---

* So called probably from the circumstance related by Wood :— " The next public work at Bath was the Hospital, dedicated to St. Katherine, which was founded by seven maiden sisters, sirnamed Bimburie, and placed south of Bellinus's Tree ; to the eastward of which Tree, Thomas Bellot founded and built another Hospital."

† The whole of the Ecclesiastical system of Bath proper, was then consolidated, and the patronage vested in the Corporation, whose nominee to the Rectory appointed the Curates of the several parishes. It must be noted that Bathwick and Walcot were not integral parts of Ecclesiastical Bath, because they were not, as now, parts of civil and municipal Bath.

a lady deeply interested in our city, whose letter we are authorized to insert :—

"London: 28, Holland Park, W.;
"March 23rd, 1882.
"My dear Sir,—
"In the spring of 1878 (or autumn of 1877), I was searching at the
" Paris Archives for any records of our English Benedictine Community of Nuns.
"The authorities were most kind, and advised me to look over a confused mass
" of letters and papers, which were contained in a 'carton,' or box, such as our
" milliners use for their goods.
"It contained several 'liasses,' or separate bundles.
"One was docketted 'The papers of M. Naylor.'
"Father Placid Naylor, of the Order of St. Benedict, had served the
" Bath Mission nearly twenty years—from 1757 to 1776. He was a man of
" some private means, and, I suspect, spent far more of his own money for the
" benefit of the Order than ever was repaid to him. He went from Bath to the
" English Benedictine Monastery of St. Edmund's, in the Rue du Faubourg-St.-
" Jacques at Paris, and was there residing at the outbreak of the French
" Revolution.
"Being Confessor to the English Benedictine Ladies of the adjoining
" Rue de l'Alouette, he seems to have retired to his apartments there, for
" greater seclusion, as it was imagined that women of a foreign nation would be
" respected. But, one night, he was seized, and all his papers carried off. He
" died a natural death in January, 1794, at Paris.
"The bundle of papers are just as they were seized, or confused, by the
" ruffianly Republicans. Among them I found the account-book of Bell-Tree
" House. There is much more of it—all the tradesmen's bills, masons' accounts,
" etc., which any one can see who ever goes to the 'Archives' at Paris.
"Ever yours sincerely,
"MARTHA JERVIS."

Much as the demolition of houses such as this is to be regretted, it is
occasionally a necessity which cannot be resisted. The Royal United Hospital,
in itself an institution of no little historic interest, which now occupies the Bell.
Tree site, embodies a noble illustration of the progress which, while preserving
the continuity of that spirit of beneficence which has long characterized our
city, yet calls for occasional sacrifices. The old Rectory-House, little claim

iv. *Introduction.*

as it may have on account of its association with the city, or even with the Abbey Church with which it was connected,* is now the site of the new portion of the General Hospital which was raised by Ralph Allen and other worthies in the last century. In one respect this Hospital is unique, in so far as it is national, securing to certain classes of persons in every part of the kingdom, suffering from peculiar chronic affections, the highest benefits derivable from our healing Waters, under the direction of the most eminent and experienced staff of medical men the city can produce. In its internal economy and the general comforts assured to the patients, this institution is a model of wise administration and good management.

Of the sixteenth century we have little information of a definite character, to guide us in our researches with reference to the special objects we have in view. Many of the current traditions and stories—sad as it may have been to lose them—have already been shown to be baseless; notably that of Queen Elizabeth's alleged second visitation to Bath; her sojourn at Sir John Harington's at Kelston; her sleeping at St. Catherine's; and afterwards honouring Sherston as a guest at Barton House. All this is mere fiction. But fiction of this kind is not confined to that period.

Of late many stories, having as little truth in them as the story of Queen Elizabeth, have obtained currency with regard to events of recent times. These stories we shall have to discredit unless we would allow them to obtain general currency as facts. There is little excuse indeed for scattering broadcast hearsay stories and traditions, when a very little research would suffice to get at the facts. One such story is typical of many. Miss Strickland says † that Queen Anne, who visited Bath in 1702—her latest "Western Progress"—touched Dr. Johnson for "the Evil," on the occasion. As Dr. Johnson was not born until seven years after this period, it is needless to say the statement is erroneous. If Queen Anne did (as the Doctor says she did) touch him for the Evil, it was not during one of her "Western Progresses." If we are to be satisfied with generally accepted traditions, by all means let the story stand; but if we want facts, we must seek for them with some care and a little regard to historical accuracy.

In this essay we have done our best to examine and sift such

* We do not think this was the house occupied by the Jacobite Rector, Carte, when, to avoid arrest for treason, he jumped out of the window "in full canonicals." (Did Jacobite Rectors always sit in their own houses "in full canonicals"?) If this gentleman did occupy the Rectory House, his connection with it, we believe, was its only claim to be regarded as historic. It ceased to be occupied as the Rectory House after the death of the Rev. C. Crook, in 1838. For many years afterwards it was used as the Commercial and Literary Institution.

† Lives of the Queens of England, vol. 12, p. 115.

Introduction. v.

sources of evidence as were open to us; guided as we have been, moreover, as to locality in relation to personages, by the valuable series of Maps collected by Mr. C. P. Russell. Without such aid, it would have been almost impossible to verify a great deal of the information given in regard to the seventeenth and eighteenth centuries, centuries replete with local history and events of characteristic interest, though the interest of the former differed essentially from that of the latter.

The social life of the seventeenth century was orderly and dull. The springs were pre-eminent. Personages of the highest class visited them for all kinds of maladies. Physicians of that day were the kings of the place; occupying the best houses, (which were for the most part erected at the close of the former century,) in which they received their most distinguished patients. Some of these mansions were contiguous to the Baths, enabling the cripples and the infirm to enter them by corridors or covered ways. The whole interest of the citizens was centred, during the greater part of the seventeenth century, upon the bathing establishments. It was not until its close that the era of "dancing and dissipation" began. The new order of things grew rapidly, and soon developed that unruly element which Nash conquered and brought into subjection, in the early part of the next century.

The eighteenth century worked great changes. It was a period of transition, witnessing the demolition of the city-walls—those emblems of a past age and a past civilization—and the beginning of a new development—of a new Bath, with a vigour, a genius, and a completeness, almost unexampled in a provincial city. Although the streets were undoubtedly narrow for the most part, ill-paved and ill-kept, yet, compared with most cities of that day, Bath presented a certain kind of stately magnificence.* Besides those mansions which stood near, and in a few cases actually joined the Baths, Stall Street and Westgate Street contained houses of great dignity and architectural beauty. A few mansions of exceptional pretensions, such as Hetling House, occupied distinct sites, but all seemed to have converged towards what was (at any rate until a later period) the main attraction of the city—the Bathing establishments.

We feel sure that Lord Macaulay was deceived by the exaggerated terms in which Wood, in the preface to his Book on Bath, disparaged the lodging houses of his earlier days. Making every allowance for the difference between the present time and 150 years ago, there is no doubt the *inferior* lodgings in Bath at that time were mean—almost squalid. But the "recognized lodgings," especially those used by the wealthy and respectable visitors, were well

* Defoe confirms this statement.

appointed and comfortable. Most of these houses belonged to "citizens of renown"—men of local standing—members of the Corporation, lawyers, physicians, apothecaries, and the like. Wood, with all his ability, was vain, and he exaggerated the defects of the past, in order to render the contrast with his own work the more conspicuous. It was unfair to generalize from what was exceptionally bad, and Lord Macaulay was unfortunate in adopting Wood's representation, "to point a moral and adorn a tale."

There is no doubt that the medical fraternity of the period—including Guidott, Greaves, Peirce, Maplet, Bave, and others of the seventeenth century, were eminent and very able men. In our desire to pick up here and there a crumb of information, we have had to wade through oceans of jargon and archaic literature, in which we were nearly overwhelmed. One of the controversies of the day was between Dr. Peirce and Dr. Guidott; the former contending for bursting libations of the Waters, the latter for limiting their use almost exclusively to external application. The reflection forced itself upon us, that professional jealousy happily was confined to a past age—all professional men at the present time "loving one another as if they were one another." But the professional feeling prevalent amongst the Doctors is not the only knowledge we obtained. Dr. Peirce's book afforded us a great deal of information as to his own personal observations and experience, which may be sought for in vain elsewhere.

Bath, in the seventeenth century, during the Rebellion, had been, if not a military, at least, under the influence of Prynne and the Chapmans, a moral stronghold of the Parliament and the Puritan party. Still, it was about the first to give in its adhesion to the Restoration; and, therefore, it is not surprising that the reaction which followed that event should have been here quickly felt. The consequence was that, at the close of the century, Bath had developed a phase of society more pronounced in all the worst vices that characterized the period than any other place. There is no reason to suppose that the moral disease of the times had infected all classes, but inasmuch as the professional and trading community more or less benefited by it, they did little to check its grossness and revolting vulgarity, and hence Bath became the scene in which the worst specimens of the then "fashionable world" played the most conspicuous parts. They came here because they found, not, perhaps, greater vices than generally characterized the times, but every sort of dissipation to suit the variety of tastes and dispositions of its votaries.

Such was the aspect of Bath society when Nash came here in the early part of 1700. In it he saw his opportunity, and he quickly turned it to his own advantage. We do not grudge him any of the credit he obtained for "licking" this chaotic mass "into shape," but we wholly deny that he was entitled to be called the "maker of Bath," or even *one* of the "makers of Bath."

Nash found a seething mass of corruption which in no respect offended his sense of morality. It was the element he wanted. He did not attempt to purify it, because purification meant destruction. It was to be made subservient to his own ends. The coarse and vulgar material needed a veneering of respectability, and the rule of "Arbiter Elegantiarum" was just the thing to cover a multitude of follies and foppery. Not a vice, not a vanity, which prevailed under the unscrupulous Webster (Nash's predecessor) was repressed or discouraged. The difference was not essential, but only apparent. Even in those days the grossness and open licentiousness which prevailed might soon have provoked a reaction which would probably have produced a more healthy tone of society. This was not the object of Nash's policy. By bringing the various elements into subjection and throwing over them a cloak of order and mock dignity, he gave a certain durability to them. What might have been an accidental or a mere passing phase of violent reaction against a rigid Puritanism, became an *institution*, the effects of which at the time were lamentable, and the memories which survived are prejudicial to the city to this day.

Goldsmith's "Life of Nash" is a vast apology. Reading between the lines, he seems to say how heartily ashamed he was at having to whitewash the subject of his memoir, for the sum of £15.* True, Nash curbed the duellist, and he ruled the "Gothic haughtiness" of his noble subjects with firmness, and waged a successful war against "white aprons," the wearing of which was always a *casus belli*, no matter who the noble ladies might be who donned them. He brought the rude and boisterous beaux into a state of docile obedience, and for a time there was no one his "will to dispute," and, as Goldsmith says, he resembled a "monarch of Cappadocia, whom Cicero somewhere calls, the little king of a little people."

The fact is that Bath became a hot-bed of gambling and every species of swindling. When Goldsmith comes to the dispute between Wiltshire, the lessee of the then Assembly Rooms, and Nash, one feels for the author of "The Vicar of Wakefield" having to travel over such marshy and unwholesome ground. He "stooped" but not "to conquer" in such a task. Imperial laws were made to restrain the gambling which had become a national scandal, but Nash audaciously defied them, and invented new games to evade them. A

* The sum which, by agreement, he received from the Corporation.

more pitiable narrative than Goldsmith's description of Nash's later career it would be difficult to imagine.

Whatever may have been the good side of Nash's disposition, it wholly failed to counterbalance the sinister and evil influences of his position and character, especially after the Wiltshire affair.

Goldsmith's closing sketch of Nash is a sad and dreary record of impotent senility, without a single incident to afford any satisfaction or pleasure. Alternations of hope, cowardly fears, and scoffing, characterized the latter days of the King of Bath. The last ten years of his life showed that he had not only outlived his power and influence, but that he was neglected, despised, and almost left to starve. The inference is clear—the moral obvious. If Nash made Modern Bath, Modern Bath valued the service at an allowance of ten guineas per month for a few months before he died, when the helpless monarch could no longer earn an honest guinea at E. O. or Faro, or any other game of his own inventing. When he died, the same bounteous dispensers of the city's gratitude and liberality—the Corporation—"voted Fifty Pounds for the purpose of burying their sovereign with *proper respect*"!!

It may be, as some contend, that Nash was in some sort a benefactor to Bath; that society, in its then loose and disorganized condition in this "focus of fashion," needed a strong man of the type of Nash to prevent its lapsing into a state of irrepressible debauchery and open licentiousness. Be this as it may, whatever truth there may be in the argument, we deny that a man is entitled to be regarded as the founder of the city of Bath, because he showed some of the qualities which enabled him to deal with exceptional people in still more exceptional times.

It must be remembered that, contemporaneously with Nash and his "little kingdom," men of great public spirit and high moral principles here resided, and that a large portion of society never recognized Nash's sway; and that the climate of Bath, and the natural beauty of the country around, were irresistible inducements to the enterprizing to make a great and beautiful city such as Bath has become.

We do not expect all our readers to agree with us in our estimate of Beau Nash. Few of them probably have ever taken the trouble to read Goldsmith's Life, or to discover anything about him. They have formed a sort of general conception of the man—that he was an impudent charlatan, with a large admixture of generosity, good nature, and benevolence. A diligent enquiry would confirm the first part, but would dispel the remainder of this

Introduction. ix.

estimate, and such readers would, perhaps, be no longer under the delusion that Bath was, even in Nash's own day, so deeply indebted to him for inestimable services and favours.

Modern Bath is really the work of Ralph Allen and John Wood. The latter built Allen's town-house first, and then his grand mansion of Prior Park. These works afforded striking examples of Wood's genius and practical ability. If Wood had not been the chronicler of his own achievements in what Mr. Earle calls "mountebank diction," it is possible his works might have found a clearer and a better exponent, and future generations would have appreciated his service to Bath more distinctly than they have done. The works of Wood, both father and son, were the result of well-considered plans and arrangements, the ichnography of which was calculated with close regard to unity of design and systematic regularity.

Ralph Allen was the inventor of the cross-post system, a fact which in itself entitled him to be regarded as a public benefactor; and, coming to a later period, it is not a little singular that the next advance in the development of the modern postal system is due to Palmer, another Bath worthy, who originated the mail-coach system, which, necessarily involving the making of good roads and the opening up of frequent and easy communications throughout the kingdom,* was the beginning of a new civilization—a new national life.

There was, then, *pari passu* with Nash and his doings, and altogether apart from them, a community whose pursuits were rational and respectable, and who, not despising the right use of pleasure, had no sympathy with gambling and the other vices associated with it. When Wood designed and built modern Bath, he evidently did not think he was preparing a grand resort for future generations of gamblers, but a residential city, the beauty of which is still unsurpassed, whose salubrity is beyond all question, and whose advantages none can doubt. When he and his no less able son died, their mantle descended, not unworthily, upon Baldwin, who built the Guildhall and the Pump Room, and to whom we are indebted for the important and now integral part of the city—Bathwick, which was partly completed at the close of the last century. The design was never quite carried out, but so far as the architect's plan was accomplished, it has the merit of completeness and no little architectural grandeur.

The Bathwick Estate, together with Wrington and Burrington, in the

* It is a singular coincidence, that whilst Ralph Allen may be regarded as the founder of the improved postal system, the founder of the Ocean postage system in our own day should have been Sir Samuel Cunard, Bart., who resided here for a long time, and whose daughter married Major R. S. Allen, a descendant of Ralph Allen's brother, Philip Allen.

x. *Introduction.*

lovely vale of Wrington, near the Mendip Hills, in Somersetshire, belonged to the Earl of Essex, by whom, in 1726, it was sold to Sir William Pulteney, the famous statesman and rival of Sir Robert Walpole. In 1742, Pulteney was created Earl of Bath. Having no surviving issue at his death, in 1764, his estates devolved upon his brother, General Harry Pulteney, who distinguished himself at Dettingen and Fontenoy. The general dying the year following without issue, the estates devolved upon Frances Pulteney, daughter and sole heiress of John Pulteney, Esq., uncle of the Earl of Bath. She married William Johnstone, Esq., M.P., of Westerhall, Dumfriesshire, who assumed the name of Pulteney. He was created a Baronet. One daughter was the issue of this marriage— Henrietta Laura Pulteney, who was created Baroness Bath, in 1792, and Countess of Bath in 1803. She married, in 1794, Sir James Murray, Bart., who also assumed the name and arms of Pulteney. On the death of the Countess of Bath, without issue, in 1808, the Somersetshire property devolved by remainder upon the Earl of Darlington, afterwards first Duke of Cleveland, K.G., of the present creation. Pulteney Bridge was begun by Lady Bath's father, then Mr. William Johnstone Pulteney, and completed by Lady Bath. This, in fact, was the first work undertaken in connection with Baldwin's building-scheme in Bathwick.

The connection of the City with Bathwick, which, before the construction of the Pulteney Bridge, was accessible only by a series of ferries, was an important event. The addition of so picturesque and lovely a suburb may be regarded as the completion of the general outline of the city, with ample scope for future development and improvement. There is little of historical importance connected with Bathwick, so far as this little work is concerned, until we come to the present century. The fact that it was the property of so famous a man as Sir William Pulteney, Earl of Bath, to whom by the way it could have been but a small source of income, is almost its only claim to notice. It was little more than a hamlet, having but a small population. The old Church, dedicated to S. Mary, was interesting. It stood in the centre of what is now the road in Bathwick Street, opposite to Rochfort Place.

Bathwick may now be said to be the most compact parish in the city; and since the Municipal Reform Act, it has been an integral part of the Parliamentary and Municipal Borough. From the latter part of the last century to the present time, it has played its part in the city, and has been conspicuous as the favourite quarter of some of our most famous visitors. Queen Charlotte, Duke of Clarence, Louis XVIII., Charles X., Napoleon III., William Pitt,

Introduction. xi.

Wilberforce, and many other distinguished personages, chose it as their temporary home.

The growth of Bath, both as regards the extension of its boundaries and the development of its resources and institutions, is a subject of considerable interest, not only to the Antiquary and student of Topography, but to the general reader who is at all interested in its history and almost unique characteristics. If we were comparing the *renaissance* of Bath with one of those big transatlantic cities which, like Jonah's gourd, grows up in a day, we should be under the disadvantage of having all the circumstances against us. The building or the rebuilding of a city in the "New World" is a work of comparative facility. It has, in the construction, the guidance of past experience, and all the advantages of modern progress and knowledge, ripe and ready to hand. The ichnography which is to determine the character of a new city is not tentative, but may be as perfect as the plan of a great mansion—replete with all that the highest intellectual refinement and all the commercial wants of the day require, allowing of course needful scope for expansion and increase of population. If we were to take Bath as Wood left it, and compare it with any contemporary town or city of that period, it would stand the severest test of comparison. The architect's plan was much in advance of his day; but still he failed to provide for many public wants which more advanced civilization or change in the public taste would now demand.

In Wood's plan there was no Theatre,* no Concert-rooms, no Reading-rooms, no Hotels, besides other adjuncts, without which now a second-rate city would be deemed deficient in enterprise and attraction. But so far as his prescient judgment directed him, he made a city which in domestic comfort, architectural completeness and beauty, leaves little, even in the present day, to be desired. It is not an uncommon expression, indeed, that it is to be regretted that modern architects do not more closely conform to the principles and practice of the Woods—father and son.

It is, however, not merely with the external and physical beauty of Bath that we have to do. It may be said, that if that alone were our subject, we might have saved ourselves the trouble of proving what is indisputable, what everybody

---

* About 1705 a Play-house or Play-room was fitted and decorated for dramatic performances, but it was small and incommodious. A proposal was made to build a Theatre, to be placed under the direction of Mr. Hippisley, the manager of the Public Rooms, but in consequence of his death, the project fell through. Theatres at this time were illegal, but the law was not strictly enforced. Although Mr. Wood did include a Theatre in his plan of Bath, there were difficulties in the way of its adoption, and the scheme proposed by Wood to Hippisley was ultimately renewed and carried out by John Palmer in Orchard Street. (See Theatre.)

admits. Nature has, in her bounteous mood, bestowed upon this "faire citie" Springs of Thermal Waters of inestimable importance—which have been, and will continue to be, more attractive than any feature of man's ingenuity; but what constitutes the supreme importance of Bath, is the combination of this healing agent with such varied climate and all that can please the eye and contribute to the rational happiness of those who seek in the "Queen of the West" a permanent or a temporary home.

The life at Prior Park was idyllic in its cheerful though subdued grandeur. As Mr. Murch says, it was to Bath what Holland House, fifty years ago, was to London. It is a mistake to suppose that Ralph Allen was "humble-minded." If unpretentious he was dignified, and his disposition was characterized by a certain kind of pride and reserve. If he were lowly, it was the lowliness that is "young ambition's ladder." He observed a good deal of stately pomp, not so much perhaps because it gratified any innate vanity, as because having wealth he deemed it his duty to spend it. Pope when he wrote

"Let *low-born* Allen with an awkward shame,
Do good by stealth, and blush to find it fame,"

greatly offended Mr. Allen, and altered the words to "humble Allen." Allen did not think there was any real humility in boring his friends about his "low" origin, nor in proclaiming "the pride that apes humility,"—the proof of a really vulgar nature. The man who could feel a true companionship with Warburton, the elder Pitt, Pope, Hurd, Sherlock, Fielding, and that doughty lady, the Princess Amelia, must have been a man of culture and breeding. He loved Bath, and he showed the absence of "false pride," by the pleasure he felt in devoting his energies and his great intelligence to the advancement of the true interests of the city in which he had made great wealth, as well as the reputation of a national benefactor. And by the exercise of unbounded hospitality to the citizens of Bath, he has bequeathed a name revered and honoured as a citizen, as well as an unwearied philanthropist. From the portals of Prior Park, he could look down upon the less imposing, though scarcely less beautiful, edifice—Widcombe House—the creation of Inigo Jones, and the residence of that Mr. Baldwin who was the prototype—possibly much exaggerated—of "Squire Western," in "Tom Jones." This house—standing as it were in apposition to the lovely little church of Widcombe—is still one of the gems of Bath. We never traverse the lane—Church Lane—without thinking of Fielding, who lived here for a while after he left Twerton. When his wife died, he met a friend in the lane to whom he communicated the fact of his bereavement, "and now," he added, "I am come out to dissipate." Those who have read "Tom Jones," will see that the novelist must have been familiar with the scenery and the sylvan glades of Prior Park, which are so singularly picturesque and charming.

> "Scenes must be beautiful which daily viewed,
> Please daily, and whose novelty survives
> Long knowledge, and the scrutiny of years."

The contemplation of these scenes by those who know anything of their past associations raises in the mind visions of the pomp and old-fashioned stateliness which characterized the life and habits of Allen and his friends at this, now, historic mansion of Prior Park.*

The Parades have been called "the classic ground of Bath"—not without reason. There Burke spent some of his later days; there Sheridan conceived some of the scenes and characters of more than one of his plays; there Wilberforce stayed more than once; and there at the close of his honoured life, Wordsworth spent some weeks of calm tranquillity; and there many others of less importance also dwelt.

As Wood's work extended so the means of access to the city increased, and larger became the influx of distinguished visitors and residents. Queen Square, Gay Street, and the Circus were occupied by great Parliamentary Men, Ladies of Quality, *Savants*, Poets, Painters. Mr. Pitt, who represented Bath in two Parliaments, built No. 7 in the Circus, and resided there; John, Duke of Bedford, lived at No. 15, and in some measure probably, for the time, at least, escaped from the bitter vituperation of Junius.

We have said that, *pari passu* with the peculiar pursuits of the *subjects* of King Nash, flourished another class—as distinct, as separate, as were the Jews from the Hivites and the Hittites. Here the Statesman, the Poet, the Artist, lived in peace and retirement. When Pitt, in 1802, worn and wearied with the cares and responsibilities of office, came to try the effect of the Waters, "which his father had so frequently tried before him," the Bathonians could scarcely understand that the quiet, unobtrusive, dignified gentleman was the great Mr. Pitt—"the pilot who weathered the storm"—the all-powerful minister. They

---

* The best description of the building of Prior Park will be found in Mr. Wood's book, and edition, vol. 2, pages 427 to 433, showing the elevations, and giving the details of the method of construction. Mr. Allen was actuated by something more than the desire to build himself a large house. "The reflections cast upon the freestone of the hills of Bath brought him to a resolution to exhibit it in a seat which he had determined to build for himself near his works, to much greater advantage, and in much greater variety of uses than it had ever appeared in any other structure." This was the most important step taken in developing the resources of the stone quarries of Bath, and in removing the prejudice against the use of the stone, especially in London, in large buildings. Mr. Wood calls the site of Prior Park the "Widcomb of Camalodunum."

Introduction.

could with difficulty believe that he who had wielded England's power as no other minister had ever done, was the gentleman who every night sat down with his friends to a game of penny Speculation. Yet it was so, and those friends were Lord Castlereagh, Lord Malmesbury, Mr. Canning, Mr. Rose, and other great statesmen of the day, who came to advise, to cheer, and to enjoy the society of their great chief.

It may be observed, that near to Rosewell's House, of which we give an autotype, and which is "hastening to decay," Wood built Chandos Buildings and Chandos House—almost his first important work—for the first Duke of Chandos. As they were the first of his genius, so by a chronological sequence are they the first to experience the blight of time, and are now but the "light of other days." These buildings had a fine garden in front; they overlooked the City Walls,* beyond which to the west lay the Kingsmead and the open country. The erection of Westgate Buildings and the construction of the roadway in front, when the Walls and the Westgate were removed, destroyed the garden and obscured the Mansion which was then no longer "fit for a Duke."

The transition in the early part of the eighteenth century, of which we have spoken, was in no respect so remarkable as in its effect upon the intellectual and social life of Bath. In the preceding century little was issued by the local press except occasional Sermons (chiefly controversial) and a few bald treatises on the Waters.† Most of these, however, in smaller or greater numbers, have been miraculously preserved, and in their way are curious, as all local collectors attest.

It is computed that at the close of the seventeenth century the population, including visitors of all sorts, did not exceed 3,000. At the middle of the next century, it amounted to about 9,000, whilst at the close of the eighteenth and the beginning of the present century, it amounted to about 34,000 souls.‡ With the expansion of the city, about 1730, there began great activity amongst the printers, publishers, and booksellers, the social life of the city being inseparably connected with them, their art, and their enterprise.

The bibliography of Bath itself is remarkable, and a study of no small interest to those who delight in local literary lore.§ One of the great attractions to men of letters was afforded by the literary gossip of the day in Bath. The life of the place in some of its phases was a fertile theme for the Satirist, and sometimes supplied ample subject for the Homilist and the Commentator on Men and Morals. The number of Books issued by the Bath press during the

---

* Under these Walls, to the Southward, was the Gehenna of the City.
† Pierce and Guidott are exceptions.   ‡ See Appendix.
§ A valuable Essay might be written upon the subject of Bath Books and Bath Booksellers.

century is not only very large but curious; and printers and publishers alike were men of high attainments and great respectability.

The names of Frederick,* Bull, Hazard, and Leake,† were as well-known almost as the leading metropolitan publishers. They were, moreover, men of enterprise, whose shelves groaned under the big tomes and choice works of the day. One of the brightest and most satisfactory features of Bath life and society, when sources of rational enjoyment and amusement were few, was that resulting from the ample literary provision so wisely made, under admirable rules and regulations, for the public.

Those who are acquainted with the admirable little book ‡ written by the late Rev. Joseph Hunter,§ may form an adequate estimate of the intellectual life of the city, at a period, too, when dynastic troubles and political disturbances throughout the country were no trifling hindrances to national intellectual advancement.

In the Libraries and Reading-Rooms all the first men of the age almost met to exchange friendly, social, and literary intercourse. The Libraries were the Clubs, as it were—the common ground to which were attracted gentlemen of leisure and refinement, where they bought and read books, and discussed them and their authors.

If the cynical maxim be true in any sense, that life would be tolerable but for its amusements, it has, at least to Bathonians of the present day, a most appropriate application to the amusements of a former age. In Webster's time the dancing took place under a tent on the Bowling-Green to the strains of a fiddle and a stridulous wind-instrument. Some of the visitors— especially two of those ladies who were the most notorious in a notorious age of libertinism, the Duchesses of Cleveland and Portsmouth—splashed about in the Baths in a fashion which shocked the Corporation, who checked the unseemly exhibition and stopped the "vocal musick," which at times was more expressive than elegant.

Subsequently, the conduct of ladies and gentlemen was subject to regulations which in these days would not be needful for the government of big boys and girls. If Nash did throw a gentleman into the Bath for admiring his own wife whilst

---

* Frederick published Wood's first Tractate.

† Leake published some of the earliest editions of Ken's Hymns. Richardson the novelist married Leake's sister; Sheridan cultivated Leake, and, it is said, wrote one of his plays chiefly in Leake's Library.

‡ Connection of Bath with the Literature and Science of England, 1853.

§ Author of the History of Hallamshire, and Editor of vols. 1 and 2 of the Thoresby Diary.

bathing, it was the most meritorious act of his reign. But when we read of the habits of the pleasure-seekers of Nash's time, we ask what, in the present day, people mean when they talk of the good old times of Beau Nash? Lolling about in toy-shops, tea and coffee shops, eating Bath buns and drinking threepenny dishes of tea and chocolate, were pleasures not very attractive. "People of fashion" occasionally had a public breakfast, and attended the concerts, some of which were conducted by Herschel or Rauzzini; and occasionally they went to church to "kill time." The concert-breakfasts, which cost "one and twenty pence a-piece"—"a meer trifle"—would astonish some of the "dull" people of the present time, we suspect. The only pleasure-ground was the Bowling-Green, with the walks in the Garden skirting the river, about 200 yards in length. The addition ultimately of "Spring Gardens" was something; but the "life" there was not *comme il faut*. There is more real enjoyment in these "quiet" times to be realized in one day than there could have been in a whole season under the laws of Nash, when men and women "yawned their heads off" for want of "something to do," until the "witching hour of night" came when they could indulge in a game of chance, and by chance impoverish themselves for the rest of their days. If Nash could revisit us now and see our streets, our mansions, our hotels, our private gardens, our domestic arrangements, our Sydney Gardens, our Park, our amusements—free as air, and plenty of them—he would return to Hades with a feeling akin to wonder that his own times should now find a single admirer, or that any person could be found to compare the past of his own day, notwithstanding his laws and regulations, with the "Bath of to-day."

It is, if not a study, an employment infinitely amusing, to read the Satires of a past age in Bath. Life in no other place during the last century offered so many salient points for the Satirist's pen, and the result is a literature almost unique in its peculiar character. Satirists lampooned society, quarrelled amongst themselves, and lampooned each other. Nor can it be said that this literature was evanescent and lived only as long as the laugh and amusement it excited. Anstey's Poem, "The New Bath Guide," will have an enduring place in the literature of the nation. For pungency, felicity of expression, and as a truthful representation of the manners and habits of the people of Nash's kingdom, it is simply perfect.

We have, however, to boast of men and women more eminent than Anstey. Smollett and Fielding left us not merely the characters of their own vivid imaginations, but the scenes in which they played their parts were the realities the authors saw and admired. Jane Austen here also conceived and wrote her most admired fictions. Lytton wrote in Bath a portion of his latest novel, "The Parisians." Here lived Miss Burney, Mrs. Piozzi, Reade, Atherston, Haynes Bayly, and Landor. It is not a small matter that amongst painters we claim as citizens Sir T. Lawrence, Gainsborough, Thomas and Benjamin Barker, and Hewlett, whilst we may be justly proud of the three brothers, James, David, and Heywood Hardy. The late Mr. Duffield was a Bath man, *par excellence*. He married Miss Rosenberg, who survives him, and in her own line is, at this time, the head of her profession. The late Mrs. J. D. Harris was her sister, and the late Mr. G. Rosenberg her brother—both eminent in the special walk they followed. Mr. Syer, one of the most appreciated artists of the day, may be claimed as a Bath man; so likewise Mr. Hardwick and Mr. Cranch here persued their calling. Willes Madox, who died too soon for the profession of which he was a distinguished ornament, was a native of our city; and last, but not least, Mr. Long, R.A., began his distinguished career in this, his native city;—whilst the father of the President of the Royal Academy--Sir F. Leighton—was long a resident in The Circus.

After Nash's death, or rather before he died, great changes began. The system of comparatively rapid travelling changed the population more rapidly. People did not remain long enough to get imbued with Bath habits and old Bath ways. The "old coaching-days" began in Bath and ended in Bath. No city in England was more identified with the coaching system than this, and in no city was the transition from one kind of social life to another so quickly perceptible. The first mail-coach ever started in England was No. 1 mail-coach, which left "The Lamb" in the year 1784, and was horsed and driven on its first two stages by John Dover, the owner and landlord of that well-known hostelry. The scenes at The York House, The White Hart, The White Lion, The Lamb, and The Three Tuns, were of the most animated and interesting character. As team after team passed through the city in all directions, they afforded never-ceasing amusement; and visitors experienced no little diversion in watching them draw up at the hotels and in criticising the smart "tits" and the skill of the coachmen in "handling the ribbons." When this ceased, forty years ago, it changed everything, and one of the results to be especially observed is this, that what brings visitors rapidly to Bath or to any other place of pleasure or health resort, as rapidly takes them away. But rapid travelling has done more than this: it has created twenty centres of interest where only one existed before. It has brought distant places within reach of the Metropolis—distant places never heard of until the Fire-King found them out. It is easier now to reach Vienna than formerly it was to visit Edinburgh. It has become, in fact, a race

xviii.   *Introduction.*

amongst nations as well as amongst cities. But amidst all these contending elements, Bath still is beautiful Bath, claiming pre-eminence in all that constitutes the attributes of a great and noble city.

With this exordium, we invite our readers to enter our humble gallery, and if some of the portraits are drawn with a feeble hand, we must plead in extenuation of our shortcomings the difficulties of having little to guide our touch or to help us to a "good sitting." We have endeavoured to be accurate, remembering that—

"Those that paint them truest, praise them most."

We fear that some portraits may be placed in the wrong frames; and, should this be so, we excuse ourselves by the fact we have already referred to— namely, that the frames have been so subject to the "chance and change" of time and circumstances, that here and there they may have deceived not only ourselves, but also the cunning of more experienced friends whom we have consulted.

R. E. PEACH.

[We have to acknowledge our sincere obligations to Mr. Murch, Mrs. Jervis, Mr. J. N. Willan, M.A., Mr. J. W. Morris, Mr. J. C. Godwin, Major Davis, F.S.A., Mr. C. P. Russell, Mr. Willcox, Mr. W. Titley, Mr. Watts, and others, for their ready and most valuable assistance.]

[The Woodburytype on the title page is from a negative by Perren, of Milsom Street.]

Historic Houses in Bath and their Associations.

HISTORIC HOUSES IN BATH

And their Associations.

ROYAL VISITS.—It would profit our readers little if we attempted to trace any Royal visits previous to Queen Elizabeth's reign. No tangible evidence exists to show that any sovereign in modern times ever visited Bath in person until **QUEEN ELIZABETH** did so in 1574, in the course of that Royal Progress which she made to the Western part of her dominions, of which Gloucester, Bristol, and Bath were the most important cities, and experienced the largest share of her Majesty's favour.[1] Her Majesty, there is little doubt, stayed at the Royal apartments in the WEST GATE, which very shortly before had been repaired and beautified by the authorities, probably in contemplation of this visit. The "Progress" of 1574 was evidently the result of policy, which the Queen, with her characteristic astuteness, turned to good account. The record of her conduct—her frank recognition of the good feeling shown her by the people, and her marked individuality of character—accounts for much of that popularity which distinguished her reign. Whatever pleased the Bristol citizens[2] pleased her Majesty; the Bathonians had their own little prejudices, and their ways were not the ways of Bristolians, but the Queen understood their peculiarities at a glance, and at once identified herself with them.[3] She "astonished the natives" by her wonderful frills and "rubyes and dyamondes" and those "satten gownds" which she reserved for what even

[1] A full account of the Royal Progress, by Mr. Emanuel Green, will be found in the "Proceedings of the Bath Natural History and Field Club," vol. 2.
[2] Mr. Green omits the address of congratulation offered by the citizens of Bristol and the Queen's answer; perhaps he did not regard them as "authentic."

Citizens.	Queen.
"We men of Bristol, we Are very glad to see Your gracious Majestie; Good Lord! how faire ye be!"	"Ye men of Bristol, we Are very glad to see; Good lack, what fools ye be!"

[3] One part of the City, she said, was "dirty of aspect and nasty of smell."—See *Sherston.*

then was a city of polite citizens. Her affectations, her foibles, and apparent love of finery, covered a purpose [1]—they were but "outward shows,"[2] behind which posed the Queen, who never forgot her imperial dignity.[3] The expense of entertaining the Queen was large, considering the small population and limited resources of the city in those days, but it was paid without a murmur. The luxury of such a sovereign was fully appreciated, and the historical remembrance of good Queen Bess's "visitation" stands out most vividly amongst all the Royal Visits from that period until the present century.[4]

If Queen Elizabeth's visit was one of policy, that of the next Royal personage (1616), **ANNE OF DENMARK, WIFE OF JAMES I.**, was undertaken for the benefit of her health by the use of the Waters. Pierce mentions this visit; but as her Majesty did not reside in his house, the probability is that she also found accommodation at the ROÝAL APARTMENTS in the WEST GATE. At that period, indeed, the Abbey House, then the residence of Dr. Pierce, was the only one (excepting Hetling House, occupied by Sir E. Hungerford) sufficiently capacious for Royalty. In connection with the Queen's visit, Warner relates the following incident:—

"As the Queen was bathing in the King's Bath, there arose from the "bottom of the cistern just by the side of her Majesty a flame of fire like a "candle, which had no sooner ascended to the top of the water than it spent "itself upon the surface into a large circle of light, and then became extinct. "This so frightened the Queen, that notwithstanding the physicians assured "her the light proceeded from a natural cause, yet she would bathe no more in "the King's Bath, but betook herself to the New Bath, where there were no

---

[1] Sir John Harington knew his Royal Mistress well. He relates (April, 1594):—"One Sunday (April last) my lorde of London preachede to the Queene's Majestie, and seemede to touche on the vanitie of deckinge the body too finely. Her Majestie tolde the ladies that if the bishope helde more discorse on such matters, shee wold fitte him for heaven, but he shoulde walke theither withoute a staffe, and leave his mantle behind him; perchance the bishope hathe never soughte her Highnesse's wardrobe, or he would have chosen another texte." Her Majesty understood more about the uses of "deckinge the bodie" than the Bishop.

[2] "So may the outward shows be least themselves;
The world is still deceived with ornament."
Merchant of Venice.

[3] "And you shall find, his vanities forespent
Were but the outside of the Roman Brutus,
Covering discretion with a coat of folly."
Henry V.

[4] For an account of the Royal Charter, see *Sherston*.

"springs to cause the like phenomena ; and from thence the cistern was called "the Queen's Bath. It was soon enlarged, and the citizens erecting a tower or "cross in the middle of it, in honour of the Queen, finished it at the top with "the figure of the Crown of England over a globe, on which was written in "letters of gold, 'Annæ Reginæ Sacrum.'"

During the Rebellion in 1644, **CHARLES I.**, accompanied by the **QUEEN**, in passing westward stayed in Bath for a few days. He had fortified the city previously, and at this time it was held by the Royal Forces. In July of the same year, the **PRINCE OF WALES** (afterwards Charles II.), having reached Bristol on his way to Barnstaple, returned to Bath, on account of the plague which was then raging at the former city.

The visit of **MARY BEATRICE OF MODENA**, second wife of **JAMES II.**, in 1687, is full of romantic interest. Her misfortunes, her beauty, her tender sympathy with her husband in his downfall, and in his banishment, and in the painful vicissitudes to which he was exposed—all show her to have been a woman of

"Amazing brightness, purity, and truth,
Eternal joy, and everlasting love."

The Queen having had four sons, all of whom died prematurely, was naturally desirous of having a living heir. Ronchi, her chaplain, in his diary, says that he shared her hopes that the birth of a Royal Prince would "be the most fitting "antidote for extinguishing the heat which the Prince of Orange doth foment in "the country, and humble the pride of the many whom the hope of a Protestant "successor hath stirred up to oppose openly the Royal transactions." He knew of her visits to miraculous wells, and he, with others, advised her Majesty not only to go to Bath for the Waters,[1] but the Royal pair were to drink at St. Winifred's wonder-working well.[2] A miracle was hinted at by her spiritual guides. The King reached Bath August 18, 1687, and remained three days. On September 6, he returned to it from Holywell. The Queen remained here during the interval, and the whole programme was carried out ; the King and Queen returned ; the Queen to hope and pray, the King to hunt and review his troops.[3] Dr. Oliver, in his interesting work,[4] indicates some special notice by their Majesties of the Benedictine Mission, "of which the Rev. F. Anselm Williams was then the Incumbent." The Queen, the following year, bore a son, who did not prove to be "a fitting antidote" against the Prince of

---

[1] See *Dr. Pierce*, chap. 9, pages 157 to 214.
[2] This well was near Winifred's Dale, Sion Hill. All trace of it is lost.
[3] Edinburgh Review, January, 1882.
[4] Oliver's History of the Catholic Religion—Missions of Somersetshire, 1857.

Orange. Warner and other local historians say that the Queen's pregnancy was a source of so much joy that Lord Melfort erected a Cross in the centre of the Cross Bath to signalize the happy event.[1] If this be so, it was the renewal probably of an older cross, which was there a century before.

It would seem, at any rate, that the Bath Waters and St. Winifred's are responsible for the birth of the "Old Pretender," and, consequently, for the political events which directly followed from the existence of that unfortunate Prince.

The first visit of the **PRINCESS ANNE**, with her husband **(PRINCE GEORGE OF DENMARK,)** took place in 1692, during the mayoralty of William Bush. She was received by the Mayor and Corporation in a manner becoming her rank and position, and their sense of what was due to the dignity of the city. This attention gave umbrage to the King and Queen, between whom and the Princess there had been a quarrel, in which it has been generally held the Princess was technically in the wrong. She had applied to the Parliament for a settlement upon herself of £50,000 per annum, without the knowledge of William and Mary; she had, moreover, espoused the cause of Lord and Lady Marlborough. Amongst other marks of attention (says Warner) shown to the Princess during her stay, it was usual for the Corporation to attend her to the Great Church on Sundays. Their conduct was reported at Court, and the Earl of Nottingham, secretary of state, was ordered to write a mandatory letter to the Mayor and Corporation prohibiting them from continuing those marks of respect to the Princess. The letter was as follows:—

"SIR,—The Queen has been informed that yourself and your brethren have attended the "Princess with the same respect and ceremony as have been usually paid to the Royal family. "Perhaps you may not have heard what occasion her Majesty has had to be displeased with the "Princess; and therefore I am commanded to acquaint you, that you are not for the future to pay "her Highness any such respect or ceremony, without leave from her Majesty, who does not doubt "of receiving from you and your brethren this public mark of your duty.
"I am, your most humble servant,
"NOTTINGHAM."

On receipt of this letter, the Mayor dispatched it to John Harington, Esq., at Kelston, and requested his opinion and advice upon the subject. He

---

[1] Dr. Pierce, who was a contemporary witness of the event, says:—"One Mrs. Booth, of "Cheshire, brought a daughter in July, 1688. She was about eleven or twelve years old; she also "drank the Waters, and bathed, and recovered in five or six weeks so well as to dance a jigg with "great applause, at a ball, which the gentry met at. A knotted cane of her father's, which she used "to try to go with, was hung up as a trophy, upon the new marble structure in the Cross-Bath, "erected by John, Earl of Melford, in memory of Queen Mary of Modena's bathing there the year "before; it was the first, of that kind, that was hung upon it, and it continues there to this day."— *Bath Memoirs.*

recommended a compliance with the Queen's command, but suggested, at the same time, that it should be communicated to the Princess in the most respectful manner. This was accordingly done, and Anne, with great good sense, and smiling at the petty malice of the Queen, desired the Corporation to omit any mark of distinction to her in future, expressing herself as particularly anxious that the city of Bath should not incur the displeasure of the Royal pair on her account. In consequence of this voluntary relinquishment of distinctions, the Mayor and Corporation omitted to attend the Princess to the Abbey Church in procession. Determined, however, to make amends for this disrespectful behaviour which they had been obliged to adopt to the Princess, they invited her, as soon as she came to the Crown, in the address presented on that occasion, to repeat her visit to Bath. This she complied with in 1702, and was received with every mark of honour and distinction. One hundred young men of the city, uniformly clad and armed, and two hundred of its female inhabitants dressed after the manner of Amazons, met the Queen and her train on the borders of Somersetshire, and accompanied them by a road *cut for the occasion*[1] from the summit of Lansdown to the western gate of the city, where the Corporation received the Royal party, and conducted them to their apartments, in the West Gate.

The next visit we have to record is that of the **PRINCESS AMELIA**, the second daughter of George II., in 1728. Having been received with due honours by the Corporation and one hundred young men, at the North Gate, she took up her abode at the Royal Quarters—the **West Gate**. She soon showed some of her Royal mettle. Her energy and resolution almost overcame a king—King Nash—who was more absolute than her Royal father. That potentate resisted her persuasion and her threats. "One more dance, Mr. "Nash; remember, I am a Princess." " Yes, Madam, but I *reign* here, and *my* "laws must be kept." She was beaten, but she was magnanimous, good-hearted, and reasonable. At this time she was about 25 years of age, fair, and comely. She scarcely regarded the etiquette of Royalty and the conventional manners of the period in dress and personal habits. In spite of her eccentricities she was popular, and much beloved for her sympathetic and kindly disposition. Her Royal Highness liked Bath so much that she re-visited it in 1752, staying for a brief period with the Duke and Duchess of Bedford, and then resumed her old quarters in the West Gate. By this time H.R.H. had become rather *en bon point*—she drank beer like a fast young man of the present day, and took snuff like any old woman

[1] Can this be the road leading from the main road on Lansdown at right angles to Weston?

of her own day. Her costume, compared with young ladies' dresses of the present day, suggests a contrast which might be contemplated by modern dressmakers and milliners with wonder if not with advantage. She wore a hunting-cap, a laced scarlet coat, rode on horseback at a spanking pace, accompanied by her favourite groom, Spurrier ; she rose early in the morning, sat up late at night, and gambled right royally with the right royal King Nash. Her language, without being vulgar, was emphatic and not quite *comme il faut*. Mr. Hutton Perkins, who writes to Lord-Chancellor Hardwicke from Bath, on the 17th September (1752), relates the following :—

"Her Royal Highness the Princess Amelia did me the honour to speak "to me in the Pump-Room since I came, to inquire after your Lordship's health. "She hoped you were well, and asked whether you were gone to Wimple. She "comes every morning to the Pump-room between 7 and 8 for her first glass of "the smallest size, and about a quarter after 8 for a second glass, which is all she "drinks in publick. She has no doctor with her, nor makes use of any here. "Ranby is the only person that directs her. By what I can learn, her deafness "is much as it was. It is not fixt; some days she hears tolerably, and others not "so. She is very affable and civil, comes to the room at noon lately, and some- "times at nights, and plays at cards there, chiefly at commerce. She takes all "opportunity, when fair, of getting on horseback, and amuses herself almost every "day some hours in angling in the river, in a summer-house by the river-side in "the garden, formerly known by the name of Harrison's Walks, which has two "fire-places in it, and to secure her against cold, puts on a riding-habit, and a "black velvet postillion-cap, tied under her chin."

The Princess paid a final visit to Bath when she was suffering from her last illness. She died in 1786.

In 1734, his Royal Highness the **PRINCE OF ORANGE** paid a visit to our city, and resided in the **Royal Apartments** at the **West Gate**.[1] He was received by the Mayor and Corporation, and treated with every mark of respect and consideration. The Mayor and Corporation entertained him at a great banquet, and well sustained the traditional character of the city for hospitality and loyalty. The Prince, on account of whose health the visit was made, departed "with a new lease of life." In consequence of this visit

---

[1] It has been stated that the Prince lived during his visit at a house in Orange Grove, now called **Nassau House**, a statement without the shadow of truth. The Prince started for Bath on the 2nd of January, and arrived at Bath on the 5th, and was received by the Mayor, Aldermen, and Common Council. On Wednesday, Feb. 27, his Royal Highness arrived at Oxford on his return from Bath. Before leaving Bath, the Town Clerk, Mr. Webb, in his own house, close to the West Gate, delivered an address to the Prince.

and the cure of the Prince, several rows of trees were planted, and the Obelisk (designed by the Rev. J. W. Borlase, the historian of Cornwall), now standing, was erected to commemorate the event. The locality was then christened "Orange Grove," an appellation it has ever since retained. The Princess whom he married was Anne, Princess Royal of England, eldest daughter of George II., and therefore elder sister of Amelia. The Prince was amiable and kind in disposition, but devoid of ability and dignity. Lord Hervey, in his Memoirs of George II., says of the Prince :—" His body was deformed, so that if you "looked at him behind, you would say he had no head, and if you looked at "him in front you would say he had no legs." Lord Hervey says a few more things of the Prince which we refrain from repeating; though if any of our readers care to read more of him in these highly-spiced memoirs they may possibly be able to gratify the wish without difficulty.

The citizens who daily, or more or less frequently, pass through the classic Square of Wood and observe the Obelisk placed in the enclosure by Nash, perhaps, at least some of them, may still require to be told that it is commemorative of the visit of **THE PRINCE AND PRINCESS OF WALES** to Bath in the autumn season of 1738. The Prince, as everybody knows, married his cousin, the Princess Augusta, of Saxe Gotha, in 1736. They were received with loyal enthusiasm, fêted by the Corporation, and cheered by the citizens. The Prince felt as much gratitude for these evidences of the good feeling of the Bathonians as he was capable of feeling. He gave the Corporation the Loving Cup, and the portraits of himself and the Princess were also presented by him to adorn the Guildhall. The Obelisk to which we have referred was put up at the cost of Nash, on much the same principle as—

" Mr. Smith, of his great bounty,
Built this bridge at the expense of the county."

The architect was Mr. Wood, who, in his book, 2nd edition, page 436, gives all the details of the cost, the sum total being £80 15s. 7d. The poet Pope wrote the inscription, which is as follows :—

" In memory of honour conferred, and in gratitude for benefits bestowed, " on our city, by H.R.H. Frederick, Prince of Wales, and his Royal Consort, " in the year 1738, this Obelisk is erected by Richard Nash."

One would not believe that Mr. Pope was required to write such an inscription as the above. The only merit it possesses is the absence of adulation of the Prince. After all, perhaps, Mr. Pope understood best what he was expected to do, though in the correspondence (see Warner, 368, 369) on the subject he affected no little modesty. The Prince died at Leicester House, March 31, 1751.[1]

In 1740 the **PRINCESS MARY**, wife of the Landgrave of Hesse, 4th daughter of George II., and youngest sister of Amelia, accompanied by her niece, the **PRINCESS CAROLINE**, daughter of Frederick, Prince of Wales, afterwards Queen of Denmark, visited Bath. (In most of the guide-books she is erroneously described as sister of Amelia and Mary.) The pair lived at **Hetling House**,[2] with little or no state.[3]

Edward Augustus, **DUKE OF YORK**, who was the second son of Frederick, Prince of Wales, and brother of George III., visited Bath in 1761, for a considerable period, occupied the centre house on the North Parade, where he held a levee once a week. He was simple and genial in his habits, delicate in health, and died in 1767, unmarried.

In 1795, the **DUKE OF YORK** of the next generation, and the **DUCHESS**, honoured Bath with their presence, and the former accepted the Freedom of the city.

[1] "Poor Fred was alive and is dead,
And as he was alive and is dead,
There's no more to be said."

[2] Facing Westgate Buildings, with three well-pointed gables, stands the much-altered shell of the old mansion known as HETLING HOUSE. It is an age-begrimed, black, three-storied building of the sixteenth century, retaining a few only of its original and marked architectural features: amongst these are the gables, a few of the early windows, the oriel window, and the large hall. Towards Hetling Court the side of the house is crowded out by mean low-storied shops. The chief remaining feature of this once fine old mansion is the hall, now in the occupation of the Odd-Fellows. The other part of the building is used by a grocer as a store-room. The hall is about 47 feet long by 14 feet wide, and about 15 ft. high. Round a portion of the walls the old characteristic oak wainscot remains, but some of this has been painted and grained to match or defile the real and good material underneath. But the grand feature of this hall (and its nearest vieing neighbour is as distant as South Wraxall) is the beautiful fire-place, which is about 9 feet 6 inches wide and 14 feet high. The lower and bolder stone cornice is supported by two flanking circular Ionic pillars on either side, on pedestals. The upper stone cornice is supported by seven taper pilasters. The whole is emphasised in the centre by a boldly and well-carved coat of arms of the family, supported by a helmet and crest. This fire-place has unfortunately been painted, but it still retains features of worth and excellence of design, and its past history and uses alone should make the Bath people its jealous and careful guardians. The room in the roof lighted by the gabled windows is unoccupied, and at present even without access. Sir E. Hungerford, K.B., one of the members of the city, in 1625, made this his Bath Town-House. In consequence of this fact, it was always supposed that the house was built by one of the Hungerfords. Canon Jackson, however, says the arms over the mantlepiece are those of an old Somersetshire family named Clarke, by whom in all probability the mansion was erected in the sixteenth century.

[3] It may be remarked here that when Bath once caught a real live Royal party a hundred and fifty years ago, it was not so easy for them to escape; it meant a visit of some duration. Now, a Royal visit is a matter of ten hours, including the time occupied in travelling.

In the year following, the **PRINCE OF WALES** paid a similar compliment to the city, and accepted its Freedom also. The Prince of Wales on this occasion, we believe, visited Colonel Leigh at Combe Hay. The Prince was not popular in Bath, nor at this time anywhere. A Bath poet (W. S. Landor) says of him :—

> "When from earth the king descended,
> God be praised, the Georges ended."

Thackeray's mocking epitaph, however, on George IV., is, perhaps, as severe as anything that was ever written on that monarch :—

> "He left an example for Age and for Youth to avoid,
> He never acted well by man or woman,
> And was false to his mistress as to his wife:
> He deserted his friends and his principles.
> He was so ignorant that he could scarcely spell ;
> But he had some skill in cutting out coats,
> And an undeniable taste for cookery.
> He built the palaces of Brighton and of Buckingham,
> And for these qualities and proofs of genius,
> An admiring aristocracy
> Christened him 'The first gentleman in Europe.'
> Friends, respect the King whose statue is here,
> And the generous aristocracy who admired him."

In 1807, at the close of the year, His Royal Highness the **DUKE OF GLOUCESTER** (nephew of George III.) visited Bath, and sojourned some time in a simple and unostentatious style. According to custom on a Royal visit, the Mayor and Corporation congratulated his Royal Highness on his arrival in a suitable address ; and at their request he was pleased to have his name enrolled among the Freemen of the city. He occupied apartments at the **York House**.

In 1813, his Royal Highness the **DUKE OF CAMBRIDGE** arrived at the **York House**, and received from the authorities the usual compliments, together with the Freedom of the city in a gold box ; and during the same month the **COUNT DE PROVENCE**, afterwards Louis XVIII., also came hither and remained some time at **34, Pulteney Street**. Mainwaring says of these visits during the dull month :—"As much at leisure as a Bath turnspit in the month of 'July." At this period it was computed that there were in Bath not less than 3,000 of these duck-legged animals, which in the season were the valuable allies of the cooks.

On the 4th of August, 1817, the imposing ceremony of laying the foundation-stone of the Freemasons' Hall took place. The **DUKE OF SUSSEX**, the Grand Master, attended in great state, and the ceremonial was conducted with due Masonic pomp. In a cavity of the stone was placed a metal box, which contained coins of the period, and was covered with a brass plate, bearing the following inscription :—

"The foundation-stone of this Masonic Hall was laid with the usual "ceremonies, August 4, 1817, in the 57th year of the reign of his present "Majesty, George III., and the year of Masonry, 5817, in presence of the Masters "and Wardens of the Bath Lodges, his Royal Highness, August Frederick, Duke "of Sussex, being Most Worshipful Grand Master of the United Grand Lodge of "England ; and Arthur Chichester, Esq., Right Worshipful Provincial Grand "Master for the County of Somerset ; Brother Wilkins, Architect ; Walter Harris, "Builder."

The Duke re-visited Bath in 1819, to preside at the Dedication of the **Masonic Hall**,[1] which took place on the 23rd of September. Perhaps, within the memory of the oldest inhabitant of this city, there never was known so great an influx of strangers as thronged to witness this ceremony, conducted with that splendour which always characterizes the processions of the honourable fraternity. The streets, at an early hour, assumed the appearance of the greatest bustle and expectation ; at every window and house-top, in the intended line of procession, groups of spectators of every degree, from the lady of title to the humblest domestic, were situated.[2] The procession moved from the Guildhall, and passed up Broad Street, where it was joined at the **York House Hotel** by the Royal Grand Master, who walked uncovered down Milsom, Union, and Stall Streets, to the site in York Street. The assemblage consisted of members of the Grand Lodge of England, and of twenty-nine Provincial Grand Lodges, from the counties of Somerset, Devon, Gloucester, Dorset, Hants, and Warwick. The line of immense length formed by these several bodies, advanced with imposing regularity, order, and solemnity ; while the music, the banners, and the various emblems of the craft, heightened the effect of this magnificent sight, and added to the grandeur and animation of the scene. On the two following days, upwards of two thousand persons

[1] At present there are three Lodges in Bath, namely :—The Royal Cumberland ; The Royal Sussex ; The Lodge of Honour. These Lodges now meet in the building in Orchard Street, which was originally the Theatre, built by John Palmer in or about 1747, and afterwards the Roman Catholic Chapel.

[2] "All tongues speak of him ; and the bleared sights
Are spectacled to see him : Your prattling nurse
Into a rapture lets her baby cry,
While she chats him ; the kitchen-malkin pins
Her richest lockram 'bout her reechy neck,
Clambering the walls to eye him ; Stalls, bulks, windows,
Are smothered up, leads filled, and ridges hors'd
With variable complexions ; *all agreeing*
In earnestness to see him."
                                                        Coriolanus, Act ii., Sc. i.

(chiefly ladies) were admitted to view the masonic paraphernalia which were displayed "*in due form*" in the hall.¹

On the 24th, his Royal Highness proceeded, by invitation, to the Guildhall, where he was received by the Mayor and Body Corporate in their civic robes. G. H. Tugwell, Esq., addressed his Royal Highness, requesting he would be graciously pleased to accept the Freedom of this ancient and loyal city, as a proof of their respect for his Royal person and firm attachment to his illustrious House. The Freedom was then delivered to his Royal Highness in a gold box of exquisite workmanship, on the inside of which the Bath arms were engraved—the outside being beautifully chased in coloured gold, the border displaying the rose, shamrock, and thistle. His Royal Highness returned thanks to the Corporation in dignified terms.

Various festivities took place on the foregoing occasion. A Masonic ball and concert at the Lower Rooms, and a grand civic dinner at the Guildhall, in honour of their illustrious visitor, were among the entertainments of the week. The Royal Duke, on taking leave, expressed, in feeling and animated language, the extreme satisfaction he had derived from his visit to Bath.

In October, 1817, it was announced officially that **QUEEN CHARLOTTE** intended to honour Bath with a visit. The two houses, **Nos. 93 and 103, Sydney Place**, were engaged for the Royal party.

On Monday, November 3rd, at an early hour, her Majesty, with the Princess Elizabeth and suite, left Windsor Castle for Bath. They proceeded at a rapid rate. In the course of the afternoon, a vast concourse left Bath to meet the Royal party, who entered the city at half-past four, full an hour before they were expected. The Royal carriages, escorted by the 15th Dragoons, passed Walcot Church and proceeded by the York House, down Milsom Street, and through New Bond Street to Sydney Place. In the evening a deputation from the Corporate Body waited on her Majesty, who was graciously pleased to fix a time for receiving an address. The Countesses of Ilchester and Cardigan, Lord John Thynne, Major-General Taylor, and Colonel Stephenson were in attendance. His Royal Highness the Duke of Clarence had previously arrived from Lord Harcourt's seat in Oxfordshire, and occupied No. 103.

On Wednesday, the 5th, at two o'clock, the Queen was received at the Pump Room by several of the Royal household, a glass of Bath water being handed to her Majesty by John Kitson, Esq., the Mayor.

¹ The building is now used as the Meeting-House of the Society of Friends.

It may be worthy of remark, that the capacious marble font, into which the water from her Majesty's glass overflowed, was *the dome* of the old cross, which was erected in this city in the year 1616, in commemoration of the visit of the Royal consort of James the First, and was appropriated to its present use under the direction of Mr. Baldwin, when the Pump Room was rebuilt.

At two o'clock on the 6th, the Mayor, accompanied by the Marquis Camden (the Recorder), the City Representatives in Parliament, the Rector, Aldermen, and Common Council, proceeded to the Queen's residence, where the Marquis delivered a loyal address, to which her Majesty replied in person, with much dignity and expressive animation. The Municipal Body were then severally introduced by Colonel Disbrowe, and had the honour of kissing her Majesty's hand.

At six on the same evening, a public dinner was served at the Guildhall; and the Mayor was honoured with the company of his Royal Highness the Duke of Clarence, the Marquisses of Bath and Camden, the principal officers of the Royal household, and several distinguished military and naval officers, with the resident clergy and members of the Corporation. The dinner having passed with much hilarity, and the cloth being removed, a messenger arrived with a letter for the Royal Duke, the perusal of which evidently produced much agitation; and in a few minutes afterwards his Royal Highness hastened, with hurried steps, from the table. All was consternation! What could it mean? In a few minutes the Marquis Camden, in the most feeling manner, announced the death of her Royal Highness the Princess Charlotte of Wales! It has been stated that her Majesty was at a ball, at the Guildhall, when the intelligence arrived. It is almost needless to say that even if her Majesty had visited Bath for pleasure she would not have attended a public ball, either at the Guildhall or the recognised Assembly Rooms. But it must be remembered that her Majesty was advanced in years, and that her sole object in visiting the city was for the use of its thermal springs.

Notwithstanding the shock to the Royal family occasioned by the Princess's death, the declining health of her Majesty rendered a recurrence to the healing springs of this city imperatively necessary; and, accordingly, on Monday, November 24th, 1817, her Majesty was again on her way for this city, attended by the Duke of Clarence and Princess Elizabeth; and, at six the same evening, the Royal party arrived in Sydney Place. There were no public demonstrations of joy; and, although a vast concourse of the inhabitants was daily attracted by the appearance of the illustrious party, yet the most marked and respectful decorum was preserved.

The Body Corporate presented three several addresses of condolence to the Prince Regent, Her Majesty, and Prince Leopold; and the Freedom of the city was presented to his Royal Highness the Duke of Clarence, in a gold box. The Freedom of the city was likewise conferred upon the following gentlemen in her Majesty's *suite* :—Edward Disbrowe, Esq., M.P.; Major-General Herbert Taylor; Lieutenant-Colonel Stephenson; and Lieutenant-General Sir Henry Campbell, K.C.B.

On Sunday, November 30th, Divine service was performed at the Queen's residence, in Sydney Place, by the Rev. Charles Crook, Rector of Bath, and Domestic Chaplain to her Majesty. Under the expectation that her Majesty would visit the Abbey Church, the wardens, Messrs. Davis and Batchelor, had fitted up Prior Bird's Chapel as a State pew.

Her Majesty attended the Pump Room punctually every morning, at nine o'clock, being carried in a sedan-chair covered with crimson. After drinking the Waters she held a levee.

On the 21st of September, 1821, his Royal Highness **PRINCE LEOPOLD** (afterwards King of the Belgians) visited this city, attended by his secretary, **BARON DE STOCKMAR**. As soon as his arrival at the **York House** was made known, the Sheriffs (Messrs. Clutterbuck and Long) waited on his Royal Highness, on behalf of the Mayor and Body Corporate, to request that he would be pleased to accept the freedom of the city. His Royal Highness, accompanied by his Worship the Mayor, proceeded to the inspection of the different buildings; and afterwards repaired to the Guildhall, where a considerable body of citizens awaited his arrival. The Mayor then presented his Royal Highness with the Freedom of the city in a handsome gold box, which the Prince received with the most polite condescension; and replied nearly in these words :—" Mr. Mayor, though a lapse of some years may have weakened the "recollection of past events, it will, nevertheless, be present to you all that, by "one of the severest dispensations of Providence, I was for ever deprived of "domestic happiness, and removed from that high station in which I could not "but have exercised a comparative influence over the affairs of this great nation; "yet, though my destiny has been changed, my feelings of warm and sincere "attachment to this country remain unaltered: and it will ever give me the "greatest happiness to contribute, in any way, to its welfare and happiness. Mr. "Mayor and gentlemen, I thank you sincerely for the honour you have conferred "on me."

His Royal Highness then proceeded to visit the Assembly Rooms,

Sydney Gardens, Beckford's Tower, and Prior Park ; and on the 23rd, left the city on his way to Malvern. Just before leaving, the Prince received a letter in Latin addressed to him by the boys of the Grammar School, praying his Royal Highness to intercede with their master for a holiday. The Prince was highly amused, and observed that he "supposed the young rogues having "heard that he had obtained 'his freedom,' were determined that he should "petition for theirs also."

His Royal Highness expressed himself much pleased with his short visit, and observed that, with respect to the public baths, they were not equalled in splendour and convenience by any of the most celebrated on the Continent, all of which he had seen ; and the general attractions of the city drew forth his unqualified admiration.

In 1827, her Royal Highness the **DUCHESS OF CLARENCE** paid a short and private visit to Sir Hutton Cooper, in the **Royal Crescent.**

On the 21st of October, 1830, the **DUCHESS OF KENT**, accompanied by her illustrious daughter, the **PRINCESS VICTORIA**, heiress-presumptive to the Throne, arrived at the YORK HOUSE. A congratulatory peal of bells welcomed the Royal party to the city, and immediately the Sheriffs, with the Master of the Ceremonies, waited on their Royal Highnesses to request they would honour the city by inspecting the public buildings and receive an address from the Body Corporate. To these solicitations a gracious assent was given, and preparations were made for receiving the Royal party with every demonstration of respect. The Mayor and Body Corporate were in attendance, and a large assemblage of ladies and gentlemen. On the arrival of the Royal visitors at the Guildhall, the Mayor (J. F. Davis, Esq., M.D.) welcomed their Royal Highnesses to this city, in terms of warm congratulation, to which a kind and flattering reply was made. It was on the occasion of this visit that an auspicious opportunity of opening the new improvements suggested itself to the Committee, and a request was made to their Royal Highnesses that they would be pleased, after inspecting the different public buildings, &c., to make the *first circuit* of those improvements. Accordingly, on the 23rd, the Royal visitors, attended by the Mayor, the Lord Bishop of the Diocese, Lord James O'Bryen, and several other distinguished personages, with a numerous train of followers, entered at the approach near Queen's Parade ; and, after taking the circuit of the drive, her Royal Highness the Duchess expressed the gratification which she and the Princess had derived from their visit to the city, and signified her desire, that in future the newly-formed pleasure-grounds should be designated the "ROYAL VICTORIA PARK."

On Wednesday, July 19, 1843, a reception was given to his Royal Highness the late **PRINCE CONSORT** at the Bath Station, on his way to Bristol, to take part in the launch of the "Great Britain" Steamship. Preparations were made by the Mayor (John Edridge, Esq.) and the Corporation to give his Royal Highness a welcome and cordial reception. The centre of the down platform was fitted up as a drawing-room, and in this temporary room the Prince was received, and an appropriate address read to him, to which his Royal Highness most graciously replied, and then proceeded to the neighbouring city. A public breakfast afterwards was given by the Mayor at the Guildhall, and the proceedings were of the most gratifying character.

The **DUKE AND DUCHESS OF CONNAUGHT** paid a brief visit to Bath on the 20th of July, 1881.

The occasion was one of much importance and no little interest—namely, the Annual Distribution of Prizes at the Lansdown School for the Daughters of Officers of the Army, who have not been able to make adequate provision for their education. It was a peculiarly appropriate opportunity for the Prince, immediately after his marriage, to show his special interest in an institution so worthy of his sympathy as a Royal Prince and a Soldier. The occasion, moreover, was rendered the more impressive from the fact that it enabled the Prince to introduce his Royal bride, herself the daughter of one of the most illustrious soldiers of modern times—the Red Prince—to witness a ceremony simple in itself, but really one of the highest national importance. Her R.H. saw for the first time in this country, the country of her adoption, that phase of practical and helpful benevolence which marks the national character. The Royal School, in the work of education, assists a class of young ladies who have the highest claim upon the nation at large, and that too in a manner which leaves no sense of humiliation and detracts in no wise from a due sense of independence in the recipients. The soldier who dies in the service of his country has established a strong claim upon his countrymen to provide some help towards the expense of educating those loved ones he leaves behind his girls—whose chances of a high-class education are not equal to those of boys, for whom also more abundant provision has been made in other respects, and to whom a greater choice of professions is open. We say the School is practically "helpful," because it is not free; but, as will be seen, whilst giving the highest and best possible education, it does so on a scale of charges adapted to the circumstances of the parent, or parents.

The pupils are admitted on a graduated scale of payment; by election; by purchase of life presentations; by presentations for the occasion. Some elected pupils are admitted on payment of £12 per annum, others on a higher scale of payment. The expenses are met by Legacies, Sale of Presentations, Donations, and Annual Subscriptions. The fundamental rule is as follows:—

"The Daughters of all Officers in her Majesty's Army, inclusive of the Royal Marines, and of "Officers who have sold out, or otherwise retired from the service (provided those children were born "prior to such retirement), are eligible. The religious education shall be, in all cases, in accordance "with the doctrines of the Church of England and Ireland; and a Clergyman of that Church shall "be selected by the Governing Body to act as Clerical Visitor to the Institution."

To promote the increased prosperity of this School was the object of their Royal Highnesses. It was a mission becoming a soldier Prince and Princess, who can so well understand, from their own training and instincts, the value and importance of an institution such as the Royal School to those for whom its privileges and advantages are intended.

The Duke and Duchess were received with due honour, and the proceedings were conducted with skill, order, and eminent success. The Royal visitors returned to London on the evening of the same day.

The history of Royal visits to our city shows that many of them have been purely of a political or State character; whilst others—and these concern us far more—have been undertaken on the part of the Royal visitors altogether for the benefits of the Bath waters. These waters are nature's gift, which cannot be taken from us, but it certainly depends upon the public spirit of the citizens, represented by the Corporation as the trustees and legal guardians of these thermal springs, to keep them more prominently before the world. True, we have baths and appliances, which, by universal admission, are the finest in the world; but we have too long taken it for granted that in providing them, we have done all that we are called upon to do. Nothing is more probable than that at some future time we may be honoured by Royal visits for the sake of these waters. It cannot be supposed that the benefits received by various members of the Royal Family during many centuries are likely to be forgotten.

THE INNS OF OTHER DAYS.[1] The Inns of the past have no small claim to be considered "historic." They were associated with the social and commercial life of the city by special and peculiar ties ; they were the links as it were that connected Bath with every other part of the kingdom. Each Inn had its own distinctive uniform and badge for its servants and waiters, and each was connected with other Inns throughout the country, to whom it sent, and from whom it received, its guests. Each had its own peculiar method of conducting its affairs, according to the quality of its visitors and the *standing* of the house.

THE BEAR INN was for more than a hundred years the most famous in the city. Its yard and stables were parallel with the whole length of Lock's Lane (now called Union Passage), extending on the East side from the Upper Borough Walls to the corner of Westgate Street. The site of The Bear Inn and premises is now represented by Union Street. The Inn faced Stall Street, and was a capacious and comfortable house.[2] It is more widely known than any other inn from having been the headquarters of the hero in Mr. Anstey's famous Satire, "The New Bath Guide."[3] Its china was characteristic and of a most delicate texture, The Bear being pourtrayed on each piece. The last landlord by whom it was kept was HENRY PHILLOTT, brother of the Rector of Bath, of Joseph Phillott, surgeon, and of Charles Phillott, banker. When street improvements began, under the Acts of 1766 and 1789, the Inn was doomed. It was closed, dismantled, and the furniture sold about 1797. The

---

[1] The Inns of the present day which were contemporary with those here described, and others not so well known, are The Angel ; The Castle ; The Christopher ; The White Lion. The York House, and other excellent hostelries came into existence between 1770 and 1780. The Grand Pump Room Hotel may be said to be the successor of the White Hart on a larger scale.

[2] John Britton says—"It was the chief house in Bath for carriage company." Smollett, no doubt, was a guest in the Inn ; he makes *Humphrey Clinker* describe his own experiences at the famous "Bear." The Inn, with its yard, coaches, stables, horses, and men, became a great public nuisance. There was no approaching the Baths from the upper parts of the city, except through the Inn-yard, and frequently "the poor trembling valetudinarian was carried in a chair, between the heels of a double row of horses wincing under the currycombs of grooms and postillions." The removal of the premises became an absolute necessity when street improvements began.

[3] "When I came here to Bath, not a bit could I eat,
Though the man at The Bear had provided a treat."
Anstey's Bath Guide.

Bear appears first on the map of Gilmore, 1694,[1] and was removed when Union Street was constructed, about 1806 or 1807. The Lodge of Freemasons met at the Inn in the early part of the last century. This Lodge was the predecessor of the Royal Cumberland Lodge, No. 41, which has existed from that time in unbroken continuity.

THE WHITE HART appears first on Gilmore's map of 1694 on the site of the house at the "White Hart Lodgings." The success of this Inn was owing to the enterprize of MR. BROOKMAN, who was succeeded by ELEAZER PICKWICK, who had been a postboy at The Bear. He attracted a large share of stage-coach business, and The White Hart became proverbially one of the most popular Inns in the city. The waiters wore breeches and silk stockings,[2] and the women a peculiar kind of close-fitting dress and white neat muslin caps, with white "bibs" hanging from their necks; and these uniforms continued almost to the closing of the Hotel in 1864. In 1869, the premises and others adjoining were pulled down, and upon the site now stands the GRAND PUMP-ROOM HOTEL. The figure of The White Hart which was over the portico now surmounts the Refreshment Rooms opposite to the Mineral-Water Hospital.

THE LAMB INN, in Stall Street, now a grocer's shop, was also a house of great celebrity. It appears on the map first in 1771. When John Palmer originated the mail-coach system in 1784, The Lamb was then conducted by Dover and Weeks. The London and Exeter Mails, which were originally started from The Three Tuns in 1784, were, in 1787, removed to The Lamb. John Dover and John Palmer, the originator of mail, coaches, were great friends. The waiters and porters wore a silver badge upon the right arm, and the women were attired in a neat dress or uniform. The figure of the Lamb, which surmounted the entrance, is now over the entrance to a public-house called "The Lamb," in the Lower Borough Walls.

THE THREE TUNS occupied the site of Mr. Manchip's shop in Stall Street, and was an Inn of high reputation. The first mail-coach from Bath to London started from The Three Tuns, and many coaches were "horsed" from it.

[1] This is Gilmore's Map, published in 1694, for which the survey was made in 1692. It is curious that in this map, whilst of course the Inn occupies the same relative position as in subsequent maps, between The Bear and Stall Street there is a block of houses intervening, leaving a narrow passage only to the latter street. In subsequent maps, these houses disappear, and the sites are absorbed into The Bear premises.

[2] In the salad days of the late Lords Lytton and Beaconsfield, they arrived in Bath and took up their quarters at The White Hart. At dinner they appeared in black velvet *tights*, cut-away coats and waistcoats of the same, and magnificent frill shirts, black-silk hose, and polished shoes with silver buckles. The waiters were struck dumb with astonishment. "Pelham" and "Coningsby" beat them out of sight in the way of superb attire, and a waiter in those days at The White Hart required some beating.

The landlord whose name was best known in connection with it, was Mr. Ballinger.[1]

THE GREYHOUND, or, as it was at one time called, **THE GREYHOUND AND SHAKSPERE**, was a Commercial Inn. It stood in High Street, opposite Bridge Street, and was closed in 1864. It is first depicted on the map of 1694. Sometimes it was called "The Dog," and by some the appellation was thought to have reference to the special animal from whose tail was to be plucked the hair which was to cure them of his bite of the previous night. The figure of the Greyhound, in a sitting position, a graceful enough object, still crouches on a wall at the back of one of the houses in Paragon Buildings, and can be seen from Walcot Street, below.

THE GUILDHALL.—The old Guildhall and Market-House, built by Inigo Jones and finished in 1625, stood in the middle of High Street, opposite The Christopher. Wood says:—" That edifice seems to have been built to " resemble, in some measure, the Stadt-House, at Delft, in Holland, erected and " finished five years before, under the direction of Cornelius Danckerts. For " it is well known, that in the year 1620, Mr. Jones surveyed Stonehenge, and, if " I am not deceived in my information, he came to Bath the same year, or very " soon after; at which time, there having been many curious workmen in the " place that had been employed on the Church of St. Peter and Paul, the " citizens embraced the opportunity that then offered, and so procured a design " of Mr. Jones, to rebuild their Market-House,[2] with a hall over it, while there " were proper artificers to execute it.

" This structure is of the Dorick and Ionick order, placed one upon the " other ; and nothing but the particular directions of an Inigo Jones could have " produced the capitals with which the upper columns are adorned.

" But the strongest circumstances to prove Inigo Jones the architect of " this Basilica, are the excellent proportions of the edifice, which is formed upon " an area of two squares and a half. The clear hall is also a figure of two " squares and a half, and so is the side front. The end front is a perfect square. " And the second order is a fifth part less in height than the rest."

In the wall of the front were stationed, in ghastly majesty, the statues of King Offa, the fabulous founder, and King Edgar,[3] the real founder of the liberties of the city. In Webster's time, balls were held in the hall on great occasions only.

---

[1] It was called originally the "Three Tuns Lodgings." The White Hart was called the "White Hart Lodgings."—See Gilmore's Map, 1694.

[2] It is obvious from this, that it stood upon the site of an edifice previously existing.

[3] These effigies are now to be seen in niches on the house, No. 8, Bath Street.

The associations of the old Guildhall are not without interest. It was identified with the public business of the city and the judicial patronage, and consequently the administration of justice. The distinguished visitors were entertained here on all public occasions with hospitality and dignity; the representatives of the city during a period of 150 years were chosen within its walls, and those gentlemen to whom was entrusted the business of the city did their work fearlessly and honourably. Bishop Warburton, when he used Ralph Allen to chide Pitt in the matter of the "Adequate Peace," made a chapter which puzzled the members of the Corporation who were not behind the scenes; but it was no small distinction, looking at the list of eminent men by whom Bath was represented during that century, that it should be able to boast amongst them the greatest orator, if not the greatest statesman, of the age. Around the Council-Hall hung the portraits of the members of the Corporation by whom Marshal Wade was elected (the fourth time) in 1741. These portraits were painted at the cost of the Marshal in 1742, and, together with his own, presented to the Corporation. The portrait of the Marshal is still to be seen on the grand staircase in admirable preservation, but the worthy Councillors—where are they?

It is not possible to look back without interest upon the history and traditions of the municipal government of the city, the political contentions, and the peaceful rivalries of public men; and the old Guildhall was associated with the most important events of which we have any definite knowledge. Those masterful Chapmans who exercised so large an influence on the fortunes of the city, sometimes sinister, sometimes beneficent, though the earliest of them was first known in the early part of Elizabeth's reign, lived almost to the beginning of the next century, and the race was perpetuated for two centuries beyond that period. Previous to 1678, we find some thirteen of the family were buried in the Abbey, which seems to have been a great charnel-house. Some of these Chapmans during the Rebellion were occasionally Royalists, occasionally Rumpers, according to the varying fortunes of the contending factions. Henry Chapman was the great political ally of Prynne, so long as Prynne was a Rumper, but his bitter opponent when he became a Royalist. Henry lived to be a Royalist, and to praise the *virtues* of Charles II. It was no longer safe to be a Rumper, but it was safe to be a lickspittle. Henry, however, was a man of mark, and he left an amusing little book—"Thermæ Redivivæ"—which gives a faithful account of the city and the springs at that period (1673). There was little to disturb the political serenity of the city from this time until the Pretender found a few partizans, headed by the historian Carte, the Rector of Bath, who proposed to proclaim him king; but the movement was never formidable, Ralph Allen having, by means never fully known, revealed the plot. Bath was, no doubt, loyal to the Hanoverian dynasty, and the Corporation, on four successive occasions (1722, 1727, 1734, 1741), elected the redoubtable Marshal Wade as one of the Members of Parliament. It was manifestly better to have him as a friend than as an enemy. It is clear that the Corporation, which, with few exceptions, consisted, from the earliest to the latest times, of men of integrity and position, discharged its duties with ability and with a due regard to the honour and the best interests of the city.

This old Guildhall, like many other old buildings, yielded to the exigencies of necessity rather than time. It had long been an obstruction to the business and traffic of the High Street, and upon the completion of the building in 1777, it was at once removed as a useless piece of antiquity. The foundation-stone of the new structure was laid the 11th of February, 1768; but in consequence of the refusal of the householders to give up their houses which stood on the site, a total stop was put to the building until 1775, when the plan was reconsidered, and being thought insufficient for the business of the Corporation, fresh designs were prepared by Mr. Thos. Baldwin, the city architect, and the building completed in 1777. It has two fronts, of which Mr. Warner says that the façade towards the Market is preferable to that facing the street. The ground floor contains the ordinary business-rooms; but on the principal storey above is the council-chamber, which opens into the banqueting-room. The great hall is a noble room, 80 feet in length by 40 in breadth, and 31 in height, containing portraits of Frederick, Prince of Wales, and his Consort, George III. and Queen Charlotte, Pitt—Earl of Chatham, Marquis Camden,[1] Anstey, Ralph Allen, and Alderman Hunt. In the Mayor's room is Turnerelli's bust of George III.; and in the council-chamber one of Ralph Allen, set up during his mayoralty. In this room also are duplicate portraits of George III. and Queen Charlotte. On the landing of the grand staircase is a fine portrait of Marshal Wade. In the

---

[1] When Camden Crescent was built, it was called *Camden Place*, after the ancestral residence of the Camden family. There was, therefore, a purpose in this. A few years ago, for some reason no one can understand, this name was changed to Camden Crescent. About the same time, Lilliput Alley was changed to North-Parade Passage, and Gallaway's Buildings to North-Parade Place. In this case, the original names which were identified with Allen and Wood (the mother of all Post-Offices was presided over by the former) were changed, as in the former instance, for no conceivable reason. It is a wanton act of folly to tamper needlessly with street nomenclature, the only effect of which is to puzzle future students of local history. What would *Sally Lunn* say if she could see her beloved Lilliput, where she invented her famous tea-cake, transformed into a trumpery *passage*?!

lobby are two busts : one of the late Sir W. Tite, M.P., and the other of the late T. Phinn, Esq., Q.C.

THE ABBEY HOUSE.—This house existed as late as 1755, when it was pulled down to make room for "modern improvements." The house, previous to the dissolution of the Monasteries, had been the Monastic House, connected with the Abbey of St. Peter and St. Paul and of the Benedictine Order, and stood upon the site of a former building of a similar character on the South side of the Abbey. The first Monastic House was destroyed when the city was sacked and burned by De Mowbray.[1] It was rebuilt by John de Villula, whose tomb was to be seen in the Monastic Church, built by himself, as late as the time of Leland. This was the Church which preceded the present building. In the earlier Monastic House, a fine collection of manuscripts and books, including the works of Abelard, one of the most famous philosophers of the twelfth century, himself a friend of Bishop John de Villula, was also referred to by Leland. Prior Bird, Prior Holway, and Charnock were no doubt associated with the same house, and doubtless added to that store of learned works, of which not a vestige has ever been traced. When the building was pulled down, in 1755, a closet was revealed, in which several vestments were found, which on being exposed to the air crumbled into fine dust.

The Abbey House to which we are referring, after the Dissolution, passed through many vicissitudes, until, in 1653 it was occupied by **DR. ROBERT PIERCE** for the reception of patients in connection with the Baths. He speaks of "the convenient situation of my house, having on one side a "Gallery and a door that goes into the King's Bath, and on the other side, "out of my Garden, a private door into the Abbey Church." It is pretty clear from this description, and from the print, No. 1, in Gilmore's Illustrated Map (see Mr. Russell's collection), that the house touched the Abbey on the western end of the south aisle, and overlooked from the upper storeys the King's Bath from the west front. The house evidently was of considerable capacity. The doctor gives the names of his principal patients, and he describes their ailments with a minuteness which would be tedious if it were not for his complacent quaintness. In 1663 he says :—

"Amongst others that greatly encouraged the drinking of the waters, was **Sir Alexander Frayser**, chief Physitian to King Charles the II. He waiting upon His Majesty and Queen

---

[1] The remote period when this occurred precluded the possibility of any minute account of it ; but the best extant is that just given by Mr. E. A. Freeman, in his History of the Reign of William Rufus and the Accession of Henry I.

"Katherine in 63, (whose Court was then at my House, the Abbey, in Bath,) I had the advantage
"of being first known to him, and it was the first time that ever he had been here. He then
"made several enquiries concerning these waters, and wrote to me afterwards about them, to which
"letters I gave answer. He from that time sent several persons (and some of great quality) hither
"and recommended them to my care, and came at length himself with his countryman, the Duke
"of Lauderdale (purposely to drink these Waters) in the year 73. The Duke, for more than
"ordinary Corpulency, and Scorbutical Distemper ; and he himself for an old cough, and Cachethic
"habit of body, and both went off much advantaged ; the Duke loosing a large Span of his Girt ;
"and Sir Alexander getting more Breath, and a fresh and better colour'd Countenance ; being pale,
"and sallow, and black under the Eyes, when he first came down. It was he that occasion'd the
"erecting of the little Drinking Pump, in the middle of the King's Bath, but done at the charge
"of the City."

BELL-TREE HOUSE and Benedictine Mission.—In the reign of Elizabeth the churches within the jurisdiction of her Charter, having previously been unjustly deprived of *all* their revenues, were consolidated, and the patronage vested in the Corporation. In consequence, St. James's was degraded to a curacy dependent upon the Abbey, and its Rectory-house was necessarily alienated. What its history may have been from that time until the period we are coming to, we cannot tell, but in 1713 the house became the property of the Bath Roman Catholics, with a ground-rent of £8 per annum, payable to the Corporation. The house occupied a portion of the site of the Royal United Hospital. At this time the Rev. Father *Bernard* Quin was "the incumbent." The history of the Mission until 1745 is one chiefly relating to the internal conduct of the house, the distinguished quality of some of its visitors, the kindly and friendly toleration of the Bath people and authorities during a time of disgraceful intolerance, and the simple every-day life of those who dwelt there. The house seems to have been used as an asylum for the Roman Catholic community who at that time came to the city, as well as a place for religious worship, the chapel being on the top storey. "During the rebellion of 1745, a fabricated letter was "forwarded to the Mayor of Bath,   *   *   *   *   *   *   and addressed, by "a supposed anonymous partisan of the rebellion, to the Right Rev. Dr. York. "It thanked the bishop for the men and money which he had *already* provided, "and for the supplies which he had promised ; and engaged to him the see "of Carlisle, in the event of the Prince's success. The mayor, satisfied in his "own mind of the forgery, waited on Dr. York, at Bell-Tree House, and was "soon convinced of the perfect innocence of the prelate, and of the malice of "the attempt on his life and character ; but, under all the circumstances of the "times, suggested the expediency of withdrawing himself, until the storm blew "over. This prudent counsel was duly acquiesced in." The Benedictine

Historic Houses in Bath and their Associations.

Mission from this time continued its labours without ostentation. In 1776, John *Bede* Brewer was appointed to the Bath Mission; in 1778 he commenced the Chapel on St. James's Parade. It was to have been opened for public worship on Sunday, June 11, 1780, but on Friday, 9th, the delegates from Lord George Gordon's association stirred up the mob; the Chapel was gutted and demolished, and all registers, archives, and Bishop Walmesley's Library and MSS. perished in the flames. The attack upon Bell-Tree House was beaten off. John Butler, the ringleader in this mob, was convicted at the following assizes at Wells, and hung on the 28th of August, at the end of Pear-Tree Lane, in Bath, without the least disturbance.[1] An action for damages was brought against the Hundred of Bath at Taunton, 30th March, 1781, and Dr. Brewer recovered £3,734 19s. 6d. He escaped himself, almost by miracle, from the infuriated rioters, was refused admission by two of the principle inns, and even at the Town Hall by the Beadles; but at last found refuge at the *White Lion*, and thence got away by a back door, across the river.

We are indebted to Mrs. Jervis (*vide* Letter, Introductory Chapter) for the discovery of all the papers that were saved,[2] from which she has made copious extracts, which are curious and interesting. They extend over a period of thirty years or more, and relate to persons, some of whom came there for economy and religious freedom, others for occasional change, others for these purposes as well as to exercise their religious opinions in peace and quietude, others who were rich—members of the old Roman Catholic families and aristocracy—to help the institution by their sympathy and their bounty. The names of the Countess of Leicester, the Pendrels, the Southwells, the Barkleys, the Arundells, the Pastons, the Doughtys, and Tichbornes, and many others, frequently occur in connection with the Accounts and in such incidents as Mrs. Jervis has collected.

---

[1] The Bath Chronicle of 15th June, 1780, gives a full account of these riots. From this account it appears that the rioters broke open the doors, destroyed the inside of the Chapel, and the materials and ornaments they set on fire on the Parade, and they were wholly consumed. It seems also that Dr. Brewer, the priest, occupied a house next door to the Chapel, which was very elegantly furnished, and was the occasional residence of Lord Arundell, of Wardour; and demolished the windows and window-panes, and threw all the furniture, linen, books, etc., into the flames, rifled the cellars, and drank or wasted all the wines and other liquors. Mrs. Mary English says -" I have heard my father say (and " his family often spoke of those times, though they occurred before his birth) that the man whom they " put to death, a poor drummer, whom the *real* instigators got to accompany them, beating his drum, " was the *most innocent* of the whole party. The real culprits were left at large, and this poor man " sacrificed to screen them - who, it is said, took no other part in the attack than beating his drum. " My father often pointed out the *White Lion* to me, and, as far as occasion occurred, patronized it " on this account."

[2] Copies of the original papers could be obtained from the Paris Archives for literary purposes, if it were desirable, but Mrs Jervis has extracted all that would be essential to an extended notice of the Bell-Tree Mission, which at some future time may be undertaken by a hand more competent than our own. It would, we think, be found that none of the papers connected with the *Mission House* were lost or destroyed.

This Mission, planted at the close of the seventeenth century, has existed in unbroken continuity to this day. Our concern, however, is limited to Bell-Tree House and its associations. The situation of the mansion was pleasant, being just within the walls, with a garden in front, and an uninterrupted view over the Ambury Mead to the south, and the King's Mead to the west.

At No. 11, NORTH PARADE.—In this house, in 1771, the EARL of CLARE[1] sojourned some years previous to that last visit of Mr. Burke's, which we have described in the next notice. The Earl was a genial, kind-hearted nobleman. He was the friend of Johnson and of Johnson's beloved friend, OLIVER GOLDSMITH. Lord Clare, on this as on former occasions, invited Goldsmith to visit him in Bath, and this was, we believe, his latest. In the same year, and at the same time, THE DUKE AND DUCHESS OF NORTHUMBERLAND[2] were at No. 10, NORTH PARADE. This was the first Duke of the present creation. He was Sir Hugh Smithson, who, after his marriage with Lady Elizabeth Seymour, whose mother, the Duchess of Somerset, was the sole heir of the Percys, assumed the name of Percy, and was created Duke of Northumberland in 1766. In Foster's "Life of Goldsmith," the following incident is related:—

"Goldsmith continued with Lord Clare during the opening months of "1771. They were together at Gosfield and at Bath; and it was in the latter "city the amusing incident occurred, Æt. 43, 1771, which Bishop Percy has "related, as told to him by the Duchess of Northumberland. The Duke and "Duchess occupied a house on one of the Parades, next door to Lord Clare's, "and were surprised one day, when about to sit down to breakfast, to see "Goldsmith enter the breakfast-room as from the street, and, without notice of "them, or the conversation they continued, fling himself unconcernedly 'in a "'manner the most free and easy,' on a sofa. After a few minutes, 'as he was "'then perfectly known to them both, they enquired of him the Bath news of

---

[1] The Earl of Clare must not be confounded with the family at present connected with that title. He was Richard Nugent, a member of an old Westmeath family, and was created Earl of Clare. The name and minor title of Baron Nugent ultimately merged into the Buckingham family. The Earl's daughter married the first Marquis of Buckingham, whose second son succeeded to the Irish Barony of Nugent and to a portion of his grandfather's estate on the death of his mother. He was an author of some repute, best known by his "Memorials of John Hampden," on which Lord Macaulay's exquisite essay was written. Lord Nugent was well known in Bath.

[2] In a little book, entitled "Memorable Houses," it is mentioned that the Dukes of Northumberland occupied a house in Westgate Street from 1683 to 1720. During that period there was no Duke nor Earl of Northumberland. The error was pardonable, because Mr. H. V. Lansdown, in his paper delivered before the Archæological Institute in Bath, in 1858, fell into a similar error, and the author of "Memorable Houses" seems to have adopted it and enlarged upon it. We can find no evidence to connect the Percy family with the house in question (See Article "Grapes Tavern").

"'the day; and imagining there was some mistake, endeavoured by easy and "'cheerful conversation to prevent his being too much embarrassed, till, "'breakfast being served up, they invited him to stay and partake of it'; but "upon this, the invitation calling him back from the dreamland he had been "visiting, he declared, with profuse apologies, that he had thought he was in his "friend Lord Clare's house, and in irrevocable confusion hastily withdrew. "'But not,' adds the Bishop, 'till they had kindly made him promise to dine "'with them.'" The Duke purchased 11, **Laura Place**, when it was in course of erection, and made it his occasional residence, until his death, in 1766.

At **No. 11, North Parade**, from Jan. until May, 1797, lived **EDMUND BURKE**. It was that brief but painful period which immediately preceded the "last scene of all." He came here, in his last illness, to try the effect of Bath air and the Baths, but only to return home, to use his own feeling words, to be "nearer a habitation more permanent." He died on July 9 of the same year. **THE RIGHT HON. W. WYNDHAM**,[1] who came to Bath at this time, says, " Feb. 4, arrived at Bath between six and seven. At Mr. Burke's, No. 11, North Parade, until bedtime. (6) Called upon Mr. Burke; went with him to *Wilberforce;* a Mr. Fuller against Dr. Priestly. Again to North Parade, when finding Mr. B. well, went to Ball to Miss Cholmondeley's. (7) Stayed at Mr. Burke's till half-past ten, he having had a return of his vomitings. I almost despair. Called again. Home—wrote letter to Dutheil. (8) Walked to Parade before breakfast to enquire after Mr. Burke. Again to Parade. Wrote till dressing for the Duchess of York; present, Lady Altamont and Lady M. Howe, Miss Cholmondeley,[2] Duchess of Newcastle, Lords Coleraine, Somerville, Northey, Fitzgerald." Mr. W. returned to London the following day.

Mr. Wilberforce, in speaking of the last interview that he and Mr. Windham had with Mr. Burke, says, "the attention shown to Mr. Burke by all that "party was just like the treatment of Ahitophel of old, 'it was as if one went to "enquire of the oracle of the Lord.'"

Bath was a place endeared to Mr. Burke by many earlier and interesting memories. *At Turley House,* near Bradford, he visited more than once his friend Mr. Atwood, whose family for two centuries had been connected with Bath. Mrs. Burke, of whom her husband spoke and wrote with such tender love and

---

[1] Mr. Windham stayed at the *York House.*

[2] This is the lady who afterwards married Lord Mulgrave, grandfather of the present Marquis of Normanby. Her portrait was painted by Gainsborough in Bath, and was sold May 27, 1882, at Christie's for 1070 gs., the purchaser being Mr. Agnew.

respect, was a Bath lady, whose father, **DR. CHRISTOPHER NUGENT**, lived at **Circus House**. After, or just before, her marriage with Mr. Burke, Dr. Nugent removed to London, and became a member of the famous Gerrard Street Club. Frequent mention is made of him in connection with Burke, Johnson, Goldsmith, Bennett Langton, Beauclerc, etc., etc.

Mr. Windham, it appears from his Diary, had been to Bath on many occasions besides that referred to above. In 1791, June 10.—" During the journey to Bath I don't think I felt quite the same as on other similar occasions. The air seemed as usual to refresh me, but I doubt if I felt the same enjoyment of the country. (12) Went to the Abbey Church. Walked after church with Wilberforce, who had arrived the night before, and whom I had called upon as he was at supper; our conversation on religious subjects. He adopts, as I understand, the Trinitarian doctrine, but not in any absurd way. I had settled with Mr. Lukin to go to Marlborough in the evening, but having in the meanwhile met with Elliot, he prevailed upon me to stay that evening, to which, indeed, I was further inclined by having received intelligence of a boxing-match that was to take place on the Tuesday, and to which I proposed to go with him. Went in the evening by agreement with him to the Duke of Devonshire's, where I settled to dine with the Duke next day, and to meet Lord Charlemont."

THE EARL OF CHESTERFIELD'S mansion (built by Wood) was in **PIERREPONT STREET**, opposite the Doric Portico. It is now divided into two (3a and 4). He was one of those who took an active part, in conjunction with the Earl of Bath, Ralph Allen, Nash, and others, who laid the foundation-stone July the 6th, 1738, in promoting the General Water Hospital, and forming its " Scheme of Rules." His name stands immediately after that of Ralph Allen. Lord Chesterfield married Melosina de Schulemburgh, natural daughter of King George I., but had no legitimate issue. The Letters to his natural son, Philip Stanhope, were, some of them at least, written in Bath. On the death of the latter, the following epigram appeared :—

"Vile Stanhope ! demons blush to tell,
 In twice two hundred places,
Has shown his son the road to hell,
 Escorted by the graces.

But little did th' ungenerous lad
 Concern himself about them ;
For base, degenerate, meanly bad,
 He sneak'd to hell without them."

THOMAS LINLEY lived at **5, Pierrepont Street**, in which house his lovely daughter, Mrs. Sheridan, was born. Linley was by trade a builder; but having studied music under the famous organist, Chilcott, he ultimately confined his attention exclusively to that profession. Linley conducted the oratorios and concerts of the city. When Sheridan became the lessee of Drury Lane Theatre, on the death of Garrick, Linley became joint patentee with him, and conducted the musical department (see article, *Sheridan*). Mr. Linley's highly-gifted son, Thomas Linley the younger, was drowned.

At **No. 2, Pierrepont Street**, the house of Mr. Spry (father of Dr. Spry, physician, a writer on the Bath Waters), from the autumn of 1780 to August, 1781, lived England's future greatest Naval Hero—**ADMIRAL VISCOUNT NELSON**.
" Unbounded courage and compassion joined,
Tempering each other in the victor's mind,
Alternately proclaim him good and great,
And make the hero and the man complete."

After distinguishing himself in a thousand ways, he in 1780 (being in his 22nd year) was appointed to command the sea part of the Expedition against Fort St. Juan, on the Rio San Juan, which runs from the great American lake Nicaragua into the Atlantic. The object of the Expedition was, by taking possession of the Fort, to cut off the Spaniards' communications between their northern and southern dominions in America. By the climate, and by his great exertions, Nelson's health became most seriously deranged, and he was obliged to be removed to the lodging-house of Cuba in his cot. Some idea may be formed of his exertions and the climatic sufferings he endured, when, as he says, he " carried troops in boats 100 miles up a river, whilst none but Spaniards since " the time of the buccaneers, had ever ascended that river." He says:—" He made " batteries and fought them," and as usual, wherever he went, he contributed largely to the success of the Expedition. On his return to Europe, he was ordered to Bath.[1] He tells his friend Capt. Locker that he is attended by Dr. Woodward, of whom he always spoke and wrote in terms of gratitude; he relates his experience of the Baths; says he is a most docile patient; that his friend is to send all his sick

[1] Captain Mark Robinson was the Commander of the *Worcester*, in which Nelson served as acting Lieutenant in 1776-7. Captain Thomas Pitt Robinson, R.N., his grandson, lived for many years at 20, Henrietta Street, and died in Bath a few years ago. Admiral JOSEPH BULLEN, who lived for many years at No. 13, Raby Place, and who died at the patriarchal age of 97, in 1858, was a Lieut. in the Royal Navy, and took part in Rodney's action, of 1782. He was personally acquainted with Lord Nelson, of whom he always spoke in affectionate terms. Admiral Bullen, besides the severe action of " '82," was under fire in some seventy "affairs," but was never touched.

friends, especially those suffering from climatic disorders, to Bath. On Feb. 15, 1781, he writes :—" My health, thank God, is very near perfectly restored, and I have the perfect use of my limbs, except my left arm." On the 21st he says to the same friend :—" I wish you had come to Bath. . . . I am sure yours is a Bath case. . . . As to my health, it is perfectly restored, although I shall remain here a few weeks longer, that it may be firmly fixed." He remained in Bath, in fact, until August, when he was appointed to the *Albemarle*, of 28 guns, and was employed in the North Sea. In 1784, Captain Nelson came again to Bath to visit his father, the Rev. Edmund Nelson, Rector of Burnham Thorpe, Norfolk, who had been ill. Writing to his brother, the Rev. William Nelson, Rector of Brandon Parva (who succeeded to the ultimate honours and wealth conferred upon his great and heroic brother), he says :—" I am happy I can say that our father never was so well since I can remember; he is grown quite lusty. His cheeks are plumped out . . . and it is all solid flesh." He then refers to his niece and expresses an intention of spending the autumn at Brandon; but in March he was appointed to the *Boreas* frigate. In September,[1] 1797, and in January, 1798, then Lord Nelson, he came most probably to visit his father, who was in declining health. After the Copenhagen affair his father was still in Bath, where he died, on the 26th of April, 1802. Lord Nelson was too ill to visit his father in his last illness, but the husband of the " Kitty " referred to, Mr. Matcham, wrote as follows to Lord Nelson, his uncle-in-law :—

" MY DEAR LORD,—
" Your good old father is very ill, and I have directions from Dr. Parry " and Mr. Spry to say to you that he is certainly in great danger. Whatever " orders you send me shall be executed.
" Believe me, my dear Lord,
" Yours affectionately,
" April 24th, 1802. " G. MATCHAM."

The Rev. Edmund Nelson was buried at Burnham Thorpe on the 11th of May.

In the " Bath Journal " of January 27, 1766, appears the following obituary notice :--" Tuesday morning, died at his Lodgings in this city, " **MR. QUIN**, the celebrated comedian, who had retired from the stage some years." There seems to have been little known locally of this famous actor, and his death, judging from this notice, excited little or no interest ; the house in which

[1] On March 20, 1797, the Corporation conferred upon Lord Nelson the Freedom of the city.

he died not even being mentioned, though there is little doubt it occurred in the same house which long before had been occupied by Lord Chesterfield in **Pierrepont Street.**[1] Quin really came to Bath for rest and tranquillity. He walked about the meadows, frequented the reading-rooms and the pump-room, where he met and conversed with the famous men of the day. In the latter, sauntering about in quiet conversation with a friend one day, a young buck put his hands upon the actor's shoulders and vaulted over his head, much to his astonishment and indignation. Turning complacently round to Mr. Quin, the buck said, "There, Mr. Quin, what would you give to be able to do that?" "Why, sir," said Mr. Quin, "I would give a thousand pounds to be able to make "half such a fool of myself!" He was buried in the Abbey, and Garrick wrote his epitaph, and, as this is in nearly every guide-book, and can be seen in the Abbey, we think it needless to quote it here. Upon the *grave-stone*, in the centre aisle of the nave, is the inscription :—

" Here lies the Body of Mr. James Quin.
" The scene is chang'd—I am no more :
" Death's the last act—now all is o'er."

Quin used to say that he did not know a better place than Bath for an old cock to roost in.

SIR WALTER SCOTT, in his early boyhood, was brought to Bath in 1777 ; he was slightly lame from a congenital affection of the foot, to cure which recourse was had, with great effect, to the *Thermal Douche.* Robert Scott, his uncle, had charge of him, and they resided at **6, South Parade.** Sir Walter never saw Bath again, though he retained "the most minute recollection of all "the striking features of the city" to his latest years. It was in Bath, where (as also with Southey), in the Old Orchard-Street Theatre, he first experienced the sensation peculiar to his imaginative nature on seeing his first play. He has himself alluded, in his Memoir, to the lively recollection he retained of his first visit to the theatre, to which his uncle Robert carried him to witness a representation of "As You Like It." In his "Reviewal of the Life of John Kemble," written in 1826, he has recorded that impression more fully, and in terms so striking, that we give it full :—

---

[1] This is partly confirmed by the following extract from Quin's will :—" Item, I give and be-"queath unto Mrs. Mary Simpson, landlady of the center house, in Pierrepont Street, Bath, One "hundred pounds, to be paid by my executors into her own hands, independent of all creditors "whatever."

Richard Lovell Edgeworth was born in this street (the number of the house we do not know), in 1744. Himself eminent, he was the father of a still more eminent daughter, Maria Edgeworth, the novelist.

"There are few things which those gifted with any degree of imagination recollect with a sense of more anxious and mysterious delight than the first dramatic representation which they have witnessed. The unusual form of the house, filled with such groups of crowded spectators, themselves forming an extraordinary spectacle to the eye which had never witnessed it before; yet all intent upon that wide and mystic curtain, whose dusky undulations permit us now and then to discern the momentary glitter of some gaudy form, or the spangles of some sandalled foot, which trips lightly within; then the light, brilliant as that of day; then the music, which, in itself a treat sufficient in every other situation, our inexperience mistakes for the very play we came to witness; then the slow rise of the shadowy curtain, disclosing, as if by actual magic, a new land, with woods, and mountains, and lakes, lighted, it seems to us, by another sun, and inhabited by a race of beings different from ourselves, whose language is poetry,—whose dress, demeanour, and sentiments seem something supernatural,—and whose whole actions and discourse are calculated not for the ordinary tone of every-day life, but to excite the stronger and more powerful faculties—to melt with sorrow, overpower with terror, astonish with the marvellous, or convulse with irresistible laughter :—all these wonders stamp indelible impressions on the memory. Those mixed feelings, also, which perplex us between a sense that the scene is but a plaything, and an interest which ever and anon surprises us into a transient belief that that which so strongly affects us cannot be fictitious ; those mixed and puzzling feelings, also, are exciting in the highest degree. Then there are the bursts of applause, like distant thunder, and the permission afforded to clap our little hands, and add our own scream of delight to a sound so commanding. All this, and much, much more, is fresh in our memory, although, when we felt these sensations, we looked on the stage which Garrick had not yet left. It is now a long while since ; yet we have not passed many hours of such unmixed delight, and we still remember the sinking lights, the dispersing crowd, with the vain longings which we felt that the music would again sound, the magic curtain once more arise, and the enchanting dream recommence ; and the astonishment with which we look upon the apathy of the elder part of our company, who, having the means, did not spend every evening in the theatre."--*Life, vol. I.*

He was particularly struck with the stone figure of Neptune, which stood at that time near the South-Parade ferry.

SOUTHEY'S early youth, too, was spent in Bath. He was brought up by his aunt, MISS TYLER, who lived in a detached house within a walled garden sloping down to the river in Walcot Street. The premises were formerly Messrs. Holmes's timber-yard, but are now in the occupation of Messrs. Hayward and Wooster, builders, and the house may still be seen. Miss Tyler was a friend of Gainsborough, who painted her portrait, which was disposed of by Christie and Manson on May 27, 1882, for 600 guineas. It was during his residence here with his aunt that Southey first enjoyed that bright evening in boyhood's life—the sight of his first play in the old Orchard-Street Theatre.[1] As he grew older, he was sent to a boarding-school at Corston, near Bath, of which the son records his father's impressions.[2]

[1] See "Life of Southey," vol. I. [2] Ibid, vol. I., Letters 1 to 15.

WORDSWORTH, the Poet, visited Bath on several occasions. In May, 1841, the poet came to Bath, on the occasion of his daughter's marriage with Mr. Quillinan at St. James's Church. On that occasion he occupied apartments at **9, North Parade**, and during his sojourn in Bath he was a constant visitor to Summer-hill, the residence of his intimate friend, Dr. Parry. In March, 1847, the poet again visited the city, and lodged in Queen Square. The late *Mr. C. Godwin*, who was known to Mr. Wordsworth, showed us a copy of his Poems, which the latter had most courteously presented to him, during his stay in Bath, at that period.

No. 7, ORANGE GROVE—now "**The Cross Keys Inn**"—in the former half of the last century was a watchmaker's shop, kept by a respectable citizen named **Lawrence**. He had two sons born in this house—**FRENCH LAWRENCE** and **RICHARD LAWRENCE**. French was a distinguished politician, the friend and executor of Edmund Burke. Dr. Richard Lawrence was the last Archbishop of Cashel, having succeeded Archbishop Brodrick, father of the former Rector of Bath, who became Viscount Midleton.

NASSAU HOUSE—a modern name—in the **Orange Grove**,[1] has been erroneously described as the residence of the Prince of Orange. The mansion was most probably first occupied by the nobleman who built and designed it—about 1730—the **EARL OF CORK AND BURLINGTON**.[2] The Earl was a man of taste, an architect of no mean pretensions, as this edifice attests. Lord Cork was the friend and companion of Pope, who, in his "Epistle to Richard Boyle," says :—

" Who then shall grace, or who improve the soil?
Who plants like Bathurst,[3] or who builds like Boyle?"

After the Earl of Cork and Burlington's death, the house became the Bath residence of the **EARL OF HOWTH**, about 1780. Lord Howth's daughter, Lady Frances St. Lawrence, married, in 1808, the Rector and Archdeacon of Bath, the Rev. J. Phillott. Lord Howth was maternal grandfather of the present **Earl of Cork and Orrery**. There was also a house situated on St. James's Rampier (part of the site of R.U. Hospital)—the design and architecture of which were also attributed to the Earl of Cork and Burlington—occupied by **DR. BAVE**, a physician of great eminence. He was born at Colen, in Germany, in

---

[1] The gabled houses on the south side were built in 1706.
[2] The Earl of Cork and Burlington died in 1753, when the English honours became extinct, the Irish honours devolving upon his kinsman, the 5th Earl of Orrery, who thus became Earl of Cork and Orrery, from whom is descended the present Earl of Cork and Orrery.
[3] Earl Bathurst, who planted Oakley Park, near Cirencester.

1588. Dr. Guidott describes him in very laudatory terms, and wrote his Latin Epitaph in the Abbey. The tablet cannot be found. Bave seems to have been one of the "old school," dressed in purple velvet and fine linen, gave "himself airs," strutted like a dandy, which he affected to be, but no doubt was a man of ability and great benevolence.

The **EARL OF SANDWICH** occupied Nos. 14 & 15, Orange Grove in 1794. The character of Orange Grove has been greatly changed. It was at one time, when the trees were standing, and it was intersected only by neat paths, a little *russe in urbe*. Several of the houses were, as we have shown, occupied by high-class residents, and others were highly respectable Boarding-houses, where visitors were "taken in and done for," in a sense not conformable to modern usuage. In 1838, the trees were cut down, and the carriage-road constructed to the North Parade. *Macadam* has superseded the shady groves, and the whisperings of lovers have given place to the perpetual clatter of wheels. Where formerly stood the **LOWER ROOMS**, and on the identical site, we have the **ROYAL LITERARY AND SCIENTIFIC INSTITUTION**,[1] in which the exertions of the *toes* have given place to the exertions of the *head*; where quiet contemplation prevails, instead of the mirth of the days when Mrs. Piozzi, in 1819, at 80 was equal in agility to the youngest of her guests assembled to do her honour on her birthday. (See Note on "*Nash*," for an account of duel in the Grove.)

BATH ABBEY.—When **Wells** successfully re-asserted her claim to become the residential city of the Bishop, **Bath**, though nominally (as it continues to be) the titular head of the United See, was administered by a **Prior**, who was also the chief of the monastic order. The Prior, there is little doubt, lived in the monastery. The Reformation not only brought this to an end, but destroyed the continuity of even the semblance of an ecclesiastical establishment. The result was, for a time at least, that, after the unjust spoliation by the king, the incumbent was dependent for his income, either on his private fortune, or gifts, offerings, and such other small legal pickings as remained, amongst which were the fees for interment in the Abbey.[2] Persons in former days had an irresistible fancy for "snug lying." Personal distinction in itself was not necessary to

[1] The origin of the Institution is given in the late Rev. J. Hunter's little work "The Connec-tion of Bath with the Literature and Science of England," and a more recent account will be found in "Rambles about Bath."

[2] In 1666, **ANTHONY Á WOOD** compiled an account of the mural tablets and other memorial stones to persons most of whom were, up to that period, interred in the Abbey. This account was deposited in the Bodleian Library, Oxford, but not published. **Mr. John Godwin** has carefully tran-scribed Wood's record, and in 1881 printed a very small number of copies for personal friends. From this account, it appears that as early a period as 1666, as many as 390 tables and stones were counted of persons buried (and of others not buried) in the church. About the time when interment at

obtain the privilege of sepulture in the Abbey; the sole qualification was the ability of the survivors to pay a lumping fee. The source of revenue gradually resolved itself into the ordinary official fees and pew-rents, the latter of which only necessity in such a church as the Abbey can justify. In the list of Rectors a great many were local men, nominees of the Council, and we do not remember any, except the *Rev. Joseph Glanville*, writer on "Witchcraft and Apparitions" (1666—1684), and *Carte*, the historian, who emerged from local obscurity. In later days, the Rectors of Bath have been men of high social position, distinguished by zeal, ability, and the highest attributes of Christian gentlemen :— Dean Law, the Hon. and Rev. W. J. Brodrick[1] (afterwards Dean of Exeter and Viscount Midleton), Bishop Carr (formerly Bishop of Bombay), the Rev. Charles Kemble, and Canon Brooke. Mr. Kemble was a man of singular energy and force of character. To him we are no doubt indebted, first, for that work of restoration and reconstruction, which involved an outlay of £30,000, of which at least one half he contributed himself;[2] and then for purifying the Abbey as a charnel-house. However much one might differ from him on many points, no fault could be found with him as to his habit and prudent method of giving. The name of CHARLES KEMBLE will occupy a prominent if not the very first place amongst the benefactors of Bath, and they are many. It was, however, not only with regard to the Abbey and its restoration he made his influence felt. He took a warm interest in all important institutions, on which he brought his vigorous judgment to bear. On all

interments were forbidden by law, about 40 years ago, 580 tablets and about 750 stones were counted. Assuming that a large proportion of persons were interred to whom no memorial was raised, it is probable that from first to last 2,500 persons were buried in the building. A correct copy of the inscriptions upon the floor now covered by the seats has been made by Mr. Russell, and a list of all the tablets upon the walls.

[1] Shortly after the appointment of the Rev. W. J. Brodrick to the living, his attention was called to the fact that the only place of sepulture provided for parishioners of the Abbey parish was within the walls of the church itself. He at once took steps to remedy this evil by establishing at his own cost the "Abbey cemetery," and thus rescuing the sacred edifice from its character as a charnel-house. The last interment in the church was on the 29th Jan., 1845.

[2] This little work has to do with Historic Houses and their Associations, and takes no note of the ecclesiastical history, as such, of the city, a subject which may be dealt with at some future time in a separate paper. Still, it is not possible to avoid incidentally referring to men who, whilst their lives and primary labours have been identified with ecclesiastical functions, have left their mark upon the temporal and secular history of the city. When the Abbey was in the course of erection, the monastery and the revenues of the Abbey were surrendered to Henry the Eighth, and the edifice was left a mere shell; and as to revenue there was not so much left as a mere endowment for a parish rectory. The Abbey was partly roofless, and only by the munificence of Bishop Montagu, Bellot, Pelling, and others, was it rendered fit for public worship as late as 1616. In the year 1573, under letters-patent of Queen Elizabeth, the several parishes of the city were consolidated into one rectory, with the vicarage of Lyncombe and Widcombe appended, and the incumbent of the Abbey was instituted as Rector of Bath and Vicar of Lyncombe and Widcombe, each several parish being under the charge of a curate. By the same letters-patent, its patronage was vested in the Corporation, and exercised by that body until the passing of the Municipal Corporation Act in 1836. In June, 1837, the advowson was sold for £6,330, to the late Rev. Charles Simeon, in whose Trustees it is now vested.

occasions when a firm hand and a clear head were necessary to guide the counsels of important public movements, he was ever ready with his purse and his co-operation. It may be said that he exhausted himself with details connected with public business which inferior men could have done equally well; but if he once set himself a task he allowed no one else to perform it. · If wealth did exercise any prejudicial effect upon his character, it was that occasionally he seemed to think that what he could do by the aid of wealth, others might do with equal facility without it. He thought so little of wealth in itself that he appeared to be unconscious of its power and importance.

On the north side of the Abbey, previous to 1830, there stood a congeries of mean parasitical houses. They seemed as if they clung to the Abbey, and were making ineffectual efforts to climb its venerable sides. The history of them is as follows :—In 1584 a *Sir Richard Meradith* was presented to the Abbey Rectory. A corrupt stipulation was made to the effect that he should grant a lease to the Mayor and chief citizens of *all* the property belonging to the five churches, their church-yards, lands, rents, issues, and profits, including even obventions and oblations, reserving nothing for himself but the vicarage-house of *Stalls*. This lease was made for 50 years, if the lessor should so long live, under the yearly rent of sixty-two pounds. Availing themselves of this opportunity to apply the lands belonging to the churches to their own use, the Mayor and chief citizens immediately began to erect mansions [1] upon the consecrated ground for the residence of themselves and their connections. *Stalls* churchyard was covered with houses and the Abbey Church polluted, disgraced, and spoiled by the mean residences of private individuals being attached to its august walls.[2] From this period Stalls Church declined; service was discontinued there; neglect permitted time gradually to crumble it into ruins; its remains were removed, and even the remembrance of its exact site is lost and forgotten.[3] Nor was this all, for so completely did these buildings cover the ground that all egress from the church-yard was blocked, *and a common passage was made through the north aisle of the Abbey*. To remedy the evil, Marshal Wade took a most active part, contributing very "bountifully" towards meeting the expense incurred, in making an alley of "communication between the Walks and the pump," which was called **Wade's Alley**.[4]

---

[1] A photograph from an old print is published by Cloakley.   [2] Warner, p. 241.
[3] Warner, p. 241.   Since Warner wrote, a crypt of well built masonry was discovered under the premises now occupied by Mr. Winstone opposite the Grand Pump-room Hotel, and there is little doubt it formed a part of Stalls Church.
[4] Wood, p. 329.

The unreformed Corporation were engaged from 1823 until 1834 in clearing away these vile deformities—the cost of doing which was £10,640.

"The citizens of Bath, with vast delight,
To hide their noble church from vulgar sight,
Surround its venerable sides with shops,
And decorate its walls with chimney-tops."

No. 14, Abbey Churchyard was the Bath residence of **MARSHAL WADE**, who represented the city in several Parliaments. There is every reason to believe that the Marshal was much liked in the city, and rendered the Hanoverian cause, of which he was such a resolute champion, popular. Whatever he might have been when repressing the Stuart insurrections, he showed little of the coarseness and austerity of manner to the Bathonians which were said to characterise him in his military commands. There was a bluff, good nature about him in his intercourse with the citizens; and he certainly exhibited no little generosity in the support he rendered to the local charities and the various institutions of the city. We are left in doubt as to the precise nature of the services he entrusted to Ralph Allen; but whatever they were, the Marshal was duly sensible of their importance and of the manner in which they were performed. In that little post-office in *Lilliput Alley*, where Allen was a clerk, some grave political conspiracy was first revealed, with so much care and circumspection, that in all probability it enabled the Government to take timely measures of precaution; and, if we are right in supposing that the facts brought to light occurred after the first ineffectual Jacobite rising, it is probable that any contemplated renewal of that attempt[1] was prevented.[2] The Marshal died in 1748.

The houses on that side of the Abbey Churchyard were much deeper than they are at present, extending some feet into Cheap Street, then a narrow, irregular street, and which was made what it now is when street improvements were made in the early part of the century.

"**GRAPES TAVERN**," **Westgate Street.**—This house is sometimes called "*Northumberland House*," but for what reason we cannot tell. We can find no trace of its connection with the family of Percy. There are other traditions relating to this house, but little information on which any reliance can

---

[1] In "Memorable Houses" it is said that Ralph Allen's services to the Government had reference to "the '45." This is absurd, as by that time he was over middle age, and had long been rich and famous.

[2] It is said that the discovery was connected with a supply of arms and ammunition for those who were favourable to the cause of the Pretender, but it is only conjectural.

(To go Opposite Page 39)

be placed. About the time which may be called the *Renaissance* period—*i.e.*, from 1720 to the close of the century—this, with the other old mansions in the same locality, was greatly altered, the old front having been removed and the present substituted. Mr. H. V. Lansdown,[1] who had given much study to the old mansions of the city, had not the courage to dismiss the Northumberland theory, which is quite incompatible with what he says afterwards with better reasons :—" It is " probable that, before that time (1720), the house belonged to the Earl of Bath, " as the *Roman Eagle* appears on the escutcheons in the interior; and this privilege " of bearing the paternal coat of arms was granted to Charles, Lord Bath's son, for " his great services at Vienna in 1683, for which services he was created Earl of " Lansdowne."[2] The only evidence as to this connection of the Grenville family with this house is the heraldic device, and it seems very likely that, Sir Bevil's son having selected Bath as the place from which to derive his title, and the associations of his gallant father with the city having especial attraction for for him, he would make it the place of his occasional abode. No reference is made in any historical record of any interest having been taken by the family in the city.

At present, the chief feature of this interesting house is preserved in the plaster ceiling of the drawing-room, to which Mr. Lansdown refers. It is a geometrical, elaborate, and fantastical ribbed piece of skilful plasterer's work, similar to ceilings at Wraxall and other Jacobean manor-houses. It is contemporary most likely with the gabled eastern end of the house, the northern end of which faces Westgate Street. Its date is probably about 1680 to 1700, and it may be that the northern front was altered on a later occasion; but this plaster ceiling is very beautiful, exhibiting birds and heads in low relief, and is well worth a visit. (See articles, " *Goldsmith*," and " *Duke of Northumberland*.")

LONDONDERRY, or ROSEWELL'S HOUSE.[3]—Beyond the West Gate of the old city walls—now destroyed—and on the west side of **Kingsmead Square**, stand the remains of an almost unique type of the Muscular Architecture of the

---

[1] The Monument on Lansdown was erected in 1720, by George, Lord Lansdowne, grandson of Sir Bevil Grenville, and nephew of the Earl of Bath (Sir Bevil's eldest son). The Earldom of Bath became extinct in 1711, and in December of that year the Barony of Lansdowne was conferred upon the above-mentioned George Grenville, who died without male issue in 1734. Neither Warner nor Wood makes it clear who this Lord Lansdowne was by whom the Monument was erected. It should be mentioned that Johnson thought him worthy of a place in his "Lives of the Poets."

[2] This is an error. He was not created Earl of Lansdowne, but was called to the House of Peers in his father's Barony of Grenville of Kilkhampton in Cornwall, in 1696. He was made a Count of the Empire. He succeeded his father as Earl of Bath in 1701, and was accidentally shot the same year.

The Earls of Bath have been as follows :—Philibert de Shaunder (1), Bourchier (5), Grenville (3), Pulteney (1).

[3] See Frontispiece.

early part of the immediately past century. It is now a sooty-coloured three-storeyed dwelling; its main and most elaborate though narrowest front is facing the square, its length facing Kingsmead Street. The other faces are of a mean character. Considering its interesting past history and its connection with those who had more than a local celebrity, its present humbled use may almost be said to be a desecration, as it now serves as the abodes, on the flat-system, of several families of a lower class. The chief front is divided vertically into three main divisions, by means of slightly projecting pilasters. The curved-pediment grouping of the central part is rather an unusual feature, whilst the architraves of the windows are elaborated by the still lingering scrolls and men supporting pilasters of the Elizabethan era. On the ground floor is the porticoed main entrance.

The window architraves of the flanking divisions are also well and characteristically moulded, and the keystones of the middle storey have well-modelled and finished heads, carved in high relief; those of the upper storey have rather heavy and obtrusive-looking cornices. Over the top window of the central division, the cornice bears a shield, on which is carved the *rebus* of a *Rose* and a *Well*, to indicate the connection of the *Rosewells* with the house; this shield stands on a base, which bears the date 1736.

The elevation facing Kingsmead Street is of much greater length than that facing the Square, and notwithstanding the many obliterative and destructive alterations of the varied owners and residents since the Square was occupied by the wealthy, it still bears evidence of its original importance and skilful design. On each of the two upper floors there are eight recessed and well-moulded window-openings, the third and sixth from either end being emphasised by large scrolled terminations. A good projecting cornice completes this elevation.

But little remains of the corresponding internal completeness of this interesting house. The humbler and lesser requirements of its various occupants have from time to time destroyed its ichnography. The oak staircase, however, is the original one—wide, easy, massive, and good.

At one time, this house had a considerable garden attached to it in the *King's Mead*, which had an unobstructed breadth to the river.

The house has been known under various names:—*Londonderry; Rosewell's House;* and *Chapman's House.* Its associations are varied and interesting. It was built in 1736 by a rival of Wood, a Bristol architect, named *John Strahan*, for T. Rosewell, who was, we believe, a builder by trade. He disposed of the house in 1744. Besides many occupants of local celebrity, it was rendered more famous by being selected as the residence of *Bishop Butler*, author of " *The*

Analogy of Religion," who died in it in 1752. *Dr. Abel Moysey*, a celebrated physician, lived here. His son was President of the Bath General Hospital in 1784, Mayor of Bath in 1792 and 1810, and represented this city in Parliament in 1774, 1775, 1780, and 1784 to 1790. The late Archdeacon Moysey was his grandson. There is no evidence of any of the Chapmans having resided in the house, and we cannot explain the connection of the name with it.

No 13, KINGSMEAD STREET, occupied by Messrs. Green and Marsh. There is nothing in the architectural features of this house, or in its history, to connect it with any known interesting associations. But in one respect it gives rise to some speculative assumptions, and that is the series of exquisite medallions, which we will endeavour to describe.

The internal evidences of the importance and taste of an early owner or occupier of these premises marks a period of the Renaissance of ceramic or plastic art, about contemporary with *Wedgwood* and *Flaxman.*

The room at the rear of the premises is well-modelled. On the North side are two large oval medallions, symbolical of Autumn and Winter.

Over the door is an allegory which is difficult to make out—a lion on what appears to be rockwork immediately over the architrave; or possibly it may be a crest, the wreath, if it be a wreath, being partly obliterated.

On the South, corresponding with those of the opposite side, are two lozenge medallions, symbolizing Spring and Summer, and two smaller oblong panels denoting sacrificial subjects.

The Eastern side has two similar lozenge medallions, which may be Hebe and Pomona, and two smaller oblong medallions, both of which derive their inspiration and design from Cupid and his Loves.

The centre is occupied by a large mirror frame embedded in the wall in similar style, and into which are incorporated six classical figure-subjects.

On the West side are two lozenge medallions of dancing-girls. Two small mirror frames and two oblong medallions of Europa and the Bull, a square Bacchanalian subject, and a well-modelled group of the death of the stag, and two subjects of Cupid and the golden apple and the burning torch.

The Ceiling is well designed in low relief.

The subjects are executed in plaster, and are very suggestive of Wedgwood and Flaxman. May it not be probable that when Wedgwood was here with his wife this house was then drawing towards completion, and that to shew the special aptitude of the ceramic art for decorative purposes, he walked down from his "show-rooms" in Westgate Buildings, close by, and executed these very medallions?

In 1772-1773, **JOSIAH WEDGWOOD** established a branch business here for the sale of his Pottery. Mrs. Wedgwood, it appears, was a martyr to chronic rheumatism, brought on "from her residence in newly-built houses." In April of 1772, Wedgwood, accompanied by his wife, came to Bath by slow stages. "The show-rooms in **Westgate Buildings**,[1] which Mr. Bentley had chosen "early in the year, were not yet opened,[2] and such time therefore that Wedgwood "could spare from attending the invalid to the pump rooms or in country drives, "was devoted to their preparation, and of this we have some interesting "particulars." In a letter from Wedgwood to Bentley, dated from Bath, June 2, 1772, he writes:—" Though the season is now nearly over, yet there seems (to "me at least) a good deal of company here; and I wish you would enable us to "open our Rooms, as I have found some of my good friends here would "bestow some pains in advertising for us. These good folks will stay a week or " 10 days here, if you could but send us something worth shewing immediately, " but we must not baulk the thing in its first starting—Green Bayze—we shall "want a good deal & the lowest we can buy here is 2/4. I have a notion you " buy it much cheaper about 18d P. yd . . . . Yellow paper for a back " ground for the black Vases, & the colour (we none of us know what it is) we " put behind the pebble Vases; we must trouble you to send it as there is none " to be got here at any rate. . . . The carpenters are more expeditious than " I expected & will have things so forward in another day or two, that we could " open the Rooms if we had anything to shew. We have recd the packages you " mention, but those I understand are only Pebble Vases & painted Deserts, we " must have all the Gimcracks in the useful ware, gems, Pictures, flowerpots, &c. " &c., in short it is our united opinion that we should not open at all till you " enable us to make a very complete shew, for there are tolerably decent shops " enow here already—we found Mr. Palmer—and Mrs. Chatterly here. It was " currently reported in Staffordshire, that Mr. Palmer was trying here to establish " a warehouse of his goods. He is gone home this morning, Mrs. Wedgwood " and I took him a few miles on his way, but have not heard anything of this " design from him or Mrs. Chatterly, but I think we can know from the latter if " there is any truth in it." ("*Meteyard's Life of Wedgwood*," vol. 2, pp. 270—271.)

[1] This disposes of the statement in "Memorable Houses" that Wedgwood's show-rooms were at 1, Milsom Street. We suspect it was Palmer (Wedgwood's unworthy rival) who lived there and who is referred to above.

[2] The "Bath Chronicle" of the period announces in an advertisement that the show-rooms are "opened at Mr. Ward's," but the number of the house is not given.

In **Chapel Court**, once a fashionable quarter, when visitors liked to be near the Baths, there is a house in the north-east corner of some dignity still, though defaced, dirty, and inhabited by several families. The house was the residence of the fastidious **HORACE WALPOLE**, in 1765. One cannot pass through this now dingy Court without noticing this fine mansion, possessing as it does all the characteristics of the best houses built in Bath during the early part of the last century.

BEAU NASH.—Having endeavoured in our Preface to analyse the character of Mr. Nash, we shall limit the notice in this article to a few of the "associations" connected with the monarch of pleasure. We know he was born at Swansea, Oct. 16, 1674; that his father was a man of respectability; that he sent Richard to the University, that he became an idler, gave his father trouble, and anxiety, and showed few qualities of a redeeming character. Goldsmith[1] puts the case with his usual neatness.[2] Mr. Nash first tried the Army; but it interfered with his pleasure. We suspect that fighting was to be done at that time, and we know he was too humane for *that*. At any rate, he gave up the army. It would be a mistake to say that he studied law; he did not, though he made a pretence of doing so, whilst he was really going through an arduous preparation for those regal duties which he was afterwards called upon to perform.

Dr. Cheyne said Nash had no father; but he certainly had, and the only touch of nature he ever evinced was when the Duchess of Marlborough once twitted him with the obscurity of his birth, and compared him to *Gil Blas*. He said, "Madam, I seldom mention my father in company, not because I have any "reason to be ashamed of him, but because he has some reason to be ashamed "of me."[3] We know that the special training of Mr. Nash made some progress by the fact that when William III. was entertained by the members of the Middle Temple, he was then so far advanced *in the law* as to be chosen Master of the Ceremonies. Goldsmith assures us that Mr. Nash had "some virtues," one

---

[1] Life, p. 9.

[2] In the Preface we have stated that Goldsmith received £15 from the Corporation to write the Life of Beau Nash. The statement is not a new one; it was made and published many years ago by Dr. Tunstall, whose alleged authority was the minute-book of the Corporation. On examining that book (which we ought to have done before printing the sheet), no such statement can be found. It is clear from Goldsmith's "Life" that he sold the copyright to Newbery, the publisher, in St. Paul's Churchyard. The name of *Frederick*, a local bookseller, is also in the title-page, and it is not unlikely he may have negotiated the purchase. The following is a copy of Goldsmith's receipt for the money he received for the copyright, and, as Mr. Foster observes, "it appears quite a surprising performance for "fourteen guineas":—" Receiv'd from Mr. Newbery at different times, and for which I gave receipts "fourteen guineas, which is in full for the Copy of the Life of Mr. Nash. Oliver Goldsmith."

[3] Life, p. 7.

of which was that "he never went in a dirty shirt to disgrace the table of his patron "or his friend." Mr. Nash's virtues, he assures us, sprung from "an honest, bene- "volent mind," and his vices from "too much good nature;" so that good nature is the parent of vice. What we cannot understand in Goldsmith's definition of Nash's virtues and vices is that they seem so much alike, and both proceed from what appears to us to be one and the same cause, as it is difficult to perceive the distinction between an "honest, benevolent mind" and "good nature." As a rule, Nash tried to evade the payment of his just debts, and when he exercised his great spirit of benevolence, he did so by borrowing the means from others, whom he never repaid. Perhaps this may be the difference between a "benevolent "mind" and "*too much* good nature."

We do not go so far as to deny that Mr. Nash did not seek to promote benevolent objects in the city in which he acquired such unwonted ascendancy; but we unhesitatingly affirm that his efforts have been greatly exaggerated, and his motives attributed to pure benevolence rather than to policy. Reference to Wood will show that many private individuals, whose names scarcely survived the occasion, collected larger sums for the Hospital than Mr. Nash. Yes, but then he abolished duelling,[1] white aprons,[2] coarse manners, and top-boots. So far, he has fairly earned all the credit to which such an achievement entitles him. He went with the times, and although public opinion generally was bringing about a great social change in the habits and manners of "fashionable society," it required more than ordinary moral courage to attempt to put down duelling and bullying in Bath at that time, and Nash showed not merely courage, but tact, wisdom, and persistency. There was once a king upon whom Divine commands were laid to do certain great things. His name was *Jehu;* he slew the prophets of Baal; put an end to Jezebel; smote the house of Ahab; and shewed in various ways his zeal for the Lord. But he spared the groves and left a few abominations in Bethel and Dan. These were his own cherished vices and sins. The king of Bath warred against the "violent man;" but the groves of gambling and the golden calves of sharping and swindling were left to disgrace the city, in spite of

---

[1] In the early part of his reign, a duel was fought by torchlight in the Orange Grove between a gamester, named Taylor, and another, named Clarke, in which Taylor was run through the body, but lived seven years after, but the wound breaking out afresh, he died. This incident caused a great deal of public indignation, and Nash saw in it a favourable opportunity for repressing the custom of duelling and wearing swords within his dominions. Great monarchs, and great ministers too, are occasionally led to adopt a particular line of policy by some toward or untoward occurrence. These two stupid and (perhaps) drunken ruffians quarrelled and fought at midnight: one all but received his immediate *quietus;* the other, it appears, was disquieted for life in his conscience, and died in poverty and contrition. Here was a fine basis for a *peace policy;* not "peace at any price," but peace, subject to the arbitration of his *puissant* majesty, King Nash. It consolidated his kingdom.

[2] See Goldsmith, p. 36.

special enactments, laws, public opinion, and common decency.[1] Nash found the pigeons; Wiltshire plucked them. They shared the plunder until they quarrelled about the spoil, and then occurred the lawsuit and the *exposé* and the disgrace.

Well, then, Nash was a devout man—also on Jehu's principle :—he went to church, held the basin, looked sleek and solemn, and then in private scoffed at all things sacred and holy.[2] He was a profligate; and although he never spoke the truth, he deceived no one, for the truth was never expected from him. It was only when by accident he spoke the truth that he deceived, for nobody believed him. His jokes were bad, his wit worse; he swore like a drayman; and when not in fear of death he blasphemed, but his fits of contrition excited contempt.[3]

In the "London Magazine," 1745, appears the following :—

"I cannot quit Mr. Nash without observing, to his honour, that he is no less a promoter of "public charity than a hero in every diversion. You see him as complaisant and diligent with the "basin at the Abbey, to collect alms for the Hospital and charity children as he is busy in getting "subscriptions for balls. His memory, perhaps, will be revered and loved from the good accruing "from the General Hospital, which he zealously forwards, and hath already brought to some perfec-"tion, long after his foibles have been passed over by the humane, and his favour has ceased to be the "ambition of the king and gay."

Such was the impression at the time. Mr. Nash knew the importance of simulating a virtue if he had it not. He knew how to make the best of both worlds. At any rate, he tried.

We have in vain endeavoured to discover where Nash lived when he arrived in Bath in quest of a kingdom, about 1705; but Wood leaves us in no doubt as to the houses which he afterwards occupied :—

"Thomas Greenway, after building a house in Saint John's Court so profuse in ornament as to "tempt the King of Bath to make part of it his palace, particularly applied himself to small orna-"ments in freestone, such as crests, vases, fruits, etc., and several that served their apprenticeships to "him pursued the business, till they brought it to such a perfection as to merit public encouragement, "and render their works a rising branch of the trade of Bath."

The house referred to at present is called the "*Garrick's Head*," and is a very ornamental building, erected about 1720. The *atrium* of the Theatre occupies almost the whole of the ground floor of the eastern part. The six windows above, and also the five windows of its southern front, have unusually boldly moulded architraves, and the cornices of these windows merge into and are

---

[1] See Wood, chap. 7.
[2] Goldsmith's Life, pp. 56, 57, 66.
[3] Ibid, pp. 174, 175; and Appendix in Rambles about Bath, p. 499.

incorporated with the main cornice above, which is a somewhat eclectic and unusual feature in classic work. The main cornice is above, and in three of its members is a handsomely carved one. The windows of the attic on both fronts are also boldly treated. The balustrade which crowned the fronts is taken away, but the corner pedestals remain. A much finer treatment is obtained in the design of this house, than in the usual classic and prevailing style. A fair bust of Garrick, by *Gahagan*, completed in 1831, surmounts the doorway of the Inn. The old staircase remains, and the room on the first floor partly so, but the various changes and vicissitudes of the house during the past century have destroyed its ichnography. The interior is characterised by none of the superior details and arrangements which distinguishes the work of Wood. When Nash left this house, it was for a time occupied by the famous **Mrs. Delany.**

Wood also refers to the next and latest house occupied by Nash—the house now with a tablet upon it as follows :—

"St. John's Court is likewise new ; it is fifteen feet broad, contains four houses, and was "formerly the *town mixen*, till the Right to the land was recovered, in favour of St. John's Hospital. "In the *return* of the building of this court, next Barton Lane, there is a *fifth* house which makes the "*present* habitation of the King of Bath, whose *former* palace, to the south of it, is so profuse in "ornaments, that none but a mason to shew his art would have gone to the expense of those "Inrichments."

This extract clearly shows that Nash lived first in the house now called "*The Garrick's Head*," and from what follows that he then removed to the house we are about to describe. It seems probable that, as Wood states the fact in his first edition, p. 97, published in 1743, Nash did not occupy the former house very long. He died Feb. 3, 1761, aged 87.[1]

This "fifth house" is a three-storeyed building, the plan of which is a simple parallelogram, and it originally stood alone. The six windows occupying its eastern aspect have remarkably plain architraves compared with those of the adjoining building, in fact the treatment of the three fronts which now remain, shows that the architect must have been restricted in his desire for elaboration. The entrance-door casing, however, on the south side, has been emphasised by skilful and beautiful ornamentation ; and the purity of its classic detail is far in advance of the work of most of the contemporary architects. The basement still retains evidences of large kitchens, and the ample demands of the culinary

---

[1] Corporation Minute-Book, 1761, Feb 14, Atwood, Mayor. "Shall the funeral of Mr. Nash "be defrayed at the expense of the Chamber at a sum not exceeding Fifty Guineas, under the "direction of Mr. Mayor and Mr. Chamberlain? Yes, 20. No, 1."

Feb. 20. "Shall the offer of Mr. William Hoare of a portrait of Mr. Nash's picture, to be set "up in the Townhall be accepted, with the thanks of the Corporation for the same? Yes, 20."

art. The ground-floor is occupied as a furniture-store. The first floor retains its old wainscoting and ornamental cornice in the large room, which is 25 feet 6 inches by 19 feet; adjoining is a smaller room, and above on the second floor are 3 small chambers.

Note.—Mrs. Delany (*née* Berry) was the great-grand-daughter of Sir Bevil Grenville. She was frequently in Bath, and has recorded her impressions and experience of Bath society at its most brilliant period. She was a well-bred, as well as a high-born lady; frank, genial, and generous. On one occasion she resided in Gallaway's Buildings; on another, on the South Parade; but her longest residence was in the house we have referred to as Nash's mansion in *St. John's Court*—" *The Garrick's Head.*" **Lady Llanover** has edited the Memoirs and Journals of Mrs. Delany in 6 vols. 8vo.

Weymouth House.—The Bath Town-House formerly of the **THYNNE** family. At the end of Mr. Murch's pamphlet on *The Elder and the Younger Pitt*, it is stated that "the title depends upon the property." This implies that the Marquis of Bath holds his title by tenure, which cannot be the case; no titles being held now by any other tenure than creation or hereditary descent. *Weymouth House*, moreover, was occupied by **VISCOUNT WEYMOUTH** in the last century, but it is more than doubtful whether any Marquis of Bath (as such), the first of whom was created in 1789, ever resided at Weymouth House at all.[1] When this Lord Weymouth was created **Marquis of Bath**, his son became Lord Weymouth, and represented the city till his father's death, in 1796, and was succeeded in the representation by his brother, **Lord John Thynne**, 3rd son of the first Marquis, who sat until 1832. It does not follow that a nobleman must hold property in any place from which he takes his title. With the exception of Pulteney, Earl of Bath, not one of the other eight Earls possessed property in the City. Pulteney had held the estate of Bathwick only a few years before he was created Earl of Bath.

SIR WILLIAM HERSCHEL.—It would not be too much to say that of all the men who have distinguished themselves in Bath, of whom we are enabled to give a goodly list, no one is entitled to higher praise or deserves warmer admiration than William Herschel. Scarcely any man ever rose to such eminence with so many difficulties to overcome, by his own unaided genius, cheerful persistency of purpose, and never-failing courage, as he. A

---

[1] The Viscount Weymouth, who, in the earlier part of his life, occasionally lived in this house, was born in 1734. Macaulay says of him : " Weymouth had a natural eloquence which astonished those who knew how little he owed to study. But he was indolent and dissolute, and had early impaired a fine estate with the dice-box, and a fine constitution with the bottle." He died in 1796, seven years after he was created Marquis of Bath.

foreigner, with even little education in his own tongue, accustomed to many privations in his early youth, and apparently with little more culture in his ostensible profession of a musician than he had acquired in the rude school of a military band,[1] he came to Bath in 1766, when he was 28 years old, to seek his fortune. With no patrons, none of the adventitious aids of a local reputation, being also ignorant of the language (except what he may have acquired by his short residence at Halifax), and without experience of any kind, he yet, by his simplicity, his noble nature, and the knowledge he displayed both of the theory and practice of music, soon established a name in this, at that time, pre-eminently practical school of music. We know little of the manner in which he attained to the excellence he exhibited in the profession; but we may assume, from what we know of him in his more prominent and important character of an astronomer, that the labours he had given to the mastery of this abstruse study had been previously applied to his earlier pursuit, by which he long subsisted, and through which it may be said he attained to that higher and more enduring fame as the *Royal Astronomer.* The peculiar characteristic about Herschel was that he neglected nothing. As a teacher of music, as a leader of the orchestra, as the organist of the *Octagon,* he did all things well and diligently. It was this faculty of concentrating all his attention upon what he was doing at the time, which enabled him to pursue the calling by which he lived and to make it subservient to that which was, after all, the great work of his life, and which resulted in practical discoveries and scientific triumphs which are for all time. It appears to have been the great sustaining enthusiasm, the calm contentment, and the never-ceasing labours of William Herschel, that excited the loving admiration of his sister, **CAROLINE HERSCHEL**, and which prompted that helpful co-operation which was the pride of her life, and of the importance of which she scarcely seems to have entertained a thought. She was content to look upon him and encourage him. In fact, she may be compared to the satellite, whilst he was the brightest planet in the firmament.

[1] "In the review of the 'Memoirs and Correspondence of Caroline Herschel,' in the *Athenæum* of this day, it is said that William Herschel 'could not bear the hardships he had to endure (in the band of the Duke of Cumberland's army), so that the parents quickly sent him away.' It was related by the Duke of Sussex to Professor Sedgwick, and by Professor Sedgwick to me, that William Herschel had deserted his military band, and that on the occasion of his first presentation to George III., the king drew from his pocket and presented to Herschel a free pardon for desertion.

"On matters of Astronomical Science the Duke of Sussex was entirely in the king's confidence. "I have seen in his possession several papers of observations, comparisons of clocks, etc., in the hand writing of George III.

"In the year 1846 I saw Miss Herschel at Hanover; she was as active as could possibly be expected from a person of her age, 96, and was still most enthusiastic on Astronomy and precise in her enquiries about some publications in which she had been concerned. -G. B. AIRY.

"Royal Observatory, Greenwich; Jan. 29th, 1876."

In comparing Herschel with many other great men, it must be remembered that he not only entered upon this most difficult astronomical investigation and study, but that he had to invent and fashion the very instruments needful for his purpose; and in this he may be said to have made a double discovery—a discovery that is the basis of all subsequent improvements in telescopic appliances.

When Herschel first came to Bath in 1766, he and his sister took apartments at **No. 7, New King Street**, and, so far as Bath people knew, he was a simple professor of music, though there is no doubt he was also engaged in his astronomical studies. After remaining here for a short time, they removed in 1774 to **Rivers Street**,[1] on the upper side, then more open to the country. It was during his residence in this street that the incident occurred,[2] which first introduced him to Dr. William Watson (afterwards Sir William).[3]

This occurred at his residence in Rivers Street, which was soon changed (1780) for **19, New King Street**. At the back of this new residence there was a neat, sloping garden and a fairly open country. It is incidentally mentioned "that "here many interesting discoveries, besides the *Georgium Sidus*, were made." Caroline mentions in a note, that "in this house the *Georgium Sidus* was dis-"covered, 1781. Here the forty-foot was finished, which revealed two more "volcanic mountains in the moon, 1789." She adds:—

"Since the discovery of the *Georgium Sidus* (*Uranus*), March the "13th, 1781, I believe few men of learning or consequence left Bath before they "had seen or conversed with its discoverer, and thought themselves fortunate in "finding him at home on their repeated visits. Sir William Watson was almost an "intimate, for hardly a day passed but he had something to communicate from the "letters which he received from Sir Joseph Banks and other members of the "Royal Society, from which it appeared that my brother was expected in town to "receive the gold medal."

1 The number we cannot tell. Mr. Monkland, in his *Literature and Literati of Bath*, pt. 1, says Herschel lived at 13, Kingsmead Street, which is an error.

2 "About the latter end of this month (Dec., 1779), I happened to be engaged in a series of "observations on the lunar mountains, and the moon being in the front of my house, late in the evening "I brought my seven-feet reflector into the street, and directed it to the object of my observations. "Whilst I was looking into the telescope a gentleman, coming by the place where I was stationed, "stopped to look at the instrument. When I took my eye off the telescope, he very politely asked if "he might be permitted to look in, and this being immediately conceded, he expressed great satisfaction "at the view. Next morning the gentleman, who proved to be Dr. Watson, jun. (now Sir William), "called at my house to thank me for my civility in showing him the moon, and told me there was a "Literary Society then forming at Bath, and invited me to become a member of it, to which I readily "consented."

3 Sir William resided at 21, Pulteney Street for some years, and died in 1824.

Speaking at this time, 1781, of future prospects, it will be seen that after he had become to some extent famous, and after the public recognition of his services had been duly made, he stuck to his original profession. His sister says :—" Now a very busy winter was commencing ; for my brother had engaged "himself to conduct the oratorios conjointly with *Rauzzini*,[1] and he had made "himself answerable for the payment of the engaged performers, for his credit "ever stood high in the opinion of everyone he had to deal with."

It seems indeed probable, that, until he finally left Bath to take charge of the Royal Astronomical Establishment at Datchet, he had no other source of income than what he derived from the musical profession.

RALPH ALLEN[2]—born in 1602 at **St. Blaizey**, in **Cornwall**—came to Bath a youth, early in the 18th century, and obtained an appointment in the Post-Office. His aptitude for business, his intelligence, rectitude, and foresight, quickly led to his advancement to the Postmastership. That he rendered important services to the Government is certain, and that **Marshal Wade**, on behalf of it, recognized and rewarded those services, is equally certain. It is more than probable that the commands of the Government were laid upon Allen, and that they extended over a period of time and were not limited to a single event, as is generally supposed. Be this as it may, he established his reputation for prudence and loyalty, and laid the foundation of that career of prosperity and usefulness which has so long been the theme of well-deserved praise and honourable pride in all writers on local topics. He married *Miss Earl*, the natural daughter of Marshal Wade, who, no doubt, for the remainder of his life gave his son-in-law the aid of that powerful influence which he exercised so well and so bountifully on the city of his adoption. We have not space, even if we had the materials, to add new facts to the comparatively simple life of Ralph Allen. But it has always appeared to us that Warner, and all the guide-writers, and even Mr. Kilvert, in his exquisite Essay, have not dwelt with sufficient emphasis upon Mr. Allen's services to the nation at large, whilst they have been too solicitous to vindicate his memory from the petty slanders of such men as Thicknesse on the ground of an unscrupulous desire for the acquisition of wealth.

We cannot too highly extol the virtues of the man : his warm but unostentatious benevolence ; his never-ceasing energy in promoting the interests of the

---

[1] Rauzzini was an eminent professor of music.

[2] An admirable portrait is photographed by Cloakley, and the same artist has also published a photograph of the Tram-Road from Combe Down to the Stone-yard on the banks of the Avon.

city, of which he may be said to have been one of the makers; his noble hospitality to the great and good, to the stately and the simple. These were graces of character—the natural manifestations of a kindly, genial, and refined nature. But we should rest Mr. Allen's claim to universal gratitude and admiration upon a broader basis than that of philanthropy and personal qualities of head and heart. Ralph Allen was a pioneer in the cause of civilization and advancement. By organizing and perfecting the **Post-Office Cross-Post System**, he became a public benefactor—one of that band of men through whose public services England has become what she is. It is enough that Allen conferred immense advantages upon the nation; that he was the precursor of that system — the postal system—which unites every class—poor and rich, high and low, Whig, Radical, and Tory—in its unqualified praise, and which is deemed worthy of the admiration and imitation of the civilized world. Only a churl of the type of Thicknesse would sneer at such a man as Allen because he had honourably acquired riches, by his head and by his genius, and spent them with a lavish hand upon all that was good and noble. The statesman, the warrior, the lawyer, may become rich amidst the applause of the taxpayers; it will be a bad day for a nation when the inventor and the wise promoter of great national benefits are alone to be regarded as unworthy of a nation's gratitude.[1]

In the old Post-Office, which stood in that quaint **Alley**, called **Lilliput**, Allen thought out and perfected his scheme; close to that corner he raised up that beautiful residence, the remains of which may be seen now if our readers will seek out and enter that narrow passage near Mr. Archer's Wine-Vaults, at the west end of the North Parade. When it was built it was the *Postmaster's House*. The reader will be good enough to exercise his imagination in removing those ugly surroundings, and thus to conceive, "in the mind's eye," the old English garden, which included a portion of the old bowling-green, and stretched to the east and the north, and then, contemplating the present hideous buildings, with Hamlet exclaim, "To what base uses we may return!" It was a pretty picture—a picture associated with a great public work, and with the memory of the man who wrought it.

The vulgar story of Allen calling in Wood to show him his wealth, by way of convincing him of his ability to build **PRIOR PARK**, the extent and grandeur of which had been indicated to the great architect, is a foolish romance. If such a scene had occurred, Wood would have told the story himself in the last edition of his work. Mr. Allen was a gentleman, and in that great mansion he

---

[1] We hope on a future occasion to attempt a brief Biography of Ralph Allen.

dispensed its honours with the ease, the bounty, and the dignity of a prince. Of his public life in Bath, we really know less than is desirable and attainable, and we have not space to add to it. He was bounteous in his gifts, and foremost in promoting all the institutions of the city. Like all men of eminence who take an active part in local matters, and who at the same time ally themselves with a political party, he did not escape censure and criticism. He was the *Coryphæus* of the Corporation, which, in consequence, was dubbed the *One-Headed Corporation*. He might have been their chosen representative in Parliament; he preferred choosing the representatives himself, and wisely and well he chose.[1] He committed some errors of judgment, but no one accused him of self-seeking. He treated Pope with infinite respect and consideration, who, for some real or fancied wrong, insulted the man whose salt he had eaten, and who, in all the attributes of a gentleman, was as superior to the poet as the poet was superior to him in genius.[2] He loved the city in which he had acquired wealth, and he lived in it to the end of his days, having apparently no other ambition than to strengthen its institutions, and to leave Bath, which he had found mean and unsavoury, sweet, bright, and beautiful.

We can form some clear idea of the enterprise which Allen exhibited in developing the stone quarries upon his estate, and the importance at such a period in Bath of the supply of stone which they afforded when the city was growing as if by the enchanter's wand. Richardson, in his Continuation of Defoe's Description of Bath, gives us a graphic account of the Stone Yard and the Tramway, connecting it with the Combe Down quarries.

Allen's Stone Yard, 1761. "Tour in Great Britain," 4 vols., 12mo., 1761. Written originally by Defoe, in 1724-25-27, vols. 1, 2, 3, re-published by Richardson, the Novelist, in 1762-69-78:—

"The stone yard of this great because good man, who may be styled the Genius of Bath, is on "the banks of the Avon. In it is wrought the freestone dug from the quarries in Combe Down, which "is another part of Odin's Down, purchased by him. He has likewise a wharf to embark the same "stone in unwrought blocks, which are brought down from the quarry by an admirable machine, that "runs upon a frame of timber of about a mile and a half in length, placed partly upon walls and partly "upon the ground, like the waggon-ways belonging to the collieries in the North of England. Two "horses draw one of these machines, generally loaded with two or three tons of stone, over the most "easy part of the descent, but afterwards its own velocity carries it down the rest, and with so much

[1] See Article, "*Earl of Chatham*."

[2] The usual story is that Pope wished his friend Mr. Allen to grant him the use of Hampton Manor, to which he proposed bringing Martha Blount, whose relations with Pope were said to have been of a questionable nature. Now it this imputation had then not been conclusively disproved, as it has been since by the late Mr. Dilke, Pope, with his knowledge of Allen's character, is not likely to have preferred any such request. It is not difficult to conceive, from the conduct of the Poet on many occasions, that he had taken offence at some trivial annoyance, and resented it in the manner with which we are familiar.

"precipitation that the man who guides it is sometimes obliged to lock every wheel of the carriage to
"stop it, which he can do with great ease by means of bolts applied to the front wheels, and levers
"to the back wheels. The freestone can be carried by the Avon to Bristol, whence it may be
"transmitted to any part of England, and the new works of St. Bartholomew's Hospital in London,
"as well as the Exchange of Bristol, are built with stone from Mr. Allen's Quarry."

Mrs. Chandler, in her poetical "Description of Bath," thus mentions the machinery referred to :—

". . . . Here is seen the new-made road and wonderful machine,
Self-moving downward from the mountain height,
A Rock its burden of a mountain's weight."

As Allen had attached himself to the political fortunes of Marshal Wade, so he became an equally ardent adherent of Mr. Pitt. Two caricatures of the period show that, however submissive his colleagues of the Council may have been, he was not without his detractors, who held him up to ridicule by the method then more powerful than the Press itself—the pencil of the caricaturist. These two prints touched both Mr. Allen and Mr. Pitt acutely, both of whom[1] were unusually annoyed by the two prints, a description of which is attempted in a *foot-note* to article "*Earl of Chatham.*"

No. 6, HENRY STREET was the residence of the Rev. **JOHN GENEST, M.A.**, who compiled "*Some Account of the English Stage, from the Restorations in 1660 to 1830,*" in 10 vols., 8vo. It is little more than a List of Plays, Actors who have played in them, and Theatres in which the drama has been played in London and Bath, but with no literary disquisition. No special mention is made of the Bath Theatre, nor its associations with the great actors who have made it famous or have been made famous by it.

DUKE OF CHANDOS. Almost the first patron of Wood was the first Duke of Chandos, for whom he built **Chandos House**, opposite to the northern end of Westgate Buildings. This house must have been a bright and beautiful residence, standing in its own court, with little or no obstruction between it and the open country. It suffered prematurely from the removal of the city walls and the consequently rapid increase of buildings around it. The house has lost a good deal of its original stately exterior. That part of Bath, indeed, in which Wood first exhibited his genius and his versatility of resource has long shown symptoms of decadence and dinginess. We believe that both the first and second Dukes occasionally resided in Chandos House, but the third and last Duke never.

[1] See Article, "*Earl of Chatham.*"

DUKE OF KINGSTON.—The house built for this nobleman stands opposite to the Kingston Baths, and from 1875 to 1880 was used as the *Free Library*. The Duke was the last of his race, and on his death his estate passed to a collateral branch through the female line, the representative of which, whose name was Meadows, assumed the name of *Pierrepont*, and was created **Earl Manvers**. The Duke possessed a considerable estate in Bath. He also possessed a very beautiful wife, whose early habits were not quite what they should have been. Before she married the Duke, she had contracted a "Fleet marriage," and her loving husband, being still alive, prosecuted and convicted her of bigamy. It is doubtful whether the Duke ever lived in the house. The greater part of the estate—which devolved upon Lord Manvers—was sold a few years ago. The Kingston Arms are carved on the pediment of the house.

GENERAL WOLFE.—At **No. 5, Trim Street,** near **St. John's Gate** or **Trim Bridge** over the door of which is still to be seen a group of warlike emblems—lived General Wolfe. He had seen much service, when, enfeebled in health and seeking rest, he came to reside in Bath. It was in Bath where the first intimation reached him that he was chosen to command the Expedition against Quebec. Who does not remember Lord Chatham's despair, when, having invited the hero to dine with him, instead of the prudent, reserved commander, he found the man to whom he had entrusted England's honour and glory, apparently a vain-glorious boaster.[1] Wolfe, in fact, was like Nelson, with whom he has been compared - a man whose one idea was "duty," a man of burning zeal, who, when not weighted with responsibility, said foolish things, but who in the face of "duty" never *did* foolish things. Short of stature, spare and attenuated in person, he seemed to be on land what Nelson was at sea—an instinctive hero. His death in action, and the enthusiasm which sustained him in his agonies, remind one very much of the death of Nelson.

---

[1] "After Wolfe's appointment, and on the day preceding his embarkation for America, Pitt, "desirous of giving his last verbal instructions, invited him to dinner, Lord Temple being the "only other guest. As the evening advanced, Wolfe heated, perhaps, by his own aspiring "thoughts, and the unwonted society of statesmen, broke forth into a strain of gasconade and "bravado. He drew his sword, he rapped the table with it, he flourished it round the room, he "talked of the mighty things which that sword was to achieve. The two Ministers sat aghast at an "exhibition so unusual from any man of real sense and real spirit. And when at last Wolfe had "taken his leave, and his carriage was heard to roll from the door, Pitt seemed for the moment "shaken in the high opinion which his deliberate judgment had formed of Wolfe; he lifted up "his eyes and arms, and exclaimed to Lord Temple: 'Good God! that I should have entrusted "the fate of the country and of the administration to such hands!'"—*Mahon's History of England*, vol. 4, pp. 162-3.

The name and literary fame of **RICHARD BRINSLEY SHERIDAN**, Dramatist and Statesman, have been associated with Bath and its past history during its most brilliant epoch. We cannot assign to him any definite place of abode, though there is little doubt that in his many visits to Bath he resided on or somewhere near the Parades, and not unlikely at the house of his wife's father. The society of Bath was evidently the subject of his study, his wit, and his dramatic genius. It is said, but we have little evidence besides this "*it is said*," and the probabilities of the case to prove it, that he was a constant *habitué* of **Leake's Library**, and that much of his literary work was executed in the Reading-Room of that famous Bibliopole. Nothing is more probable than that he, with his acute critical faculty, should have relished the scenes of which he was an observer, and in which he evidently played his own part. He had an eye for beauty, and if he fought for one so lovely as "Delia" and wrote elegant verses in her honour, one cannot blame him much, when we remember the gentle and lovely woman who was the theme of general praise and esteem. There is no reason to suppose that Sheridan did not treat his wife with great personal tenderness; but a woman so gentle and susceptible must have had much to endure from a man whose habits were irregular, and whose career was characterized by all the mad eccentricities of the period, to say nothing of his habitual impecuniosity. He was born in 1751, and was therefore three years senior to **ELIZA ANN LINLEY**, born at 5, Pierrepont Street, in 1754, to whom he was married in 1773. She was the daughter of Mr. Linley, of whom we have written. Miss Linley was a woman of exquisite beauty and sweet disposition— the "fair maid of Bath," the enchantress, whose voice and execution were the admiration of her age; her songs and ballads were like

"Little dewdrops of celestial melody."

She was in the front rank in her own particular line. She died at the early age of 38, leaving one son, **Tom Sheridan**. He left three daughters and one son, namely :—*Mrs. Norton*, afterwards *Lady Stirling-Maxwell; Lady Dufferin*,[1] afterwards *Countess of Gifford;* the *Duchess of Somerset*, who, as *Lady Seymour*, was "The Queen of Beauty" at Lord Eglinton's Tournament, in 1839; and *Mr. Sheridan*, of Frampton, Dorset.

Wood Street, so named in honour of John Wood the *Elder*. At No. 1, the first **Earl of Hardwicke** resided, about 1760 ; and some years later his second son, **Charles Yorke**, who also attained to the Chancellorship, and just before that event, took up his abode in the same house. He had impaired his health by hard drinking, and derived much benefit from the Waters. The circumstances

[1] Mother of the present Earl of Dufferin.

under which he accepted the Seals were said to have reflected upon his honour, in the then state of parties. The patent of a Peerage, as Lord Morden, was made out, but before it was actually conferred, he died by his own hand. It will be remembered that the Lord Chancellor, at this time, 1770, was *Lord* and then *Earl Camden, Recorder of Bath*, whose son, the Hon. John Jeffreys Pratt, was the honoured representative of this city in Parliament, from 1780 to 1794.[1] He lost the Seals through the alleged duplicity of the *Duke of Grafton*. After they had been offered and refused by Lord Mansfield, they were offered to Charles Yorke, a good lawyer and an ambitious man.

"After struggling with all the convulsions of ambition, interest, fear, honour, dread of abuse,
"and, above all, with the difficulty of refusing the object of his whole life's wishes, and with the
"despair of recovering the instant if once suffered to escape, Charles Yorke, having taken three days
"to consider, refused to accept the Seals of Chancellor. Mr. Conway acquainted me, in the greatest
"secrecy, that the Duke of Grafton, dismayed at Yorke's refusal of the Great Seal, would give up
"the Administration. Not a lawyer could be found able enough—or if able, bold enough—or if bold,
"decent enough—to fill the employment. Norton had all the requisites of knowledge and capacity,
"but wanted even the semblance of integrity, though for that reason was probably the secret wish of
"the Court. He was enraged at the preference given to Yorke ; yet nobody dared to propose him,
"even when Yorke had refused. Sir Eardley Wilmot had character and abilities, but wanted health.
"The Attorney-General, De Grey, wanted health and weight, and yet asked too extravagant terms.
"Dunning, the Solicitor-General, had taken the same part as his friends, Lord Camden and Lord
"Shelburne. Hussey, so far from being inclined to accept the office, determined to resign with his
"friend, Lord Camden, though earnest against the dissolution of the Parliament. Of Lord Mansfield
"there could be no question ; when the post was dangerous, his cowardice was too well known to
"give hopes that he could be pressed to defend it. In his exigence, Grafton's courage was not more
"conspicuous. His first thought, without consulting the King's inclination, was to offer the Adminis-
"tration to Lord Chatham or Lord Rockingham ; but inclining to the latter. He had desired Mr.
"Conway to come to him in the evening and meet Lord Gower, Lord Weymouth, and Lord North,
"in the most private manner, for consultation. Conway went away in haste to Court, promising to
"return and dine with me, that he might consider what advice he would give to the Duke at night ;
"but what was my astonishment, when, in two hours, Mr. Onslow came and told me that Mr. Yorke
"had accepted the Seals ! He had been with the King over night (without the knowledge of the
"Duke of Grafton), and had again declined ; but being pressed to reconsider, and returning in
"the morning, the King had so overwhelmed him with flatteries, entreaties, prayers, and at last with
"commands and threats, of never giving him the post if not accepted now, that the poor man sunk
"under the importunity, though he had given a solemn promise to his brother, Lord Hardwicke, and
"Lord Rockingham, that he would not yield. He betrayed, however, none of the rapaciousness of
"the times, nor exacted but one condition, the grant of which fixed his irresolution. The Chancellor
"must of necessity be a peer, or cannot sit in the House of Lords. The Coronet was announced to
"Yorke ; but he slighted it as of no consequence to his eldest son, who would, probably, succeed his

---

[1] On his father being created an Earl in 1784, Mr. Pratt sat as Viscount Bayham, and succeeded his father in 1794 as Earl Camden. He was advanced to the dignity of a Marquis in 1812, and was Recorder of Bath until the Municipal Reform Act was passed. The son, George Charles, Earl Brecknock, represented Bath at intervals from 1799 to 1835, being then summoned to the House of Lords in his father's Barony of Camden. The portrait of Charles, first Earl Camden, adorns the banqueting-room, in the Guildhall.

Historic Houses in Bath and their Associations. 57

" uncle, Lord Hardwicke, the latter having been long married, and having only two daughters. But
" Mr. Yorke himself had a second wife, a very beautiful woman, and by her had another son. She,
" it is supposed, urged him to accept the Chancery, as the King offered, or consented, that the *new*
" peerage should descend to her son, and not to the eldest. The rest of his story was indeed
" melancholy, and his fate so rapid, as to intercept the completion of his elevation.

" He kissed the King's hand on the Thursday ; and from Court drove to his brother, Lord
" Hardwicke's—the precise steps of the tragedy have never been ascertained. Lord Rockingham was
" with the Earl. By some it was affirmed, that both the Marquis and the Earl received the unhappy
" renegade with bitter reproaches. Others, whom I rather believe, maintained that the Marquis left
" the House directly ; and that Lord Hardwicke refused to hear his brother's excuses, and retiring
" from the room, shut himself into another chamber, obdurately denying Mr. Yorke an audience. At
" night it was whispered that the agitation of his mind, working on a most sanguine habit of body,
" inflamed of late by excessive indulgence both in meats and wine, had occasioned the bursting of a
" blood-vessel ; and the attendance of surgeons was accounted for by the necessity of bleeding him
" four times on Friday. Certain it is that he expired on the Saturday between four and six in the
" evening. His servants, in the first confusion, had dropped too much to leave it in the family's
" power to stifle the truth : and though they endeavoured to colour over the catastrophe by declaring
" the accident natural, the want of evidence and of the testimony of surgeons to colour the tale
" given out, and which they never took any public method of authenticating, convinced everybody
" that he had fallen by his own hand—whether on his sword, or by a razor, was uncertain."

" *Horace Walpole's Life of Geo. III.*," vol. 4, *pp*. 48 *to* 53.

On the right-hand side of St. John's Gate, in Trim Street, there stands a very handsome house, with highly ornate windows and a pediment. This house was the property and residence of **Dr. French Lawrence, M.P.**, of whom we have already made mention in connection with his brother and father (7, Orange Grove).[1]

No. 7, John Street was the residence of an eccentric Bathonian named **Fleming**. He wrote *Tim Ginnadrake*, and a *History of Bath*, now scarce, though it possesses no considerable merit. The two daughters of Mr. Fleming here also conducted a very famous *Dancing Academy*.

The upper part of *John Street* terminates in a large house, in which, Mr. Lansdown informs us, there resided a firm of famous *Milliners*—the **Misses Hoblyn. The Duke and Duchess of York**, about 1794, or 1795, visited these ladies' establishment, and from that time it became the rage. The Misses Hoblyn

---

[1] Mr. Monkland says :—" Dr. French Lawrence, LL.D.—a scholar, a senator, an eminent
" civilian, and the intimate friend of Edmund Burke—was the eldest son of Mr. Richard Lawrence, a
" watchmaker, and member of the Bath Corporation. He was born April 3rd, 1757. He was a man
" highly esteemed for his talent and integrity ; in 1797 he was appointed Regius Professor of Civil Law
" in the University of Oxford. Among his published works, which were much distinguished, were
" 'An Ode on the Witches and Fairies of Shakspere,' and 'A School Exercise,' written when at
" Winchester, and thought so good as to be set to music by Linley, and performed as an Oratorio in
" London. Many of the papers in the 'Rolliad' were written by him, as were some of the Proba-
" tionary Odes, etc. He was also the author of a volume of 'Remarks on the Apocalypse ;" and, as
" the executor of Burke, was a joint editor of his works. He wrote an Elegy on the Death of his
" Father."—" *Literature and Literati of Bath*," *vol.* 1.

saved a large fortune. The Duchess, it was said, was a very untidy "dresser;" perhaps these dexterous ladies improved H.R. Highness's taste and her "top gear."

SHERSTON, whose name has been associated with the **Charter of Queen Elizabeth**, and under which either in 1591 or 1596,[1] he was the first Mayor,[2] is said to have lived at **Barton House** in John Street, which runs parallel with the eastern side of Queen Square. Sherston was chosen by his colleagues of the Corporation as one of the Representatives in four consecutive Parliaments, namely 1596, 1600, 1603 and 1605; this favours the presumption that the first Parliamentary Election under the Charter occurred in 1596. The story of the Queen visiting him at Barton House is a fable. We can find *no record of there having been any house on the site other than that now standing*, and it is obvious that such a house was wholly inadequate to the residential requirements of a man of the fortune and position of William Sherston. There is no proof that he lived in this cottage, and we do not believe any can be adduced. It rests upon no other testimony than the fact that Sherston was the occupier of the estate on which the cottage stands; and it is more than probable that it was a little cottage in which the business of the farm was conducted, and nothing more. Sherston resided at *Swainswick*, and during his Mayoralty, his official residence would be in the Guildhall of the period. This Guildhall was superseded by the one designed by Inigo Jones. Under the Charter, special powers were granted to build a new Guildhall. The history of the Charter is simple enough. All the adroitness imputed to Sherston may be true, but there is no proof of any abuse of his power intrinsically afforded in the text of the Charter. If we received the stories of Sherston as true, we should have to conclude that it was obtained by elaborate and deliberate fraud. Queen Elizabeth's ministers were not likely to be imposed upon; nor indeed is there a single clause in the document which denotes anything more than a very simple matter of business in every particular. Wood, it is curious to observe, alleges that, in his own day, the Charter occasioned some trouble from doubtful jurisdiction, but the doubt arose from time having rendered it uncertain as to whether a portion of the territory in Walcot really came within the scope of the Charter, a remedy for which was easily obtained in the reign of George III.

[1] It is a matter of doubt whether the Charter came into practical operation earlier than 1596, even locally.

[2] Sherston was one of the representatives of Bath before the Charter, in 1583. The fact, that, no intermediate election being recorded between 1587 and 1596, seems to favour our theory as to the Charter.

When we read the several accounts of this Charter,[1] the circumstances connected with it, and the objects it was intended to secure, we cannot help feeling surprised that so able a local historian as Mr. Warner should have given perpetuity to Wood's infatuated nonsense. Barton Farm was close upon the confines of the old city boundaries, and the enlargement of those boundaries of necessity incorporated the lands occupied by Sherston, and *extended* the jurisdiction and liberties of the local government, which in itself was not only necessary, but secured immense advantages to the city. The Ecclesiastical lands, which had formerly been under an independent jurisdiction and enjoyed certain especial immunities, were brought within the perambulations and control of the corporate government. It follows as a matter of course that in all arrangements of this nature some individual is likely to derive especial advantages. That Sherston was a shrewd, able man, is certain. As a clothier he had done much to develop the trade, and to make Bath the centre of it. He was, in truth, just one of those men of whom we have types in every age, who leave the stamp of their individuality upon the institutions and the history of the places with which they have been connected. Neither Wood nor Warner advances one iota of evidence to show that Sherston's transactions were otherwise than honourable, or that they were not conceived in a spirit favourable to the interests of the city.[2]

Warner says :—

"By the above-mentioned charter, the city not only gained a confirmation of its former franchises, and an addition of rights and privileges, but also a considerable extension of its ancient jurisdiction. Hitherto its own walls, which did not include more than fifty acres, had been considered as limiting the authority of its mayor and justices ; but by the description of the metes and boundaries in Elizabeth's charter, it is evident that a large sweep of new territory was then added to the city, and the jurisdiction of the corporation made to embrace the whole farm of Berton, the privileged lordship of the dissolved priory, and a large part of the parish of Walcot. This acquisition seems to have been effected by the management of Mr. Sherston, who, being at that time tenant of Berton demesne (of which he became absolute purchaser in the year 1621), and owner of other property about Bath, contrived to procure the boundaries of his own tenures to be inserted as the limits of the city ; but aware that an immediate exercise of this novel jurisdiction might possibly awaken enquiry into the legality of it, 'the corporation,' observes Mr. Wood, 'were wise enough to be silent in their claims, till the memory of man from the date of the charter was 'quite worn out.' The extension, indeed, with regard to the priory, was formerly so strongly opposed by the lords of that privileged manor, that they would not permit the mayor of the city so much as to set his foot on the abbey land ; and it was but lately that the magistrates of Bath began

[1] See *Charter, Appendix* in *Warner*, p. 81.
[2] See *Hyde's Award*, 1619, *Appendix* in Warner, p. 93.

"to claim jurisdiction over the farm of Berton, and the other part of the county of Somerset that lies within their common perambulations."[1]

Sherston died in 1621, and was buried in St. Michael's Church—"in the "chancell on the east wall." This Church *preceded* Harvey's wretched structure, which was built in the elder Wood's time, and received his well-merited condemnation. It was pulled down, when the present church was erected on its site, in 1837.

WOOD, JOHN, the Elder, resided in the **centre house** on the north side of **Queen Square.** No more appropriate residence could have been chosen. To his creative genius we owe the square, and it was fitting he should be surrounded by the work he had brought into existence. He also built himself a **Villa at Batheaston,** near the Church. An eagle in stone is on the pediment, and the house possesses many of the well-known characteristics of Wood's style. At a later period he removed from 24, Queen Square, to **41, Gay Street,** which is at the corner of Old King Street, and really forms a portion of Queen Square. It is almost impossible to say anything of Wood without saying too much; but his works speak for him *in stone* more eloquently than the ablest pen can express in words. Wood was a self-made north countryman, and the fact is borne out by a few peculiar expressions in his diction. He died in 1754. His work on Bath, on the preface of which **Lord Macaulay** based his description of Bath, was published in 1742, in 1 vol. He died in Queen Square, May 23, 1754.

WOOD JOHN, the Younger. Less is known of Wood the Younger than of his father. *He never wrote a book,* though presumably he revised the second edition of his father's work on Bath, published in 1765, in 2 vols. He completed the **Circus,** which his father designed; he was the architect of **Camden Crescent,** and if we wanted an epitaph to sum up his work and the result of his genius we should say, "**HE BUILT THE ROYAL CRESCENT.**" He resided in his father's house, **41, Gay Street,** and at his father's villa, at Batheaston, in which he died, 1781. In the edition he issued of his father's work, after quoting the former preface to which we have referred, he draws a contrast between the Bath then described and the Bath of his own day, and this we quote :—

[1] "He (Sherston) having then rented Berton farm, in the parish of Walcot, of the above-mentioned Edmund Colthurst, just before he sold it to Sir George Snigge, Berton-House was the first that was honoured with the new regalia of the city; and by the artifices of Mr. Sherston, the whole farm was included in the perambulation which the citizens were then empowered for the time to come to make. The site of the priory was taken into the same perambulation; and the court of record, as well as courtleet, then granted to the corporation, were extended over the precincts of the dissolved monastery, notwithstanding the rights and privileges of that house had been sold to Mr. Colles by King Henry VIII. in the year 1542.'—"Wood's Essay," p. 203.

"As the new buildings advanced, carpets were introduced to cover the floors, though laid with the finest clean deals, or Dutch oak boards ; the rooms were all wainscoted and painted in a costly and handsome manner ; marble slabs, and even chimney pieces, became common ; the doors in general were not only made thick and substantial, but they had the best sort of brass locks put on them ; walnut tree chairs, some with leather, and some with damask or worked bottoms supplied the place of such as were seated with cane of rushes ; the oak tables and chests of drawers were exchanged, the former for such as were made of mahogany, the latter for such as were made either with the same wood, or with walnut tree ; handsome glasses were added to the dressing tables, nor did the proper chimneys or peers of any of the rooms long remain without well framed mirrors of no inconsiderable size ; and the furniture for every chief chimney was composed of a brass fender, with tongs, poker and shovel agreeable to it.

"Beds, window curtains and other chamber furniture, as well woollen as linen, were, from time to time, renewed with such as was more fit for gentlemen's capital seats, than houses appropriated for common lodgings ; and the linen for the table and bed grew better and better till it became suitable even for people of the highest rank.

"With all this increase of goodness in the furniture of the Bath houses, and with the addition of screens and many other useful things, lodgings received no advance during the seasons ; the seasons, however, were almost every year lengthened ; and when the Lodgings were abated, it was only the price of the principal rooms that was reduced, and that was lowered from ten to seven shillings and sixpence a week for each room.

"To make a just comparison between the public accommodations of Bath at this time and one and twenty years back, the best chambers for Gentlemen were then just what the garrets for servants now are." (This, be it remembered, was in 1765.)

If any proof were wanting of the truth of this representation, the houses on the Parades, and in Gallaway's Buildings, and the earlier buildings of the Elder Wood would amply supply it ; but we contend that the comparison drawn is between houses not of the same relative class of an earlier date, but of an inferior class altogether. See Preface to " Rambles about Bath," last edition.

Mr. Wood was a county magistrate and was highly esteemed. The career of these two eminent men extended over a period of sixty years.

MRS. PIOZZI, as Mrs. Thrale, had visited Bath, with her husband, on many occasions. After Mr. Thrale's death, she, in 1781, adopted Bath as her permanent residence.

The house, **No. 8, Gay Street**, with the floral decorations, built for **Mr. Gay**,[1] who was the owner of much property in the city, was, after a short time, fixed upon as her residence, and she certainly kept it alive with her revels and her parties. As a recent writer says, "She was in a perpetual state of "rampant senility." In 1819, she gave a grand ball at the Lower Rooms to celebrate the 80th anniversary of her birthday, and led off the ball with her nephew, *Sir John Salusbury*. All the incidents of Mrs. Piozzi's life are so well known that nothing new can be said. We have, indeed, in the *Autobiography*,

[1] Mr. Gay was M.P. for the city in 1727, and Lord of the Manor of Walcot.

edited by *Mr. Hayward, Q.C.*, little new in connection with her life in Bath. Her energy, love of pleasure, affectation, good nature, wit, and sprightliness, rendered her popular. Nobody could understand why she married Piozzi, amiable and estimable as he seems to have been.[1] She wanted some one to domineer over, to reverse the order of things, and Piozzi was more submissive than Thrale. It was in 1776 that **Dr. Johnson** visited Mr. and Mrs. Thrale, who were then residing on the North Parade. The Doctor made his quarters at **The Pelican Inn**, in Walcot Street. This inn is now called *The Three Cups*.[2] At that time, Walcot was a bright suburb of Bath.[3] The character of the street is changed completely. Then there was a series of good villas extending from *The Pelican* to Walcot Church, each standing in its own grounds, with sloping gardens to the river. The verdant hills on the opposite side were not built upon, or only partly so, the road was wide and well kept, and Walcot Street, therefore, was the *locus in quo* of wealthy citizens and residents. *The Pelican* in 1776 was an inn for the "quality," and Dr. Johnson, fond as he was of Fleet Street, selected it as a quiet retreat. He was free from the "young bloods" of the day at *The Bear* or *The White Hart*. Walcot Street changed its character when the lower were abandoned for the higher levels, and when Bathwick superseded the older streets about the time to which we are referring. **Boswell**, as we know, visited Dr. Johnson in April of the year 1776, and he also found good quarters at *The Pelican*.

[1] Her own family were incensed with her, and an estrangement ensued. Johnson said she had done everything wrong since Thrale's bridle was off her neck. But this was an exaggeration, arising probably from the fact that the Doctor's influence over her had diminished. Piozzi, it is clear, behaved with admirable disinterestedness, and conducted his *capering* little wife's pecuniary affairs with prudence.

[2] There was a "Three Cups," in 1771, in Northgate Street, as, in the *Bath Chronicle* of Dec. 5th, of that year, the following announcement appears : —" The modern Colossus or Wonderful Giant, " which has been exhibited at the 'Three Cups,' in Northgate Street, has been removed to a more "genteel and airy room, at 'The Rose,' in Avon Street." The deduction from this is that Avon Street was a "genteel and airy street" in 1771. In 1882 its gentility would have to be determined by a community of the sweeping fraternity, and its airyness by those who are obliged occasionally to go through it. Our Northgate citizens would be not a little indignant to have their locality and their *status* compared with Avon Street and its denizens.

[3] The Villas were built upon the sites of the Cloth Factories after the decline of that industry in Bath.

THE EARL OF NORTHINGTON and EARL CAMDEN.—It was said that Ralph Allen refused to become one of the representatives of Bath in Parliament, but that he took care to choose the members himself; that is, he exercised unbounded influence over the Council; he was its "one head." It may be well to see how he used his power. Allen, we know, was a warm adherent of the Hanoverian dynasty. He was attached to it by ties of interest, conviction, and personal connection with Marshal Wade. The Marshal,[1] as the representative of Bath, from 1722 to 1748, (the year of his death,) had little sympathy with any particular shade of politics which existed amongst the "Revolution party";[2] he cared for the dynasty and for that alone. The Marshal was much more than the representative of the city in Parliament; he was its fast friend; he lived in it and loved it, and identified himself with its local institutions. So long as the Marshal lived, Allen seems to have contented himself with giving him and his colleague a steady and loyal support. The Jacobite and the High Tory party were relatively small and insignificant, but the great Whig party was split into two separate factions, and the conflicts in Parliament were almost limited to those two sections, Allen choosing the section which was led by William Pitt, in opposition to Walpole.

At the general election of 1747, *Marshal Wade* was again chosen a representative of the city, in conjunction with **ROBERT HENLEY**, who was descended from an ancient Somersetshire family. Henley's father was Anthony Henley, a man of great distinction, the friend of Dorset, Sunderland, Swift, Pope, and Arbuthnot. Generous and bounteous, learned and witty, he was one of the most popular men of his time. He represented Andover, and afterwards, till his death, Melcombe Regis. Considerable wealth came to him through his wife, who was sole heiress of the Hon. Peregrine Bertie, second son of Montague, Earl of Lindsey. Robert Henley was the second son of the marriage, and was born in 1708, ultimately succeeding to the family estate,[3] on the death of his elder brother, Anthony. Educated at Westminster and Christ Church, he was entered of the Middle Temple and called to the bar in 1732. Handsome in person, jovial in habits, he used to pass his vacations at

---

[1] It should be mentioned that the house in the Churchyard in which he lived was designed by the Earl of Cork and Burlington.

[2] A term applied to the political party favourable to the Revolution of 1688, the Hanoverian dynasty, and to Whig principles.

[3] "The Grange," Hampshire. The original mansion was built by Inigo Jones. When the property passed into the possession of the first Lord Ashburton, he pulled down the old house and built the present magnificent mansion on the site.

Bath, and was one of the best known of the fashionable men at "The Bear." He was the gayest of the gay in the Pump-room in the morning, and amongst the most jovial of the topers in "The Bear" at night. His briefs at this time did not give him much trouble, but he cultivated the friendship of the Bath citizens, and was singularly popular. Lord Campbell relates the romantic story of his courtship and marriage, which is very similar to that previously told by Lord Henley,[1] in his "Life of the Earl of Northington."

There was at Bath, for the benefit of the waters, a very young girl of exquisite beauty, who from illness had lost the use of her limbs so completely that she was only able to appear in public wheeled about in a chair. She was the daughter and co-heiress of Sir Jno. Husband, of Ipsley, in Warwickshire, who was the last male of a time-honoured race, whom Dugdale states to have been lords of that manor in lineal succession from the Conquest. Henley, struck by the charms of her face, contrived to be introduced to her, when he was still more fascinated by her conversation. His admiration soon ripened into a warm and tender attachment, which he had reason to hope was reciprocated. But it seemed as if he had fallen in love with a Peri, and that he must for ever be contented with sighing and worshipping at her shrine, when suddenly the waters produced so effectual and complete a cure, that Miss Husband was enabled to comply with the custom of the place by hanging up her votive crutches to the nymph of the spring, and to dance the "Minuet de la Cour" at the Lower Rooms with her lover. Soon after, with the full consent of her family, she gave her hand to the suitor who had so sedulously attended her. To the end of a long life, she continued to enjoy a most perfect state of health, and their affection remaining unabated, she gave him that first of human blessings—a serene and happy home.

They were married by Henley's old schoolfellow, Bishop Newton, at the chapel in South Audley Street. After describing his settling in London and the family property descending to him, the memoir goes on:—

"After his marriage, Henley continued to go frequently to Bath, carrying "his wife along with him. He now led comparatively a sober life, but "occasionally he would indulge in his old convivial habits, and, by his toasts and "his stories and his very agreeable manners, he ingratiated himself so much with

---

[1] The Earl had eight children—three sons and five daughters. Only one son survived his father, and he seems to have been a man of unusual promise. His abilities were considerable and his manners popular. In 1783 he was appointed by the Coalition Ministry Lord-Lieutenant of Ireland. The daughters all formed high alliances, but they all died without issue except the Lady Elizabeth, who married Sir Morton Eden, who was raised to the Irish Peerage by the title of Lord Henley. His son (who wrote his Grandfather's Life) married the sister of the second Sir R. Peel, and left by her a son, the present Lord Henley.

"the Mayor and Common Council, forming a very small corporation, with the
"right of returning Members to Parliament exclusively vested in them, that they
"made him their Recorder, and agreed to elect him at the next vacancy one of
"their representatives ; being swayed, perhaps, not merely by his personal good
"qualities, but the prospect of his being now able to show his gratitude for their
"kindness to him. Accordingly, on the dissolution of Parliament, which took
"place in the summer of the year 1747, he was elected a representative for Bath
"along with Field-Marshal Wade."

It is certain that he had ingratiated himself with the Marshal and Ralph Allen, and although he never distinguished himself as a speaker, he was a good lawyer and a fair debater. He was subsequently Solicitor-General to the Prince of Wales (afterwards George III.). In Nov., 1756, he succeeded Murray[1] as Attorney-General to the Crown, and on Dec. 2 in the same year, on the issue of a new writ, was re-elected. In the following year he was made Lord Keeper by Pitt (by whom he was succeeded in the representation), an office which rendered his seat vacant and precluded him from sitting in the Commons, though it did not involve a peerage. In 1760, the Lord Keeper Henley was elevated to the dignity of Lord Chancellor and the Earldom of Northington. He held the Great Seal nine years, in two reigns (Geo. II. and Geo. III.), and during four administrations.

Marshal Wade died in 1748, and was succeeded in the representation by **SIR JOHN LIGONIER**, a distinguished military commander. Sir John was re-elected at the general election in 1754. In 1757 he was created an Irish Viscount; at the following general election, in 1761, he was re-elected in conjunction with the same colleague, Mr. Pitt; and in 1763 he was made a Peer of the Realm as Earl Ligonier, when **SIR JOHN SEBRIGHT, Bart.**, was elected.

EARL CAMDEN.—The connection of this eminent man with Bath was of long duration, and reflected the highest honour upon the city. We cannot discover whether Lord Camden occupied a private residence, but we are inclined to think that, like Lord Northington, he continued the habit of going to the famous hostelry, **THE BEAR**, (which as a young barrister on the Western Circuit he adopted,) during his occasional visits, after he had become one of the foremost men of his time.[2]

[1] Afterwards Earl Mansfield.
[2] Wood, who built what is *now*, by a perversion of historical association, called Camden Crescent, named it Camden Place, which was the name of Lord Camden's place of residence. The preservation of historical nomenclature is important, except perhaps to noodles, to whom one thing is much the same as another. Camden Place was a monument to the connection of Bath with its greatest Recorder (if we except Prynne), and one of England's greatest Chief Justices and Lord Chancellors.

It was the custom for the barristers on this circuit, before and after the County Assizes, to make Bath their headquarters. They prepared themselves for the business of the law by a course of the pleasures of Bath, and afterwards compensated themselves for their arduous labour by renewing them. Charles Pratt had less inclination for the attractions of the Pump-room, and, unlike Lord Northington, none whatever for the carousing habits of the tavern. For many years—1738 to 1745—Pratt scarcely held a brief. In the following year, he greatly distinguished himself as junior to Henley.[1] He had begun almost to despair of success, and contemplated entering the Church—a proposal Henley would not listen to. By special contrivance (it was supposed) Pratt was retained in a case in which his leader, Henley, was, at the right moment, to be seized with an attack of gout. Be this as it may, "the lead "was suddenly cast upon Pratt, who opened the plaintiff's case with great "clearness and precision, made a most animated and eloquent reply, obtained "the verdict, was complimented by the judge, was applauded by the audience, "and received several retainers before he left the hall." His fame was at once established, and his progress was rapid. Pratt's first judicial appointment was that of Recorder of Bath, of which Lord Campbell makes no mention,[2] an office in which he succeeded Henley, whom he also succeeded as Attorney-General when Henley was made Lord Keeper, and nine or ten years after as Lord Chancellor.[3] These two eminent men, who were so closely connected with Bath, were also connected with Pitt. They were identified with the same political parties, and although in the earlier part of their legal careers a warm friendship existed between the two men, in later times great divergencies of opinion occurred between them on some of the great legal and constitutional questions of that momentous period, the solution of which was due in a great measure to the courage of Lord Camden, whose successors in the peerage to the third generation were politically and judicially connected with the city.[4]

[1] Lord Campbell does not say where, but we believe it was at Bristol.

[2] "Lives of the Chancellors," vol. 5.

[3] See "Charles York," p. 56, and footnote.

[4] Bath was represented by the Earl's son, the Hon. John Jeffreys Pratt, in three Parliaments—1780 to 1784, and as Viscount Bayham, 1790–94, when he succeeded to the Earldom of Camden. In 1812 he was created Earl of Brecknock and Marquis Camden. He was Recorder of Bath from 1812 until the passing of the Municipal Corporation Reform Act, in 1835. In 1818, the Earl of Brecknock, the only son of the Marquis, was elected one of the representatives of the city (1818 to 1832).

No. 7, Circus was the Bath town residence of **WILLIAM PITT, EARL OF CHATHAM.** The **Earl of Northington** and **Earl Camden** we claim to have been of and for Bath, but we cannot show that they were *citizens*. William Pitt was a citizen,[1] and proud of the city in which, from his early manhood, he had spent so much of his time, and from whose famous waters he had experienced such signal benefits during the terrible attacks of his constitutional malady. We are unable to trace where Pitt lived during any of his occasional visits to Bath, but there is no doubt that on two of his visits he was entertained by Ralph Allen at his town-house, and once, if not twice, at Prior Park. He is said to have suggested the erection of the Palladian Bridge at the lower part of the grounds in that noble domain. If anything, in the absence of positive evidence, leads us to doubt the fact, it is that Wood's exuberant fancy needed little stimulus from others. His plans were usually very complete, and in those relating to Prior Park he refers especially to the external ornate perfection of the scheme submitted to Allen, which was adopted. It is no part of our purpose to enter upon any historical or political disquisition, except so far as it may enable us to make clear the relation of Pitt with Bath, and to put into a more definite form some of the very interesting associations connected with him and with those other statesmen who either were the choice of Allen, or in the choice of whom Allen had the largest share. Allen looked after the big fish; the meshes of his net allowed the minnows to escape; he caught the tritons; he left the minnows to more degenerate times. The representatives chosen, we have shown, were some of the foremost men of the age, who thought it an honour to be representatives of Bath.

When a special vacancy occurred in the representation of the city, by the elevation of Attorney-General Henley to be Lord Keeper, Pitt was unanimously chosen as his successor. At the general election of 1761, he was re-elected in conjunction with his former colleague, *Viscount Ligonier*.[2]

---

[1] It is well known that the elder Wood designed the Circus, and that the execution of it was left to the younger. The house No. 7, with all its covenants and obligations, was conveyed to Pitt on the 3rd day of January, 1755. The property was re-sold by Pitt in 1763, the year in which the breach between him and the Corporation occurred. The house is now the property of, and is occupied by, W. Bush, Esq., formerly mayor of the city.

[2] A distinguished soldier, by birth a French subject. Not a man of great abilities, yet he had risen by steady and sterling qualities to become a Field-Marshal and a Peer of the Realm. He (then Sir John Ligonier) served under the Duke of Cumberland at Lauffeld in 1747, where he was taken prisoner. During his captivity, Marshal Saxe made overtures of peace to him, which, but for her allies, England might have listened to. In 1763, the Marshal, through an unworthy intrigue, much commented upon at the time, was removed from the Mastership of the Ordnance, a post he had filled efficiently. He was made an English Earl with a pension for life. It seems, from the position he is made to occupy in the Caricature, No. 2, to which reference is made on page 25, that the Marshal sympathised with Mr. Pitt in his breach with the Corporation. (See Appendix.)

In 1763, this nobleman having been created a Peer of the Realm, a vacancy occurred, to supply which *Sir John S. Sebright* was elected, and thus became the colleague of Pitt. We refer to the fact that Pitt, in his early political career, had joined that section of the Whigs which opposed Walpole, and that he declaimed with "unabated violence and with increasing ability" against that minister, because there is no doubt that it had much to do with his popularity in Bath, and especially with Allen and the other members of the Corporation. Pitt vehemently clamoured for war with Spain, which Walpole resisted, but Walpole, against his better judgment, was ultimately compelled to declare war, which, after all, did not arrest his downfall. Burke has denounced this war as unjust, and history has almost universally endorsed his judgment. Pitt was obliged himself to declare that the war was needless and unjustifiable. Notwithstanding, from this period (1740—1) until he became the representative of the city, he was always received with special honour by the municipal body and the citizens. His eloquence and his unswerving honesty covered a multitude of political sins,[1] and certain it is, that the admiration felt for this great man by Ralph Allen was shared by his colleagues and the citizens. At this time, a man who resisted the opportunity to rob his country was regarded as a prodigy, and we can easily conceive that the rigid integrity of Pitt altogether apart from his commanding genius, would, to a man like Allen, prove an irresistible attraction. So great, so dazzling, had become the reputation of Pitt as an orator and patriot, that he exercised an influence individually over men's minds as well as over the country generally, such probably as had never been felt before;[2] and Bath, having once set her affections on the great man, steadfastly

---

[1] Macaulay says of him—"Yet, with all his faults and affectations, Pitt had, in a very extraordinary degree, many of the elements of greatness. He had genius, strong passions, quick sensibility, and vehement enthusiasm for the grand and the beautiful. There was something about him which ennobled tergiversation itself. He often went wrong, very wrong. But, to quote the language of Wordsworth—

"'He still retained,
"'Mid such abasement, what he had received
"'From nature an intense and glowing mind.'

"In an age of low and dirty prostitution, in the age of Dodington and Sandys, it was something to have a man who might, perhaps, under some strong excitement, have been tempted to ruin his country, but who never would have stooped to pilfer from her—a man whose errors arose, not from a sordid desire for gain, but from a fierce thirst for power, for glory, and for vengeance."

[2] In 1744, the old Duchess of Marlborough died. In a codicil to her will, she left a legacy to Pitt—"I give to William Pitt, Esq., the sum of Ten Thousand Pounds upon account of his merit in the noble defence he made for the support of the laws of England, and to prevent the ruin of his country." In 1765, an eccentric Somersetshire Baronet, Sir William Pynsent, bequeathed the whole of his fortune, £3,000 per annum, to Mr. Pitt. The estate of Burton Pynsent became his residence. Sir William had no near surviving relations, and therefore Pitt could accept the bequest without compunction. Lord Stanhope says: "'There was no enemy of Pitt could whisper against him the name of legacy-hunter, since he had never once seen nor even written to Sir William. The voice of faction itself must be mute, or must acknowledge that this was an unsought tribute most

adhered to him through evil and good report, and finally chose him, through her trusted leader, Ralph Allen, as her representative in Parliament. His triumphs were the triumphs of the city; his defeats and failures were shared by all classes of the citizens as their own. The old Whigs, pure and simple, could not endure a man like Pitt, who, whilst professing the same or even a greater love of constitutional liberty, yet spurned their methods and despised their traditions. Lord Stanhope says of Pitt that he and he alone at this time (*i.e.*, about 1765), like some lofty pine-tree in the forest, soars high above the undergrowth of Rockinghams,¹ etc.

In 1754, when Pelham died, Pitt was ill in this city, and on that occasion the Corporation paid him the most marked attention. That body, with its most important member, Ralph Allen, showed the great Commoner almost regal honours. The past and the present in his conduct as a statesman to them as the elective body were deserving of the warmest approbation, and they felt great

"honourably paid to high public character and eminent public services." Notwithstanding the sharp pangs of regret and vexation occasioned Ralph Allen by the severance of Pitt's political tie with Bath, Allen felt no resentment, as will be seen by an extract from the Codicil to his Will, dated November 10, 1763—the year preceding his death :—" For the last instance of my friendly and grateful regard for " the best of friends, as well as the most upright and ablest of ministers that has adorned our Country, " I give to the Right Honourable William Pitt, the sum of One Thousand Pounds, to be disposed of " by him to any of his children that he may be pleased to appoint."

¹ The contrast between Chatham and Rockingham was expressed in a witty epigram that appeared after the latter became Prime Minister in 1765 :—
"The truth to declare, if we may without shocking 'em,
"The nation's asleep, and the minister's *Rockingham*."

Lord Albemarle, in his Life of Rockingham, of whom and of whose ability he is an ardent admirer, says of Pitt—" The effect of his eloquence is unquestioned, but his speeches have been " scantily recorded. He was at once the Cicero and the Roscius of his age—a great orator and a " consummate actor. As a member of the Cabinet, he was incredibly haughty, impracticable, and " even obstructive to his colleagues. As a leader of opposition, he was more formidable as an " assailant than faithful to his adherents or consistent in his measures. To his sovereign he was ulti- " mately harsh and subservient ; to the nation he was an energetic, but a costly and a hazardous " guide, never scrupling to arouse passion, or to incur debt where glory was to be won ' in flood and " ' field.' Finally, as a statesman, he displayed rather the accomplishments of a Bolingbroke than " the solid prudence of a Burleigh. His talent for conducting military operations blinded him to the " disastrous effects of war to his own country and to mankind. Of social improvements or financial " skill he exhibited no proofs. He rendered his country glorious rather than prosperous ; and he " bequeathed to his successors the dangerous rather than the salutary precedent of preferring ' arms to " ' the gown.' These were his defects, and they were grievous, but his virtues too were singular and " illustrious, especially if they be measured by the general standard of his age." Lord Chesterfield says of him : " His private life was stained by no vice and sullied by no meanness. His habits were " domestic, and his sentiments lofty ; his knowledge was various and his taste refined. His letters to " his nephew, Lord Camelford, breathe a noble and generous spirit, and abound in weighty sense and " graceful diction. Throughout his correspondence with his wife and his illustrious son pervades a " tenderness which shows that his arrogance was part of his theatrical rather than his natural temper. " *He was made up of contrasts. It is much easier to eulogise or to condemn him than to draw a just " portrait.* To him belongs the merit of having been the first to raise the standard of morality in " public men." Lord Stanhope, in a very elaborate and admirably written panegyric on Pitt, in one passage says :—" But that which gave the brightest lustre, not only to the eloquence of Chatham, but " to his character, was his loftiness and nobleness of soul. If ever there has lived a man in modern " times to whom the praise of a Roman spirit might be truly applied, that man beyond all doubt was " William Pitt." Similar testimony is borne to the qualities of Pitt by Lecky in his " History of " England in the Eighteenth Century."

resentment at the manner in which he was treated by Newcastle in the construction of the new Administration. They applauded his opposition to the subsidies to the German States. They adopted an address to the king on the disasters which followed the war.[1] It is clear they did not look for consistency in their idol. If he opposed at one time what he afterwards supported, they probably thought that the capacity of the man made all the difference between the soundness and the unsoundness of the policy pursued. In April, 1757, he and his colleague, the Chancellor of the Exchequer, Legge, received each the freedom of the city in a gold box for "their services to the country "during their late short administration."[2] In July following, on the elevation of Henley to the Lord Keepership, Pitt resigned Old Sarum and was unanimously chosen for Bath.

Lord Macaulay says, "This was the turning-point of Pitt's life." The disasters under the feeble administration of Newcastle had occasioned great national indignation, and the public voice proclaimed Pitt to be the man to "save the country." Up to this period, the Bath Corporation had enthusiastically supported their illustrious representative. After he entered upon the Administration—which lasted from June 17, 1757, to Oct., 1761, and in which he was practically all-powerful—he received the cordial approval and the repeated thanks of the Corporation, by whom he was elected, and of the citizens, who worshipped him. His conduct of the war, the policy of the war—indeed, every act of his public life—inspired his friends in Bath with exultant pride and commanded their unfaltering allegiance. In Oct., 1760, the Mayor and Corporation unanimously adopted the following address to Mr. Pitt and his colleague, Lord Ligonier:—

"Bath; Oct. 6, 1760.
"SIRS,—
"We, the Mayor, Aldermen, and Common Council of this city, do "transmit to you, our representatives in Parliament, our most grateful thanks, "for exerting your great abilities with so much zeal and unwearied diligence in "the service of his Majesty and our country, as hath reflected particular honour "on our city. We are convinced we should not do justice to ourselves and "brother citizens, if we did not pay that regard which is justly due to your

---

[1] In November, 1755, Legge and Pitt were dismissed from office—the former (as Chancellor of the Exchequer) for refusing to sign the Treasury Warrants for the payment of the subsidies granted, and the latter, as Paymaster of the Forces, for his fierce denunciation of the principle of subsidies.

[2] Under the Duke of Devonshire. It began in Nov., 1756, and ended in April, 1757. It was during this Administration that Admiral Byng was tried, and Pitt used the noblest efforts, in vain, to save him.

"distinguished merit, by taking the earliest opportunity of offering to you the
"same trust at the next general election; and which we hereby beg the favour of
"your acceptance of, from,
"Gentlemen,
"Your much obliged and very humble Servants."

MR. PITT'S ANSWER.
"St. James's Square, Oct. 9, 1760.

"Mr. Mayor and Gentlemen of the Corporation,—
"I am this day honoured with your letter, and cannot defer a moment to
"express the sentiments of the warmest and most respectful gratitude for such a
"fresh mark of your condescension and goodness to me, after the many great
"and unmerited favours which you have already conferred upon me.

"Happy! that my feeble endeavours for the king's service have, in your
"candid interpretation, stood in the place of more effectual deservings; and that,
"actuated by the generous motives of zeal and steady attachment to his
"Majesty's Government, you are pleased again to think of committing to me the
"important and honourable trust of representing you at the next general election.

"Be assured, gentlemen, that I am justly proud of the title of servant of
"the city of Bath, and that I can never sufficiently manifest the deep sense I
"have of your distinguished and repeated favours; nor express the respect,
"gratitude, and affection with which I remain,

"Mr. Mayor and Gentlemen of the Corporation,
"Your most faithful and most obliged humble Servant,
"W. PITT."

LORD LIGONIER'S ANSWER.
"To the Worshipful the Mayor and the rest of the Corporation of the City of Bath.
"North Audley Street; Oct. 10, 1760.
"GENTLEMEN,—
"The very great honour done me by your letter of the 6th instant
"requires my earnest and most grateful thanks. Though your noble and
"generous way of acting is no new thing to me, who have had the honour to
"represent you in the two preceding Parliaments, and have experienced so often
"your goodness to me, nevertheless I must feel a very great satisfaction at the
"approbation you are pleased to express of my endeavours to serve my king and
"country as your representative. I meet with ... atitude this distinguished

"mark of your favour. The interest and honour of your city of Bath it will be ever my study to promote.

"I am, with the greatest regard and esteem,
 "Gentlemen,
  "Your most obliged and most faithful Servant,
   "LIGONIER."

These cordial relations between the electors and the two representatives were creditable to both parties. There was neither servility on the one side nor arrogance on the other. Everything pointed to the continuance of those relations, which was indicated in the Address, and at the general election in March, 1761,[1] the two members were unanimously re-elected. Pitt had steadily maintained his war policy;[2] he was judged by it, and he was ready to stand or fall by it. The Corporation not only re-elected their members, but honoured them publicly at the Guildhall, and the citizens vied with each other in doing honour to the men, especially to Pitt, of whom they were justly proud. In Oct., Pitt was defeated in the cabinet on the question of war with Spain. In December of the same year, the following *gushing* Address was sent to Mr. Pitt by the Corporation :—

"SIR,— "Bath; Dec. 18th, 1761.

"Had it not been for the particular relation in which we have the honour "to stand towards you, we should, perhaps, have been still content, as others "are, to enjoy in silence those fervours of gratitude which every true British "heart must feel for the great, unparalleled services which you have done your "king and country throughout the course of your late ministry.

"It is true that after so ample and honourable a testimony, borne to them "by your royal master himself, it would be extremely vain in us to think that "anything could be wanting to the glory of a character thus illustriously estab-"lished. But though we can add nothing to you, we have ventured to employ "this occasion to do credit to ourselves in that light, and are most ambitious to "be seen of faithful and loyal subjects, for in these expressions of our great "regard to you, we have only presumed to follow the gracious example of the "best of kings.

[1] By an oversight or misprint, Mr. Murch gives the date as March, 1760.

[2] The term Jingo was not then known, but if it had been it might probably have served a noble or ignoble purpose, as the case may be.

"For the rest, there is no station where you can be found in which your
"country will not need and will not be sure to have your most effectual
"assistance.
 "We have nothing, sir, further to offer but our ardent prayers for your
"health, a blessing so precious and so important to the public.
"We have the honour to be, Sir,
"Your most humble and affectionate Servants."

MR. PITT'S ANSWER.

"Hayes; Dec. 22, 1761.
"MR. MAYOR,[1]—

"I have received the particular honour of a letter signed by you, sir, and
"by a great many other gentlemen of the Corporation, containing the most
"condescending and endearing remarks, marks of personal regard and favour
"towards me, and at the same time bestowing on such inconsiderable efforts as I
"have been able to exert in the service of my king and my country—testimonies
"of so distinguished and honourable a nature, that I only accept them with a
"confusion joined to unceasing gratitude.

"Allow me, Mr. Mayor, to entreat that you will please to communicate to
"the other gentlemen of the Corporation these my most unfeigned and
"respectful acknowledgments, and to assure them of my ardent and continual
"wishes for the prosperity of the City of Bath, and for the particular welfare and
"happiness of the several members of that ancient and considerable Corporation.

"I am, with the warmest sentiments of regard and respectful considera-
"tion, sir, your most obedient and most obliged humble Servant,

"W. PITT."

This correspondence, it must be remembered, followed the energetic
counsels given by the Minister to the King, as to the expediency of a declaration
of war against Spain on account of the "family compact,"[2] and her equivocal
conduct towards those with whom we were at war, and it leaves no doubt that
the great minister felt that in resigning office he had the sympathy and confidence
of those from whom that address came, whatever it was worth.

The war against Spain which Mr. Pitt urged in vain in October of

---

[1] At this time, Alderman John Chapman.

[2] With reference to which, as Lord Stanhope says, "the commencement of the war of succes-
"sion was never yet so fully vindicated as by the conclusion of the family compact." *History of
England*, vol. 4, p. 234.

1761, and which his prescience had foreseen as inevitable—was declared by Lord Bute, in Jan., 1762, three months after Pitt quitted office. It seems probable that this short delay and the retirement of the great minister had encouraged Spain in the insolent and offensive course she had taken against Great Britain. Be this as it may, the attitude of Spain, and her intrigues with France, if they justified war in January, equally justified it in the previous October, when Pitt "would have had the first blow, which is often half the battle." "When once "convinced of their hostile designs, why allow them further time for prepara-"tion?"—which, indeed, was just what that fatal delay accomplished. The war was declared on the 4th January, 1762, and was concluded early in 1763. Bute resigned in April. The war had been carried on languidly, and much against his inclination. Pitt opposed the peace, because he deemed it *inadequate;* it did not secure the objects for which it was undertaken. When Parliament met, he denounced the peace with vehement eloquence, but all to no purpose. Eloquence could not prevail against the corruption employed to buy over a majority of members in favour of peace.

There has been nothing to show that, as between Pitt and the Corporation, either collectively or individually, there had been any misunderstanding.[1] When the peace was concluded which Pitt had so vehemently opposed, the Corporation, at a special meeting,[2] held in May, 1763,[3] over which Ralph Allen presided, adopted the following Address. It is printed in italics, because it will be observed that on the terms of the document hinged the whole future relations of Pitt with the Bath Corporation. It is the more necessary to make this clear, because in the late Rev. F. Kilvert's paper on Ralph Allen he leaves the Address out of the Correspondence; so in like manner Mr. Murch omits it. So that in each case the reader is left in a state of utter ignorance as to the character and wording of that document which gave Pitt so much offence

---

[1] It would seem indeed that Pitt's resignation was regarded by the citizens and the Corporation as a great public calamity. It inspired Mr. T. Atwood (who was Mayor, 1756-60-66,) to write well, a stanza, which, if it does not exhibit poetic genius, perhaps faithfully expresses the feelings of his colleague:—

"Whence does the Gaul exult? Can *Broglie** boast
"At length one battle not entirely lost?
"Or has the Spaniard their alliance joined?
"Alas! much worse—our Patriot has resigned!"

* Duc de Broglie, who commanded a portion of the French Army.

[2] Of which I can find no record in the Journals.

[3] It should be mentioned here that in April of this year Viscount Ligonier (in the Irish Peerage) was created an English Earl. His seat being thus vacated, two candidates were proposed—Mr. Long and Sir John Saunders Sebright, when the latter was elected.

and led to the termination of his political connection with a city in which he had received so many proofs of the confidence and admiration of all classes.

"*TO THE KING'S MOST EXCELLENT MAJESTY.*

"*We, the Mayor, Aldermen, and Common Council of the ancient and loyal*
"*city of Bath, do beg leave to congratulate, and most humbly to thank your Majesty*
"*for an* ADEQUATE *and advantageous peace, which you have graciously procured for*
"*your people, after a long and very expensive, though necessary and glorious war,*
"*which your Majesty, upon your accession to the throne, found your kingdoms*
"*engaged in.*

"*And we take the liberty to assure your Majesty, that upon all occasions we*
"*shall be ready to give the most evident proofs of the truest zeal and duty, which the*
"*most dutiful subjects can testify to the most gracious and best of princes.*

"*In testimony whereof we have hereunto affixed our*
."*Common Seal, the 28th day of May, 1763.*"

"Hayes; June 2, 1763.

"DEAR SIR,—

"Having declined accompanying Sir John Sebright in presenting the
"address from Bath, transmitted to us jointly by the Town-Clerk, I think it, on
"all accounts, indispensably necessary that I should inform you of the reason of
"my conduct. The epithet of *adequate* given to the peace contains a description
"of the conditions of it, so repugnant to my unalterable opinion concerning
"many of them, and fully declared by me in Parliament, that it was as impos-
"sible for me to obey the Corporation's commands in presenting their address,
"as it was unexpected to receive such a commission. As to my opinion of the
"peace, I will only say, that I formed it with sincerity according to such lights as
"my little experience and small portion of understanding could afford me. This
"conviction must remain to myself the constant rule of my conduct; and I
"leave to others, with much deference to their better information, to follow their
"own judgment. Give me leave, my dear, good sir, to desire to convey,
"through you, to Mr. Mayor and to the gentlemen of the Corporation, these my
"free sentiments; and with the justest sense of their past goodness towards me,
"plainly to confess that I perceive I am but ill qualified to form pretensions to
"the future favour of gentlemen, who are come to think so differently from me,
"on matters of the highest importance to the national welfare.

"I am ever, with respectful and affectionate esteem, my dear sir,

"Your faithful friend and obliged humble Servant,

"(Signed) W. PITT.

"Lady Chatham joins with me in all compliments to the family of Prior Park."
"To Ralph Allen, Esq."

"Prior Park; June 4, 1763.
"My Dearest Sir,—
"It is extremely painful to me to find by the letter which you was pleased "to send to me the 2nd of this month, that the word *adequate*, in the Bath "address, has been so very offensive to you, as to hinder the sincerest and most "zealous of your friends in the Corporation from testifying for the future their "great attachment to you.

"Upon this occasion, in justice to them, it is incumbent on me to "acquaint you, that the unexceptionable word does not rest with them, but "myself; who suddenly drew up that address, to prevent their sending of "another, which the Mayor[1] brought to me, in terms that I could not concur in; "copies of the two forms I have taken the liberty to send to you in the enclosed "paper, for your private perusal; and Sir John Sebright having, in his letter to "Mr. Clutterbuck, only acquainted him, that in your absence in the country he "delivered the address, I shall decline executing of your commands to the "Corporation on this delicate point, unless you renew them, upon your perusal of "this letter, which for safety I have sent by a messenger, and I beg your answer "to it by him, who has orders to wait for it.

"Permit me to say that I have not the least objection to, but the highest "regard and even veneration for, your whole conduct; neither have I any "apology to make for the expression in which I am so unfortunate to differ from "you. And with the utmost respect, affection, and gratitude, you will always "find me to be, my dearest sir, your most humble and obedient servant,
"(Signed) R. Allen.
"To the Right Hon. Mr. Pitt.
"The best wishes of this family always attend Lady Chatham.
"R. A."

"Hayes; June 5, 1763.
"My Dear Sir,—
"I am sorry that my letter of the 2nd inst. should give you uneasiness, "and occasion to you the trouble of sending a messenger to Hayes. I desire "you to be assured, that few things can give me more real concern, than to find "that my notions of the public good differ so widely from those of the man "whose goodness of heart and private virtues I shall ever respect and love. I "am not insensible to your kind motives for wishing to interpose time for second

[1] Alderman Samuel Bush.

"thoughts; but knowing how much you approve an open and ingenuous
"proceeding, I trust that you will see the unfitness of my concealing from my
"constituents the insurmountable reasons, which prevented my obeying their
"commands in presenting an address, containing a disavowal of my opinion
"delivered in Parliament relating to the peace. As their servant, I owe to these
"gentlemen an explanation of my conduct on this occasion, and as a man not
"forgetful of the distinguished honour of having been invited to represent them,
"I owe it, in gratitude, to them, not to think of embarrassing and encumbering,
"for the future, friends to whom I have such obligations; and who now view
"with approbation measures of an administration, founded on the subversion of
"that system which once procured me the countenance and favour of the city of
"Bath. On these plain grounds, very coolly weighed, I will venture to beg
"again that my equitable good friend will be so good to convey to Mr. Mayor
"and the gentlemen of the Corporation my sentiments, as contained in my
"letter of the 2nd instant.

"I am ever, with unchanging sentiments of respect and affection,
"My dear sir, most faithfully yours,
"W. PITT.

"Prior Park; June 9.
"MY DEAREST SIR,—
"With the greatest anxiety and concern, I have in obedience to your
"positive and repeated commands executed the most painful commission that I
"ever received.

"Upon this disagreeable occasion, give me leave just to say that, however
"different our abilities may be, it is the duty of every honest man, after he has
"made the strictest enquiry, to act pursuant to the light which the Supreme
"Being has been pleased to dispense to him; and this being the rule that I am
"persuaded we both govern ourselves by, I shall take the liberty, not only to
"add, that it is impossible for any person to retain higher sentiments of your late
"glorious administration than I do, nor can be with truer fidelity, zeal, affection,
"and respect than I have been, still am, and always shall be, my dearest sir,
Your most humble and most obedient servant,
"(Signed) R. ALLEN.

"To the Right Hon. Mr. Pitt.
"The best wishes of this family wait upon Lady Chatham."

Lord Stanhope thinks the word *adequate* slipped into the Address without design or the intention of conveying a meaning of especial significance. If it be so, it is singular that a word should have been used which, in itself, is so plenary in the sense it bears, and at the same time is the very converse of that which Pitt had used over and over again to characterize the peace—*inadequate*. It is not surprising that he should have regarded the Address with scornful indignation, not simply as approving the peace, but as by implication reversing all the judgments the Corporation had passed upon his previous policy and conduct. The word was "untoward," and Pitt thought that not only the word, but the whole Address, was the artful work of Bishop Warburton.[1] Pitt sold his house in the Circus at the close of the year, and, although he visited the city again in 1766 for the use of the waters, he does not seem to have renewed his intercourse with his former friends. He retained his seat until 1766, when he was created Earl of Chatham,[2] the dignity of Baroness Chatham having been already conferred upon his wife, Lady Hester Pitt (sister of the Earl Temple). The events were not without their amusing features, and in a book of this nature, the history of the caricatures relating to the *contretemps*, of which mention has been made, may appropriately find a place.

Ralph Allen, it needs not again to be proved, was a man who exercised great influence for good. It may be safely asserted that he was incapable of committing a sinister or unworthy act. His errors sometimes arose from his generous disposition, and it will be seen from the rupture with Pitt how sensitive he was and how much he suffered. There is no doubt that the Corporate body of the period deferred to him on most public matters in which he felt an unusual interest, but it does not appear from the Minutes of the Council, that he was a regular or even a frequent attendant at its meetings. Yet there remains the fact that the municipal body, from the circumstance that his authority and

---

[1] Bishop Warburton, who married Gertrude Tucker, Mrs. Allen's niece, had received his Bishopric from Pitt, and having promoted a similar Address from his own Chapter, the only Chapter in the Kingdom from which a similar Address was sent, it was natural that the Bishop should have been suspected of being "the power behind the throne" who had prompted Allen. The Bishop denied the accusation, but it is fair to presume that as he was constantly at Prior Park, he may have made known his intention of sending an Address and the sense of it, and thus unintentionally, or it may be too adroitly, influenced Allen's judgment. The Bishop wrote to Pitt, whose reply left a wound which troubled him not a little: "I will only venture to observe, my Lord, that the Cathedral of "Gloucester, which certainly does not stand alone in true duty and wise zeal towards His Majesty, has "however the fate not to be imitated by any other Episcopal See in the Kingdom, in this unaccustomed "effusion of fervent congratulations on the Peace."

[2] In an amusing passage in Barry Lyndon, Thackeray puts some trenchant remarks into the mouth of his hero with regard to the Seven Years' War in which he had taken a part, and concludes by a short reference to the "Marquis of Tiptoff" and Lord Chatham: "Though a Whig, or, perhaps, "because he was a Whig, the Marquis was one of the haughtiest men breathing, and treated com- "moners as his idol, the great Earl, used to treat them—after he came to a coronet himself—as so "many low vassals who might be proud to lick his shoe-buckles."

influence were so much deferred to, was nicknamed "The One-headed Corpora-
"tion," and that he assumed on this particular occasion the sole responsibility for
the fatal composition. The transaction no doubt excited much animadversion and
public dissatisfaction, which found expression in two humorous but somewhat coarse
caricatures of the day. In the first of these, dated 1763, the central figure is a
large head—an admirable portrait—of Allen; perched on it is a raven who is
croaking "poor Raafe, poor Raafe;" Allen is holding a scroll in his hands, on
which the word "Adequate" is conspicuously written. A bishop (Warburton) in
full canonicals is whispering into Allen's right ear, "'Tis I did this great work
"for you!" The devil, however, who is close upon the bishop's back, says,
"No, no, friend, 'twas I, the father of political lies, that first thought
"of *Addressing!*" to which Coward replies, "Don't drive me, St. John,[1] I'll
"go graze on the Common or in **PRIOR PARK**." In the right-hand upper
corner is a portrait of Lord Ligonier, and in the left a portrait of Pitt.
Around the figure of Allen are gathered the members of the Corporation, each
in the character which symbolized his calling. The death's head and gallipots
signified the several medical men. The wagon—Walter Wiltshire, carrier; the
horse's head—John Glazier, coachman; greyhound's head—Sir John S. Sebright,
M.P.; the ass's head—Leonard Coward; the bishop—Bishop Warburton; the
double-faced head—Ald. Biggs, lawyer; the clock-face—French Laurance, watchmaker; the E. O. Tables—J. Leake, publisher; the latticed window—Axford,
glazier[2]; the lock—Hales, ironmonger; the £500 and doll—Davis, jeweller and
toyman; the inkpot—Clutterbuck, the town-clerk, who is exclaiming, "What is
"all this *clutter* about"; the soldering-irons—Atwood, glazier[3]; the hoop—
Milsom, cooper. To the left stands the figure of Falstaff, whose identity[4]
is not so certain. He is very angry, and evidently was a man who thought
he did well to be angry. From the part played by Thicknesse in Bath about
this time, and from a close study of the character of the man, we feel almost certain that he it is who is intended to be represented by Falstaff. It is
the more probable from the language he is made to use, "Damn 'e for a set of
poltroons, I'll drive you from hence with this dagger." The sturdy, thick-set

[1] St. John was apparently a citizen who exercised some influence upon Coward; there was no person of the name in the Council.
[2] Axford Buildings are so called after the worthy Councillor.
[3] Atwood was a man of considerable wealth and local importance. He possessed a pretty villa at Turley, in which he is said to have entertained Romaine, and, at a later period, the great Burke himself. Henry Atwood, the last male representative of the family, died at Cranley House, Weston Road, on the 13th of December, 1814.
[4] We are indebted to Mr. T. W. Gibbs for the clear identification of the figures in the group, except Falstaff.

figure, the attitude, and the true nature of Thicknesse's courage, are all so admirably depicted in the Falstaffian figure. It is difficult to conceive any "outsider" in Bath at this period who combined in himself so many unamiable qualities as Philip Thicknesse. The caricature gave deep pain to Allen, because it imputed to him gross dissimulation—which was utterly foreign to his nature, and he was so little accustomed to be chidden by his Bath friends. Bishop Warburton thought it not beneath his dignity to write to Pitt to vindicate himself from the implied charge of duplicity, or, what was worse, treachery, and complained of the character he is made to assume in the caricature. Shortly after the first caricature appeared, the second was published, "A Sequel to the "Knights of Baythe, or the One-headed Corporation." The Committee is here represented, the members of which are most likely discussing Pitt's reply. Allen is presiding. After others have spoken, he is just saying " An Adequate " Peace merits an Adequate Address," when the curtain is drawn aside by a character whose identity we fail to recognise, who says, " I'll show them in their " proper colours," and there stand Bishop Warburton, Pitt, Ligonier, and the redoubtable swash buckler Falstaff. The Bishop says, " And I must have a " stroke at 'em." Falstaff says, " They should drink the Waters, for the Body " wants cleansing, by G——." Pitt exclaims, " Let who will represent such " Wretches, I wont." Ligonier put in, " Faith, Brother, they deserve to have no " Members at all." Underneath the picture the following lines are printed :—

> " See *Liberty's* Champions still loyal and true,
> " Displaying the tricks of poor R——h and his crew ;
> " Who thinking to shew himself *courtly* and civil,
> " Is eagerly riding *post-haste* to the *Devil!*
> " ' My friends (Hark, he crys) of this wise *Corporation,*
> " ' This *Adequate Peace* deserves *Congratulation.*
> " ' His *Lordship* by me too his compliments sends,
> " ' And promises shortly to make you amends.' "
> " Then to it they go, but, ye Gods ! such a Thing
> " Was never presented before to a ——— ;
> " For *Reason* her sentiments wisely expresses—
> " A *Peace* that is patch'd should have patch'd-up *Addresses.*"

Allen retired from the Council and died the year following. He had served the city as no other man could have done, and the treatment he received in this matter was but a very ungenerous return.

At 6, **WALCOT TERRACE**; at 9, **ROYAL CRESCENT**; at **THE LODGE**, Bathampton;[1] and at **THE HERMITAGE**; in the order in which we give them, lived, at various periods, **PHILIP THICKNESSE**, a man of

---

[1] Now occupied by Mr. Ross.

whom that accomplished gentleman, the Rev. Joseph Hunter, said he had attained a "bad eminence." Sir Bernard Burke, in his "Landed Gentry," says Philip Thicknesse was "a celebrated writer." Thicknesse tells us himself that he "was late Lieut.-Governour of Landguard Fort, and unfortunately the father of "Lord Audley."[1] Family History will irrefragably show that Philip Thicknesse belonged to a distinguished and highly respected family of Staffordshire and Lancashire, and the life and career of Philip will prove that in him that family had one who by no means added to its respectability. We have tried to form a dispassionate and just estimate of Philip Thicknesse as a "literary character," and to do this it was necessary to read his works. In our desire to extend our knowledge of Thicknesse's writings we derived little edification, whilst our impressions of his personal character were deepened. A man may be a charming writer and at the same time a very bad man; Thicknesse attained to a "bad eminence" in the various characters he assumed. Milton says—

> "Satan exalted sat, by merit rais'd
> "To that bad eminence,"

and we really cannot find in Philip Thicknesse a single merit, except of that kind which Milton describes.

It would be exceedingly difficult, if not impossible, to discern, within the scope of the investigations needed for this work, the record of any man so utterly devoid of every generous and manly quality as the subject of this notice. It is not that he was ill-natured, or envious, or unamiable *merely*—he was all these; but he was rancorous, uniformly vindictive, slanderous, and malicious. And it must be observed that when he gave utterance to his "sentiments" on his opponents, or deliberately committed them to paper for publication, he did so after long reflection, and in many instances after he had been through the ceremony of forgiveness and reconciliation with them. There would be some allowance to be made for a man of this kind, if he lacked the capacity of discerning the difference between good and evil. Thicknesse showed that he had a clear perception of the difference, especially when an opponent got the better of him. Some compensation might be derived from reading his works, if they possessed satirical humour, or real sarcastic force; but they are dull, ponderous, stupid, egotistical diatribes, abounding in libellous, coarse, indecent, and revolting ribaldry, unredeemed by a single generous thought or a well-expressed sentence. We should like to believe that the love he professed for his

[1] The misfortune seems to have been on the side of the son.

eldest brother, George Thicknesse,[1] High-Master of the Charter-house, was real, if he did not so irresistibly prove that such a feeling was foreign to his nature.

Philip Thicknesse was the third son of the Rev. Ralph Thicknesse, of Farthinghoe, Northamptonshire. Born in 1719, he was in due time placed in the Marines, rising to the rank of Captain. About 1750, through the interest of his family, he was appointed to the Governorship of Landguard Fort, on the Coast of Suffolk, and in that capacity he exhibited not merely a total unfitness for command, but some of the worst traits of his character. One of the officers in command of a regiment of volunteers was a Col. Vernon, (nephew of the famous Admiral of that name, whose heir he was,) afterwards Lord Orwell and Earl of Shipbrook. With him Thicknesse quarrelled. In the first instance the Governor was strictly in the right; but, not satisfied with the support he obtained from **CHARLES TOWNSHEND**, then Secretary at War, he showed the Minister's private letter to "everybody," to show his victory over his opponent.[2] Then again, by way of annoying the Colonel, he put up on his own private dwelling, which stood opposite the Colonel's mansion, a Wooden Gun, with offensive lines under it, for the purpose of reflecting upon Vernon's courage and honour. The Colonel becoming a candidate to represent Bury St. Edmunds in parliament, Thicknesse issued the most libellous and shameful handbills reflecting upon the Colonel. For these he was prosecuted, fined, and imprisoned for one year. He admits that he was the libeller, but protests that the prosecution should have been called a *persecution*, inasmuch as one witness, he alleges, swore to a fact he could not have had any knowledge of, though the fact was true! In certain cases, in which he affected a great zeal for reforms in the garrison in some small matters, he succeeded only in picking quarrels with everybody about him. Every person with whom he thus gets at loggerheads is a *wretch, an infamous person, a scoundrel,* or something only to be described by even stronger terms. Happily for Landguard Fort, he was permitted to retire, as he says, by "Lord Rockingham "(during his virtuous administration) with a recompense of two thousand four "hundred pounds from the present possessor, Capt. Singleton"! This was in 1763.

[1] Mr. Monkland, in his amusing book, "Literature and Literati of Bath," says: "*Ralph Thicknesse* died suddenly while performing some of his own music at a concert at Bath." Ralph Thicknesse here referred to was brother of Philip, and was a man of distinguished parts, as many of the Thicknesses were. The family is represented in Archdeacon Thicknesse, whose name was Coldwell, and who married the only surviving child (Anne) of Ralph Anthony Thicknesse, Esq., of Beech Hill, M.P. for Wigan, and assumed the name of Thicknesse.

[2] In a copy of Thicknesse's Memoirs, with notes in the handwriting of that excellent man, Dr. Harington, one of them on this fact is "shameful conduct"!

The account which Thicknesse gives of his first marriage, when he was 42 years old, is the most shameful narrative ever penned by any man of himself. Under a feigned marriage he seduced the woman, who he expected was rich, in order that he might make his own terms with her parents before he really married her! Her name was Lanove, her father being the grandson of a French Protestant Refugee. Thicknesse brought his wife to Bath; after giving birth to three daughters, she died (and two of her children also) of what was then called "Pelham sore throat." The rest of this part of his Memoirs is sickening from the revolting selfishness which it reveals.

After the death of Thicknesse's first wife, he, according to his own story, at the suggestion of a learned and indecent old Judge,[1] made love to a widow lady named Concanen,[2] who was willing to marry him if a little longer time only were permitted her to forget the *sainted* and departed Concanen. It is well to mention here that the narrative is preceded by the writer's views and feeling on religion. Being a Whig, and an advocate of liberal government, he denounces everybody who does not agree with him, and amongst others Burke, who was pleading the cause of the Dissenters and Roman Catholics with his usual power and earnestness. Thicknesse blended his piety with a good deal of dirty morality, which reveals the character of the man. In telling the story of this courtship, Thicknesse seemed to think it a fine joke. The widow, however, was unequal to the task of a courting match with the gentleman, for he goes on to tell his readers that when Lady Elizabeth Touchet (sister to the Earl of Castlehaven and Baron Audley), and heir-presumptive to the latter title, heard of this courtship, she thought she would rather marry him herself, which she did. As the gallant gentleman puts it,—"So I left the widow to finish her second mourning, and was soon after married to Lady Elizabeth Touchet."[3] By this lady he had two sons, George and Philip, and two daughters. Of the sons we shall see more; the

---

[1] The Judge suggested to him as an infallible method of winning the widow, who lived on the South Parade, to "get into the lady's bedroom, put on his night-cap, and look out of window when the walks are full of company."

[2] Widow of Matthew Concanen, who is mentioned in "The Dunciad," Pope satirizing him as a pretender—
"Cook shall be Prior, and Concanen, Swift!"
Concanen was an Irishman, by profession a lawyer, but took to journalism, and imagined himself to be a *Swift*. He was author of several dull and dead scurrilities, and in a paper called *The Speculatist*, he attacked Pope, who in another reference to his assailant says—
"True to the bottom see Concanen creep,
"A cold, long-winded native of the deep."

[3] November 10, 1749. Her ladyship's brother, the Earl of Castlehaven, dying in 1777, the Barony of Audley descended to her elder son, George, who married Elizabeth, 2nd daughter of Lord Delaval, and by her had two sons and one daughter. The elder succeeded his father, 1812, the younger was never married, and was killed at the battle of Copenhagen. The title is now in abeyance.

daughters being brought up in the Roman Catholic faith, they were sent to a Convent[1] in France. Thicknesse quarrelled with both his sons, and assuming that *all* the blame was on the part of the young men, what can be thought of a father who, to the end of his days, held up his children to contumely and execration? But, taking Thicknesse's own account of the quarrel with his sons, it is clear that if any fault was attributable to the sons, it was a fault that a good father would have corrected with "*good counsels, which are chains to grace.*" At the age of 19, George became Lord Audley, and Philip inherited part of the personal property of his late uncle, the Earl of Castlehaven.

First, Thicknesse promotes a quarrel between the brothers, and the father accompanies the younger son (then about 17) to a magisterial bench to swear that the elder brother had set him upon a runaway horse with the wicked intention of killing him, in order that he might obtain his fortune; the charge was unquestionably suggested by the father, and was a shameful falsehood. Then the two brothers, after a while, became reconciled, and the father on every occasion applied to them the vilest and most opprobrious epithets. It is not easy to discover from Thicknesse's tumid and envenomed narrative what were the ostensible grounds of his animosity against his sons, but it is almost certain that the real cause arose from his inability to help himself to their fortunes. The elder son, whether blamable or not, bore his father's abuse and malignity in silence. The younger, on one occasion, acting under advice, repelled, in an affidavit, certain statements made by his father. One statement made by the father, with an ingenious but ineffectual attempt to obscure the facts, will exhibit him in his true colours. Thicknesse at

---

[1] The elder daughter was sent to the English Benedictine Convent, at Pontoise united, on account of poverty, with the English Benedictines of Dunkirk. The United Community, which came over to Hammersmith during the French Revolution, now reside at St. Scholastica's Abbey, Teignmouth, which was built for them by the Countess English, sister of A. H. English, Esq., Coroner for the City of Bath. The papers are now in the Archives at Versailles.

1769. February 24. Came for Noviceship, Mrs. Elizabeth Thicknesse, aged 18 last August.

Le Mardi, 20 Juin, 1769, a reçue l'habit religieux, Dlle. Elizabeth Thicknesse, Fille de Messire Philippe Thicknesse, et de My lady Elizabeth Touchet, née à Turnam-Green dans la Province de Middlesex, en Angleterre, le 15 Aout, 1750. Elizabeth Thicknesse, ditte en religion Sœur Anne Marie.

(Témoins qui ont signé leurs noms.)
    Marie Anne Clavering, Abbesse.
    Henry Verme, Directeur.
    D'Amoinville, Curé de N. Dame.
    L. Havard, Prêtre.
    Jacques Mather, Curé de S. Vincent.
    F. de Jerningham.
    Henry Belasyse.
    Charles Belasyse.

Dame Elizabeth was professed on 31 July, 1770, there being only one additional witness – Bermingham Chanoine. In 1789 she went to the English Benedictines in the Rue de l'Alouette, Paris, with a pension of 600 francs per annum.

this period lived in a small house he called **The Hermitage**[1] (in the grounds of which he tells us he buried his last surviving daughter by his first marriage). The younger son, on his father announcing his intention of going abroad, was willing to purchase the property, and the amount agreed upon was £500; not having the money, and being only 18 years of age, he gave his father an acceptance for the amount. Some time after, having the money, he paid the £500, together with another £100 as a free gift, to his father. The father craftily availed himself of the son's inexperience to retain the acceptance. When a few years had elapsed, and after the son had expended much money upon the house, he allowed his father to repurchase his former residence on repayment of the £500. The father then claimed payment of the acceptance! The son denied at first that he had given any such acceptance, but after a while, he remembered the transaction. Thicknesse held up his son to scorn and contempt, though he does not deny, what indeed was abundantly proved, that he had received £100 over and above the amount for which the document was given! The son, Philip, joined the Independent Nonconformists, and his father, actuated by those enlightened principles of which he so often boasted—his attachment to liberal government and his love of pure Protestantism and generous toleration—after exhausting his rich vocabulary of epithets against this unhappy son, crowned them all with the terrible charge of "Independency"! He occasionally met his match. Once Dr. William Falconer condescended to crush him.

His most terrible and doughty antagonist, however, was Dr. Mackittrick, who had added the name Adair[2] to his patronymic. Thicknesse was an empiric. He advocated the use of a peculiar cordial or ætherial spirit, which was made by *Tickell*, who then resided in Bath; it was a nostrum in which he affected great faith, and *profited* by the sale of it. He wrote the Valetudinarian's Guide, in which he prescribed opium and rolling the patient upon a barrel in cases of bilious disorders. His books of Travels, when they do not verge

---

[1] The Hermitage is situate between the west wing of Lansdown Crescent and Somerset Place. Thicknesse, writing to a friend, describes the place as a spot of exceeding loveliness. As a matter of fact, it was a very mean wretched place. He offered to let it unfurnished at a rent of £30 per annum, and furnished at £37 10s. During the lifetime of Lady Elizabeth he resided at No. 9, Royal Crescent, except when he was at Landguard Fort. The Hermitage, as it is now, is a very different place.

[2] Adair exposed with crushing force and ability the pretension of this charlatan. Thicknesse, in his Memoirs, had nothing worse to say of Adair than that he had changed, or rather added to, his name; yet for this there is no language too strong for him to use against his antagonist. In 1790, Adair, under the name of *Benjamin Goosequill*, criticised Thicknesse's Memoirs, published in 1788. He laid bare the character of Thicknesse with richly deserved severity; showed up his malignity; his ignorant empiricism; his treachery; his false scholarship; his foulness to his sons, who, if they were not good, had before them an example which accounted for the fact. In the

upon indecency, are sickening in their egotistical references to himself. He wrote a *Bath Guide* in 1778, in which he abused poor Mrs. Catherine Macauley, the author of the History of England, as if she had committed a crime. He was by turns "capricious, gloomy, and resentful." He boasted that enemies were more useful to him than friends, because it enabled him to vilify them in pamphlets, and then he derived a profit by compelling his "friends" to buy them, under a feeling of terror lest they might be the next victims of his malignity. Poor Gainsborough had the misfortune to be numbered amongst his friends. Thicknesse wrote a sketch of Gainsborough's career, in which he endeavoured by "inuendo"—to use his own word—to show that the great painter owed all success to him, and though it is pretty clear that Gainsborough despised him, and that his intolerable tyranny had much to do with driving the artist out of Bath, yet Thicknesse did observe a little prudence by not coming to a rupture with his friend, but he made up for his "Christian" forbearance by vilifying Mrs. Gainsborough, who was a careful woman and protected her husband's interests (he himself was a careless man) against the rapacity of the man, whom, with Scottish shrewdness, she[1] saw through and utterly distrusted and despised. Thicknesse married as his third wife Miss Ford, niece of Sir Richard Ford. She was a woman of great beauty, and of varied accomplishments as a writer.[2] Mrs. Thicknesse survived her husband thirty-two years, dying in Edgware Road, London, June 20, 1824. Thicknesse, always embarrassed by debt, relieved Bath of his presence, which for years had become a nuisance, and went to Boulogne in 1791. At the close of 1792, when about to start for Italy,

---

closing Vol., Thicknesse retorts in language so virulent, in defamation so abominable, that the Volume was suppressed, perhaps in consequence of his death, which occurred in 1792. Adair, in reference to Thicknesse's quarrel with his sons, wrote the following :—

"THINK what you PLEASE about your SON,
 But ne'er DIVULGE your thoughts ;
 For NATURE says, you ought to HIDE,
 And not EXPOSE HIS FAULTS.

 Suppose the ' WRETCH'S ' conduct should
  Our tend'rest feeling shock,
  The WORLD will only SMILE, and say
  'THE CHIP IS LIKE THE BLOCK.

  Know, then, and knowing, pray be still,
  (Thou base, malignant elf,)
  That HE, who'd make his SON a KNAVE
  Must be a KNAVE HIMSELF."

Dr. Mackittrick Adair died at Harrowgate, April 24, 1802.

[1] See Gainsborough.

[2] She was the author of "Sketches of the Lives and Writings of the Ladies of France," in 3 vols. London, 1778-82. She had a son, Capt. Thicknesse, R.N.

he died suddenly. The first clause of his Will runs thus :—" I leave my right "hand, to be cut off after my death, to my son, Lord Audley ;[1] I desire it may be "sent to him, in hopes that such a sight may remind him of his duty to God, "after having so long abandoned the duty he owed to a father, who once *so* "*affectionately loved him.*" It is strange, indeed, that any father should boast that he once *loved* a son ![2] The end of the man was worthy of his life. He carried his resentment beyond the grave itself.

MAJOR ANDRÉ, 23, CIRCUS.—John André, a British officer, of French extraction, educated at Geneva, and originally intended for a commercial career, entered the army in 1771, at the age of 20. At the outbreak of the American War, he was sent to Canada, and taken prisoner at St. John's, but, being exchanged, in 1778, he joined Sir W. Howe's force at Philadelphia, and it was he who, to infuse cheerfulness into the troops who were beginning to feel the dispiriting influence of inactivity, got up a remarkable *fête* called the *Mischianza* (Medley). It consisted of every sort of knight errantry, fantastic dances, processions, and elegant amusements. Captain André was the life and soul of the affair. The "gayest of the gay"; the brilliant, handsome, fearless young officer, destined in all probability to high distinction and command, met with that fate which even his enemies regretted, and his friends and the British Nation universally deplored. But the life-long bitterness—the loving sorrow—was reserved for his mother and sisters, who, residing at 23, Circus, devoted the rest of their lives to works of charity, in a spirit of meek endurance and resignation, and in memory of one whose life was so joyous and whose death was so tragic.[3] André, who was equally distinguished for his love of art and literature, as for his gallantry and chivalrous character,

---

[1] Lord Audley died at the age of 61 in August, 1813, at his seat, Sandridge Lodge, Wiltshire.

[2] As a proof of malignity, and coarse and radically vulgar nature, Thicknesse, after his quarrel with his son, to inflict pain and mortification upon him, put up a board over his own window with the following inscription upon it—"Boots and shoes mended, carpets beat, etc., etc., by P. Thicknesse, father of Lord Audley."

[3] "The execution of Major André is, indeed, one of the saddest episodes of the American war, "and in the judgment of many it left a deep stain on the reputation of Washington. The victim was "well fitted to attract to himself a lively romantic interest. Though only twenty-nine, he had already "shown the promise of a brilliant career. He was a skilful artist, and the singular charm of his "conversation, and the singular beauty of his frank, generous, and amiable character, endeared him to "all with whom he came in contact, and was acknowledged by not one more truly than by those "American officers with whom he spent the last sad days of his life. Nothing could be more dignified, "none courageous, more candid, and at the same time more free from everything like boasting or

had been engaged for some years to Miss Honora Sneyd, a lady of great beauty and accomplishments. It should be mentioned that after General Howe retired with his forces from Philadelphia, André was attached to the force under General Clinton at New York, to whom he was *aide-de-camp*, and adjutant-general. The event which led to his death may to some of our readers not be without interest :—

"The Americans had a strong fortress at West Point, on the Hudson river. It was one of the
"most important places in the country, and its acquisition was anxiously desired by the English.
"Possession of West Point would have given them command of the Hudson, up which their ships of
"war could have sailed for more than a hundred miles. But that fort, sitting impregnably on rocks,
"two hundred feet above the level of the river, was hard to win ; and the Americans were careful to
"garrison effectively a position so vitally important.
"In the American army was an officer named Arnold, who had served, not without distinction,
"from the beginning of the war. He had fought in Canada when the Americans unsuccessfully
"invaded that province. His courage and skill had been conspicuous in the engagements which led
"to the surrender of Burgoyne. He was, however, a vain, reckless, unscrupulous person. He had
"by extravagance in living involved himself in debt, which he aggravated hopelessly by ill-judged
"mercantile speculations. He had influence with Washington to obtain the command of West Point.
"There is little doubt that when he sought the appointment it was with the full intention of selling
"that important fortress to the enemy. He opened negotiations at once with Sir Henry Clinton, then
"in command of the English army at New York.
"At midnight Major André landed from the boat of a British ship of war, at a lonely place
"where Arnold waited him. The conference lasted so long that it was deemed unsafe for André
"to return to the ship. He was conducted to a place of concealment within the American lines,
"to await the return of darkness. He completed his arrangement with Arnold, and received
"drawings of the betrayed fortress. His mission was now accomplished. The ship from which he
"had come lay full in view. Would that he could reach her ! But difficulties arose, and it was
"resolved that he must ride to New York, a distance of fifty miles. Disguising himself as he best
"could, André reluctantly accepted this very doubtful method of escape from his fearful jeopardy.
"Within the American lines he had some narrow escapes, but the pass given by Arnold carried
"him through. He was at length beyond the lines. His danger might now be considered at an end,
"and he rode cheerfully on his lonely journey. He was crossing a small stream—thick woods on his
"right hand and his left enhanced the darkness of the night. Three armed men stepped suddenly
"from among the trees and ordered him to stand. From the dress of one of them, André
"thought he was among friends. He hastened to tell them he was a British officer, on very special
"business, and he must not be detained. Alas for poor Major André, they were not friends ; and the

"ostentation, than his conduct under the terrible trial that had fallen upon him, and it is even now
"impossible to read without emotion those last letters in which he commended to his country and his
"old commander the care of his widowed mother, and asked Washington to grant him a single
"favour—that he might die the death of a soldier and not of a spy. At the same time it is but justice
"to remember that he suffered under the unanimous sentence of a board consisting of fourteen general
"officers, and that two of these Steuben and Lafayette were not Americans. Nor can the justice
"of the sentence in my opinion be reasonably impugned. As a matter of strict right, the American
"sentence against André appears to me unassailable, and it is only on grounds of mercy and magna-
"nimity that it can be questioned."—*Lecky's History of the Eighteenth Century*, vol. iv.

"dress which deceived him had been given to the man who wore it when he was a prisoner with the
" English, in place of a better garment of which his captors had stripped him.
" André was searched ; but at first nothing was found. It seemed as if he might yet be allowed
" to proceed, when one of the three exclaimed, ' Boys, I am not satisfied. His boots must come off.'
" André's countenance fell. His boots were searched, and Arnold's drawings of West Point were
" discovered. The men knew then that he was a spy. He vainly offered them money ; they were
" incorruptible. He was taken to the nearest military station, and the tidings were at once sent to
" Washington, who chanced to be then at West Point. Arnold had timely intimation of the disaster,
" and fled for refuge to a British ship of war.
"André was tried by a court formed of officers of the American army. He gave a frank and
" truthful account of his part in the unhappy transaction—bringing into due prominence the
" circumstance that he was brought, without intention or knowledge on his part, within the
" American lines. The court judged him on his own statement, and condemned him to be hanged
" as a spy.
" His capture and sentence caused deep sensation in the English army, and every effort was
" made to save him. But Washington was resolute that he should die. The danger to the patriot
" cause had been too great to leave any place for relenting. There were dark intimations of other
" treasons yet unrevealed. It was needful to give emphatic warning of the perils which waited on
" such unlawful negotiations. André begged that he might be allowed to die a soldier's death. Even
" this poor boon was refused to the unhappy man. Since the awful lesson must be given, Washington
" considered that no circumstance fitted to enhance its terrors should be withheld. But this was
" mercifully concealed from André to the very last.
" Ten days after his arrest, André was led forth to die. He was under the impression that his
" last request had been granted, and that he would die by the bullet. It was a fresh pang when the
" gibbet, with its ghastly preparations, stood before him. 'How hard is my fate,' he said ; ' but it
" ' will soon be over.' He bandaged his own eyes ; with his own hands adjusted the noose to his
" neck. The cart on which he stood moved away, and poor Major André was no longer in the world of
" living men. Forty years afterwards his remains were brought home to England and laid in
" Westminster Abbey."—*Mackenzie's America.* London : Nelson, 1882.

GAINSBOROUGH.—14, ABBEY CHURCHYARD ; 8, AINSLIE'S BELVEDERE ; 24, CIRCUS, were successively the residences of this eminent Painter. No adequate biography has ever been written of Thomas Gainsborough. The fact may be owing to the circumstance that, unlike Reynolds, Lawrence, or Hayden, Gainsborough did not add to his wonderful genius as a painter any great love for literature, and left little or nothing in the way of correspondence on which an interesting biography could be based. He was shy, sensitive, and retiring ; he seemed to care little for literary men, as such, and this may be accounted for by the consciousness that he was not qualified to shine in conversation with his compeers, many of whom he eclipsed with his pencil. Certain it is that Gainsborough added nothing to the literature of his art, though he has left a name immortalised in his works, the adequate description of which would form in itself a noble monument to art literature. Gainsborough was born at Sudbury, in 1727. The history of his earlier years shows that he cared little for learning, and that his every faculty was absorbed in his efforts to acquire a knowledge of his future art, which he was obliged to pursue furtively and as he best could. His youthful genius and the means he adopted for its cultivation and development appear to have been regarded by his father as sheer waywardness and eccentricity. But, in spite of all opposition, and with little else to help him besides nature and his innate love of the beautiful, he acquired that knowledge of his art which rendered him the first, or one of the first, painters of the eighteenth century.[1] What is so singular with regard to Gainsborough is the intuitive soundness of all the *methods* he adopted in the pursuit of his art. He was a born painter, and, as Sir Joshua Reynolds[2] says of him, after that interview he had with Gainsborough on his deathbed:—"Without entering into a detail of what passed "at this last interview, the impression of it upon my mind was, that his regret at "losing life was principally the regret of leaving his art; and more especially as "he now began, he said, to see what his deficiencies were, which, he said, he "flattered himself in his last works were in some measure supplied."

He married, early in life—when he was about 19—Margaret Burr, a girl of Scottish descent, pretty, lively, and, fortunately for Gainsborough, with a good deal of *canny* carefulness about her. Dr. Harington says:—"A Scotch Duke "had placed her at school, perhaps with no good intent. She was beautiful, and "when he died left her an annuity of £200 a-year." Gainsborough first tried his fortunes in London, but Thicknesse asserts he had "not formed any high "ideas of his own powers," and that he thought his chances of success were greater in the country. At any rate, he took his pretty wife to Ipswich, and there, in a small cottage at six pounds a-year, made a second attempt. It was at this time Philip Thicknesse met with him, took him under his sinister patronage, brought him to Bath, and induced him to take apartments at 14, Abbey Churchyard, at £50 per annum, but the risk was not undertaken without a strong protest on the part of the canny little wife, whose instinctive aversion to Thicknesse ultimately developed into avowed antagonism, for which she had very good reason. Thicknesse's patronage was equalled only by Rehoboam's tyranny; and

---

[1] Speaking of Gainsborough's "intuitive perception," Sir Joshua Reynolds says "He found out "a way of his own to accomplish his purpose. It is no disgrace to the genius of Gainsborough to "compare him to such men as we meet with, whom natural eloquence appears, even in speaking, a "language which they can scarce be said to understand; and who, without knowing the appropriate "expression of almost any one idea, contrive to communicate the lively and forcible impressions of "an energetic mind."

[2] Fourteenth Discourse.

at length, after vainly attempting to suppress his feelings and his disgust, Gainsborough suddenly left Bath and fled to London, where the repute he had achieved in the city of his adoption attained its full growth. In telling the story of Gainsborough, Thicknesse, as usual, has one word for his hero and two for himself. He praises Gainsborough with a sort of pitying patronage, and then gives vent, by way of relieving his pent-up wrath, to unmanly abuse of the poor little wife, because she protected the interests of her husband against the crafty patron. Thicknesse tells a story in which he tries to insinuate that Gainsborough treated him with something like shabbiness, if not dishonourably, but if Gainsborough had ever condescended to give his version of the affair, there would have appeared facts which Thicknesse did not care to tell. Gainsborough began by painting portraits at Five Guineas, then Eight Guineas, then Forty Guineas for a half-length, and One Hundred for a full-length. From the Abbey Churchyard, Gainsborough went to live in Ainslie's Belvedere, and we believe from thence to 24, Circus.[1]

Fulcher's Life of Gainsborough, written under every possible disadvantage, we must allow, gives little that is interesting as to the works that he executed in Bath. This is attributable to the fact to which we have alluded, namely, the paucity of Gainsborough's notes and correspondence relating to his professional life and experience. The reason of this may be ascribed to that sensitive, half-suspicious temperament which was peculiar to him. In the "Leisure Hour" for 1882, a series of Letters, written in the year 1769, is published. These Letters, addressed to his friend, Jackson, of Exeter,[2] are very characteristic. We regret that we are not permitted to make use of them except in piecemeal, as they bear out our estimate of Gainsborough's disposition. While they exhibit a shrewd and keen perception of art and other kindred subjects, they are erratic, and possess none of the literary polish of his great contemporary, Sir Joshua

---

[1] The late Dr. Randle Wilbraham Falconer thought it was at the house occupied by his grandfather (Dr. William Falconer), and then later by his father (the Rev. Thomas Falconer, M.D.), but this could not be, Dr. W. Falconer having been in possession of No. 29 some years before Gainsborough took up his residence in the Circus.

[2] "To the above narrative it may be added, for the information of the reader, that William Jackson, of Exeter, raised himself and his family, by his talent as a musician and an artist, much above their original position in life. His son William Jackson went to India in the Civil Service, and was afterwards sent as one of the Commissioners to China in Lord Amherst's expedition. Returning with an ample fortune, he married Miss Frances Baring, daughter of Mr. Charles Baring of Exeter. She was one of a family of beautiful and accomplished sisters, one of whom married Sir Stafford Northcote, another Sir William Young, grandfathers of the present baronets. As Mr. Jackson (of the Indian Civil Service) had no family, he and his wife adopted and educated an orphan relative of his own, William Elmsley, who became a successful lawyer, Q.C., and County Court Judge of Derbyshire. To him Mr. Jackson bequeathed his father's autobiography and many art treasures collected by him." Jackson wrote a notice of Gainsborough after his death, not in a flattering spirit.

Reynolds. These letters were written to his friend in the full confidence of friendship, and leave a very pleasant impression upon the mind as to his generous and kindly disposition.

The friendship between *Walter Wiltshire*[1] and the painter was sincere and creditable to both. The former was a man of much local reputation, trusted by the citizens, given to hospitality, and greatly esteemed for his probity and good qualities. He was generous to Gainsborough, but he affected nothing of the patron, and the return Gainsborough made to him *now* seems out of all proportion to the services rendered. But the half-dozen pictures presented to Wiltshire a hundred years ago would represent at that time a very different value from the prices they realized on the death of that excellent man, *John Wiltshire*, fifteen years ago.

The portraits painted in Bath by Gainsborough, although scattered about in various directions, are carefully preserved, and from time to time delight the eye at our public exhibitions. In Bath, besides his many exquisite landscapes, he painted Lord Clare during that visit which Goldsmith has rendered immortal. This portrait hung over the mantel-piece in the dining-room at Stowe, and was sold Sept. 14, 1848, to Field-Marshal Sir George Nugent, Bart. (Lord Clare's grandson), for £106.[2] In Bath he painted the portraits of Lord Killmorey, Foote,[3] the actor, Mr. Medlicote, Mr. Moysey, Doctor Charlton, Mr. Fischer the oboe-player (son-in-law), Mrs. Thicknesse,[4] Bishop Hurd, Sterne, Richardson, Sheridan, Burke, Lord Camden, Graves of Claverton, and above all in "pre-eminent merit," the parish clerk of Bradford, now to be seen near that other glorious portrait from his pencil, Mrs. Siddons, in the National Gallery. Here also he painted that lovely woman, Miss Cholmondeley (afterwards Countess of Mulgrave), and that not less charming *idol*, Miss Linley[5] (Mrs. Sheridan).

[1] Walter Wiltshire, the great Carrier of that day, who gratuitously conveyed all Gainsborough's pictures to London. He employed Baldwin to build his mansion at Shockerwick, and served the office of Mayor in 1780-91. John Wiltshire was Walter's grandson.

[2] As it has not been sold since, we presume it is in the possession of the family still.

[3] It is said the portraits of Foote and Garrick are not good likenesses. But, as Gainsborough said, "Rot them for a couple of Rogues, they have everybody's faces but their own."

[4] This was Philip Thicknesse's third wife, an enchanting woman. By this lady there was one son, Capt. Thicknesse, R.N., whose widow survives, and who is the possessor of this portrait—a portrait rendered the more famous because the subject of it gave the last finishing touch to the quarrel between her husband and Gainsborough.

[5] Gainsborough had a passion for music, and a story is told by Thicknesse in relation to Miss Linley, highly characteristic of the painter:—"After returning from a concert where we had been "charmed by Miss Linley's voice, I went home to supper with my friend, who sent his servant for a "bit of clay from the small beer-barrel, with which he first modelled, and then coloured her head, and "that too in a quarter of an hour, in such a manner that I protest it appeared to me even superior "to his paintings! The next day I took a friend or two to his house to see it, but it was *not* to be "seen—*the servant had thrown it down from the mantle-piece and broke it.*"

Mrs. Delany, one of the most witty and brilliant women of her day, said Gainsborough's paintings were "splendid impositions," but who now will be found to agree with her?

Gainsborough had two daughters, very beautiful women; Gainsborough himself had a handsome countenance, but there is that furtive, shy expression which was indicative of his true character.[1] His sister married the Rev. Daniel Gibbons.[2] Three of his nieces, the Miss Gardiners, were milliners—when to be milliners in Bath, with a high connection, meant a certain fortune—in Brock Street, and a nephew of the same name either founded the once-famous Northgate Brewery, or was a partner in it in its early days.

Gainsborough died at the age of 62, from cancer in the neck; almost his last words to Sir Joshua Reynolds being "We are all going to heaven, and "Vandyke is of the company." Truly, it may be said of Gainsborough that he was an honour to Bath. It is something to boast of that in this city his transcendent ability was, at any rate, partly recognized. There is no sad story of neglected genius, starving children, and selfish indifference. Gainsborough himself, it seems probable, was unconscious of the full extent of his power, which successive generations have more fully understood and appreciated.

14, CIRCUS, in 1774, was, for a brief period, the residence of the famous **LORD CLIVE**. His visit was ostensibly for the use of the Bath Waters, but the epileptic fits, induced by long exposure to an Indian clime, and by immense mental strain, precluded the use of the Waters, the ostensible object of his visit.

15, CIRCUS, was the property and residence of **JOHN, DUKE OF BEDFORD**. *Junius* said to him, in his letter, dated Sept. 19, 1769, that he was "so little accustomed to receive any mark of respect or esteem from the public, that if by accident a complimentary expression escaped him, the Duke might regard it as an insult to his understanding." The Duke and Duchess previously resided in Queen Square, and although the Duke appears to have been a man

---

[1] "Soon after Gainsborough settled in London, Sir Joshua thought himself bound in civility to pay him a visit. That painter, however, as our author told me, took not the least notice of him for several years; but at length called upon him and requested him to sit for his picture. Sir Joshua complied, and sat once, but being soon afterwards taken ill, he was obliged to go to Bath for his health. On his return to London, perfectly restored, he sent Gainsborough word that he was returned, to which Gainsborough, who was extremely capricious, only replied that he was glad to hear that Sir Joshua was well; and he never afterwards desired Sir Joshua to sit, nor had he any other intercourse with him till a short time before his (Gainsborough's) death, when he sent a request to see Sir Joshua, and thanked him for the very liberal and favourable manner in which he had always spoken of his works." —*Beechy's Literary Works of Sir J. Reynolds.*

[2] One of Lady Huntingdon's "Students," and afterwards a minister in the Connection.

94 *Historic Houses in Bath and their Associations.*

easily led away by party and by the more subtle influences of political friends, there is nothing connected with the Duke's career in Bath to justify the extremely harsh judgment of *Junius*. The Duke and Duchess were the subjects of especial attention of Lady Huntingdon, and were regarded as converts to the faith. *Junius* understood little, and cared less, about the revivalists or the revival movement in Bath, but be this as it may, he never ceased to regard the Duke as a "vessel of wrath." It was during the period when the Duke resided in Queen Square, that the Princess Amelia visited him. The Duchess was one of *The Duchesses*.[1]

4, EDGAR BUILDINGS.—In this house lived the **COUNTESS OF HUNTINGDON**; Lady Selina Shirley, second daughter of Washington, second Earl Ferrers. She was cousin to Laurence, the fourth Earl Ferrers,[2] who succeeded his uncle, Henry, the third Earl, a younger brother of Lady Selina's father, who had no male issue. Lady Selina married, on the 3rd of June, 1728, Theophilus, Earl of Huntingdon. There were two great "Revivals" in Bath during the eighteenth century, both fraught with the elements of excitement, but eminently antagonistic. The *Countess of Huntingdon* was the central figure, the source of authority and power of the Religious Revival. *Beau Nash* was the head of the other Revival; he was the king, the autocrat, the centre of authority, in the realms of fashion and gambling. To read the history of these conflicting movements is rather a wearisome task. If a casual reader were to take up "The Life and Times of Selina, Countess of Hunting-"don," he would at once come to the conclusion that he had opened a copy of the Companion to the Peerage by mistake. He would scarcely expect to read so much about *illustrious descent, high rank, brilliant positions, ancestral grandeur*, and a good deal more of that sort of locution, in connection with so much lowly piety and disregard of worldly distinctions; but so it is. The editor of the book, a cadet of the noble families of Shirley and Hastings, is deeply impressed with the fact that in proportion to his[3] kinswoman's superior rank, so was her piety and godliness above that of ordinary plebian Christians.

It would be impossible to give, in the limited space at our command,

---

[1] The Duke died in 1771. The spirit shown by the Duke during his last illness is very remarkable, notwithstanding the languor and depression attendant on the complaint (paralysis) under which he laboured, he neglected no part of his business, either public or private.—*Horace Walpole*. The Duke was the father of the Duchess of Marlborough, wife of George, third Duke of Marlborough.

[2] This was the Earl Ferrers, who was executed for the murder of his steward, Johnson.

[3] We assume the writer to be, or to have been, a man, though we are obliged to admit our ignorance of the fact.

more than a very brief account of the Religious Revival, of which Lady Huntingdon was the director, and of which Bath was the head-quarters. The movement is almost forgotten in Bath, and few traditions have survived the period. Lady Huntingdon's memory, and the cause to which she devoted her life and energies, have suffered from the ill-written "Life and Times of Lady Huntingdon," by a "Member of the Houses of Shirley and Hastings." Amidst all the exaggeration and the extravagant nonsense with which the book abounds, it is difficult to arrive at a clear and dispassionate judgment, either upon the Countess herself, or the cause with which her name is identified. The following extract will suffice as a key to the whole tenor and spirit which pervade the book throughout:—
"Wherever she was called by the providence of God, she was acknowledged as "'a burning and shining light.' *The common lights of Christians were eclipsed* "*before her*, and *even her spiritual friends could never stand in her presence, without* "*being overwhelmed with a consciousness of their own unprofitableness.*" Mr. Toplady "considered her Ladyship *the most precious saint of God he ever knew!*"

That Lady Huntingdon was a woman of energy, fervid spirit, and great piety, admits of no doubt, but when such claims are put forward as those we have quoted, they can only be regarded as presumptuous *hyperbole*, bordering upon irreverence. There was one peculiarity about this Bath Revival, and that is the fact that, so far as its religious operations were concerned, they were almost —nay, in their earlier stage, exclusively—confined to the upper classes. Around Lady Huntingdon, as the centre of the system, revolved a number of inferior "burning and shining lights." It does not appear from this "Life and Times" that there were any regular ministrations to the poor, and this may account for the fact that we do not find any instances recorded in Bath of those painful and distressing physical manifestations, which sometimes resulted from Wesley's and Whitefield's preaching elsewhere. The aristocratic converts were not apparently susceptible of the same influences and the same convulsive phenomena as the less refined and uneducated classes. If the Earl of Bath (Pulteney), who is claimed as a convert by the author of "The Life and Times," had fallen down in a convulsive fit and bitten the dust, it would have been a striking testimony to the supernatural character of such manifestations.

The Earl did not object to being regarded as one of the elect; it saved him no little trouble, but neither in his public nor private life did he manifest any of the fruits of the spirit.

"*Esse bonum facile est, ubi quod vatet esse remotum est.*"

The Earl, moreover, was a type of many others, who, from curiosity, or from a real interest in listening to the eloquence of Whitefield, attended the services in the private room of Lady Huntingdon. The Earl of Chesterfield was, in common with many others of the nobility, a frequent attendant at these private services, and the difference—according to the author of the "Life and Times"—between the two Earls, was that his lordship of Bath contributed to the funds, and allowed his name to appear, and himself to be placed in the category of saints; whilst his lordship of Chesterfield contributed anonymously, and was accordingly dubbed "an infidel," and relegated to the kingdom of Satan. The logic of the writer, if sound, is inconvenient, because the young Earl of Huntingdon was a protégé of Chesterfield's, and although a young man of ability, ambition, and fairly good character, he did not share his mother's opinions, nor did he promote her work of religious propaganda, and it must have disturbed the Countess' happiness, despite her own creed, and the assurance of her own acceptance with God, to believe that her son was no better than Lord Chesterfield, and was destined to the same everlasting wrath. The Countess of Huntingdon, shortly after marriage, was a frequent visitor to Bath. It was during these visits that she gathered round her all those eminent persons who became more or less her coadjutors in the work in which she was engaged. At first she seems to have had no definite plan, and no distinct organization. Nor, indeed, does she appear to have contemplated the establishment of a sect. The object obviously was to arouse amongst her personal friends and patrician acquaintances a deeper sense of religious responsibility, and a more earnest spirit of devotion. For some years, it is evident that the services which she instituted were limited to her own house, in London as well as Bath, and were conducted by Wesley, Whitefield, Romaine, Hervey, and others, who were especially invited to do so. In 1747 she emphatically declared that "she had impartially examined "the controversy between the Dissenters and the Church of England, and "thought it her duty to adhere to the latter." There can be no doubt that, so far at least as Bath is concerned, that these chamber-services were confined exclusively to persons of her own rank; and there is no reason to find fault with her on that account, as it is beyond all doubt that she often succeeded in compelling her noble and aristocratic friends to listen to serious discourses, who otherwise would have remained inaccessible to the ordinary ministrations of the Church.

At this period—that is, from about 1734 until the close of Lady Huntingdon's life—Bath, apart from the peculiar influence exercised by Nash upon that "little kingdom" of which he was the acknowledged sovereign, was no exception in its spiritual condition to the rest of the nation. But it is clear that whatever might have been Lady Huntingdon's influence, and the effect of her own example on the coteries of high-born dames whom she invited to hear her chosen preachers in her drawing-rooms, they had no effect whatever upon the religious life and condition of the people at large in Bath. Whitefield's [1] preaching was addressed chiefly to these limited select audiences. We read of none of those impassioned sermons to great masses of people, which were addressed to vast assemblages elsewhere, and therefore we hear of none of those exciting exhibitions of religious ecstacy and fervour, which were regarded as the evidences of supernatural conversion. The result of Whitefield's preaching to the exalted ladies who were invited to Lady Huntingdon's house to hear him, occasionally produced results less affecting, but yet not without their melancholy aspects.[2] Lords Bolingbroke, Bath, Chesterfield, and other noblemen and great ladies who came to Bath, including the Duchesses of Marlborough and Queensberry, and others, who attended the services, showed no external symptoms of conversion. They paid hollow compliments to the preachers, but those who were "infidels" remained "infidels" still, and those arrogant, self-willed Duchesses remained so to the end of the chapter. Lady Huntingdon, no doubt, was a woman of "no small mental powers, with a most ardent and somewhat "imperious character"; and though it is clear that the results of her efforts, beyond her own immediate circle of friends, was almost inappreciable in this city, yet it is equally clear that Bath was the head-quarters of the movement with which her name is, and ever will be, associated. It was here where she conferred with her ministers; from hence she issued her mandates; here she entertained

[1] "So swells each wind-pipe; ass intones to ass;
"Harmonic twang! of leather, horn, and brass,
"Such as from labouring lungs the enthusiast blows,
"High sound, attemper'd to the vocal nose;
"Or such as bellow from the deep divine;
"There Webster peal'd thy voice, and Whitefield thine." *Dunciad.*

[2] The Duchess of Buckingham (wife of John Sheffield, Duke of Buckingham, whose first husband was William Phipps, Esq., father of the first Lord Mulgrave) consented to hear Whitefield, and in a letter to Lady Huntingdon, which, as Mr. Lecky says, is "amusingly characteristic both of the "writer and of her time," she thus delivers herself:—"I thank your Ladyship for the information "concerning the Methodist preachers. Their doctrines are most repulsive and strongly tinctured "with impertinence and disrespect towards their superiors, in perpetually endeavouring to level all "ranks and do away with all distinctions. It is monstrous to be told that you have a heart as sinful "as the common wretches that crawl the earth. This is highly offensive and insulting, and I cannot "but wonder that your Ladyship should relish any sentiments so much at variance with high rank "and good breeding."
The Countess of Suffolk, the mistress of George II., attended once, and was bitterly offended, because Whitefield, who was ignorant of her presence, introduced a passage into his sermon which she construed as an attack upon herself. It was hardly fair, she thought, that her particular foibles should be exposed.

her intimate friends, whose names are more or less identified with her own in the work of proselytism. In Bath were written those letters to her ministers and friends, which are such a curious admixture of humility and aristocratic arrogance; such a wonderful combination of elements, showing a spirit of submissiveness with an unconscious tone of command. Whitefield never forgot the difference in rank between him and the lady he served; he always addressed her in his letters as "Honoured Madam," and a tone of great deference pervaded the letters of all her correspondents. She was without doubt an eminent Christian and a great patrician lady. Lady Huntingdon's creed was of the strictest Calvinistic type.[1] It was a creed admitting of no sort of doubt, and was not to be questioned. Lady Huntingdon felt no doubt on this point, why should anybody else? The doctrine of Justification by Faith alone was to her as clear as—nay, it was *the* Revelation. Sir R. Steele's *dictum* as to the difference between the Romish Church and the Anglican Church of his day, applies to the system Lady Huntingdon espoused, namely, that "the Romish Church claimed to be infallible, and the Anglican was always right." No infalliblist had less doubt about his Church than Lady Huntingdon about her Creed. It was on this matter of creed that John Wesley formally separated from Whitefield, and it was on the subject of this same revolting creed, involving a difference of opinion but not of practice, that Toplady forgot himself as a gentleman and a Christian, and abused John Wesley with all the vehemence of bitter and unsaintly acrimony. Lady Huntingdon and her friends affected, and no doubt sincerely, a great regard for Christian liberty, but they practically denied it. The faintest resistance to their commands was a proof of fatal error, and met with immediate punishment. All amusements and recreation were

---

[1] Anstey, of course, would find matter for his satirical pen in the Religious Revival in Bath.
"I am very sorry to find at the City of Bath,
"Many folks are uneasy concerning their faith;
"Nicodemus, the preacher, strives all he can do
"To quiet the conscience of good sister Prue.
"But Tabby from scruples of mind is released,
"Since she met with a learned Moravian priest;
"Who says, *There is neither transgression nor sin;*
"A doctrine that brings many customers in.
"She thinks this the prettiest ode upon earth.
"Which he made on his infant that dy'd in its birth."

"ODE.*
"Chicken blessed
"And caressed,
"Little bee on Jesus' breast;
"From the hurry
"And the flurry,
"Of the earth thou'rt now at rest.

* The learned Moravian has pirated this Ode from Count Zinzendorf's Book of Hymns. Vide Hymn 33." Zinzendorf was a friend of Lady Huntingdon's, but she subsequently quarrelled with him. Anstey rather confounds Lady Huntingdon's Connection with the Moravians, with whom at first she affected much sympathy.

proscribed. As to literature, it was repressed amongst the faithful with relentless severity, no matter how pure, how moral, how elevating, as being antagonistic to spiritual progress and true piety. The author of the "Life and Times" sums it up thus, speaking of the writers of the "Augustan Age" of Queen Anne:—
"These writers obtained great influence over the nation, and whatever good they "effected by giving currency to thought, they directed it in channels leading *from* "evangelical piety to sentiment, ethics, and taste, or to physical knowledge. "The waters were indeed clean and beautiful, but they were unhealthy, and, in "some respects, the opposite of the Prophetic stream of which it is predicated— "'Everything shall live whither the river cometh.' The most chaste and moral "of these popular works, though recognizing Christianity, are unvivified by its "spirit; and while they advocate the claims of virtue, found not their argument "on the principles of the Gospel, and teach, often not otherwise than as a "heathen would have taught, sound duties and graces rather than the 'obedience "'of faith.' The founder of Methodism was not far from the truth when he "said, 'That few things were more unfriendly to the progress of the Gospel, than "'the national fondness for Addison's *Spectator*.'" Could stupidity and fanaticism go further than this? It was written as late as 1840, and it shows that the writer, and those who sympathise with him, cannot discern the difference between things totally distinct in themselves. The human intellect needs culture, and variety of intellectual food, even as the body needs physical nurture by a variety of God's good gifts to His creatures. It would be as reasonable to assert that man must not eat, as that he should not employ his mental faculties on those pursuits and objects for which his capacity is adapted. We have experienced, as Sydney Smith says, "some of the worst evils of fanaticism two centuries ago, and "it is one of those evils from which society is never wholly exempt; but which "bursts out at different periods The last eruption destroyed both Church "and Throne with its tremendous force. Though irresistible, it was short— "enthusiasm spent its force—the usual reaction took place, and England was "deluged with ribaldry and indecency, because it had been worried with fanatical "restrictions."

If the contending forces in Bath during the past century had been differently constituted; that is, if Nash's[1] vicious rule had been met by a more

---

[1] "When Mr. John Wesley was preaching at Bath, some time before the coming of Charles, "Beau Nash entered the room, and approaching the preacher, demanded by what authority he was "acting? Mr. Wesley answered, 'By that of Jesus Christ, conveyed to me by the present Archbishop "of Canterbury, when he laid his hands upon me and said—*Take thou authority to preach the Gospel.*' "Nash then affirmed that he was acting contrary to law. 'Besides (said he) your preaching frightens "people out of their wits.' 'Sir (replied Mr. Wesley) did you ever hear me preach?' 'No,' said the

rational, manly, healthy moral system, it would have had less chance of resisting it. The fanatical denunciations which treated all amusements as wicked, and put all recreations under the one category of "frivolous and sinful," was regarded as pure fanaticism, and made no impression upon the habits and vices of the age. We have lived through two or three *revivals* within the last 30 years, but it is reserved to us in this penultimate decade of the nineteenth century to witness the worst and most contemptible manifestation of that fanaticism (combined with hypocrisy) of which we are speaking. It is something shocking to see the middling and lower classes giving up the sober and rational worship in their respective Churches and Chapels, to run after a set of men and women who have no more claim to superior sanctity, than the tub thumpers and fanatics of other days. This thing will have its day; but if through any misfortune the system should become permanent, we shall then have realized to some extent what Sydney Smith, in 1808, regarded as not impossible:—"If such, in future, should be the situation "of this country, it is impossible to say what political animosities may not be "engrafted upon this dangerous *division* of mankind into the *godly* and the "*ungodly*. At all events, we are quite sure that happiness will be destroyed, "reason degraded, sound religion banished from the world; and that when "fanaticism becomes too foolish and too *prurient* to be endured, it will be suc- "ceeded by a long period of the grossest immorality, atheism, and debauchery."

The abiding influences of Lady Huntingdon's religious operations are comparatively insignificant. The communities called after her name are few in number, and as a sect numbering few in the aggregate. But it is only just to say that, like the noble founder, those who are her followers, and who justly revere her name and memory, show in their practice and everyday lives that they are better than their creed, in the ever-abounding evidence they give of good works. Lady Huntingdon, in her mode of conducting business, was impulsive, uncertain,

"Master of the Ceremonies, ' How then can you judge of what you never heard?' 'By common re-
"port,' replied Nash. 'Sir,' said Mr. Wesley, 'is not your name Nash? I dare not judge of you by
"common report.' Nash, finding himself a very different person in the meeting-house from what he
"was in the pump-room, thought it best to withdraw.
 "Nash sometimes conversed with Lady Huntingdon on religious subjects, and was once
"prevailed on to hear Mr. Whitefield at her house. Beau Nash was congratulated on his conversion
"by his gay associates, who failed not to rally him on his turning Methodist. Verses were written
"on her Ladyship and Mr. Nash, which were fastened to the walls of the pump-room and the
"assembly-room; and printed notices were circulated in every direction, one of which was shown
"to the writer many years ago by Dr. Hawels, stating that 'The Countess of Huntingdon, attended
"'by some saintly sister, purposed preaching at the pump-room the following morning, and that
"' Mr. Nash, henceforth to be known as the *Rev. Richard Nash,*' was expected to preach in the
"evening at the assembly-room. It was hoped that the audience would be numerous, as a collection
"was intended for the late Master of Ceremonies, who was retiring from office. This profane raillery
"never discomposed the Countess, but gave great offence to Mr. Nash; and no inducement could ever
"after prevail upon him to go to Lady Huntingdon's house."—*Life and Times*, vol. 1, p. 445.

and consequently unsuccessful. She possessed none of the forethought of Wesley, and she lacked, or failed to avail herself of, that common-sense wisdom which distinguished him in the organization of his great work, and hence she failed, and her influence scarcely survived her own day. Lady Huntingdon, like Wesley, intended her labours to be in connection with, and an auxiliary to, the Church ; the result, as in his case, was the establishment of a sect. Wesley's success, so far as he succeeded in *doing what he never intended to do*, no doubt was owing to his more flexible and workable organization, and the less cold and repelling doctrines which he taught. Wesley had little private fortune, and the wealth he devoted to the cause which he directed came from his faithful band of followers. After the Earl of Huntingdon's death, in 1746,[1] the Countess devoted her whole fortune to the organization of the Calvinistic section of the Methodists. The College of Trevecca she founded in 1768, and it sent forth missionaries to every part of the United Kingdom.

It was in the year 1765 that Lady Huntingdon purchased the ground in the Vineyards, and built the house and the Chapel in which Romaine (who ultimately seceded in deference to the wishes of his Bishop) and Whitefield were the chaplains in chief. Romaine steadily "refused to be a field-preacher." The Chapel was opened on the 6th of October, 1765, and from this time until Lady Huntingdon's death in 1791, it was "supplied" by the most eminent men in the "Connection." Madan, Fletcher, Whitefield, Wesley, Shirley, Venn, and other clergymen of the Established Church preached in it. Occasionally "itinerant "labourers" were invited to preach, and to be the "bearers of grace," and amongst others one Mr. Relly, from whose discourses and letters extracts are given in "The Life and Times," but whether as examples of eloquence, or proofs of the possession of unusual unction, does not appear. Mr. Relly, in reference

---

[1] The Earl was succeeded by his only surviving son, Francis, to whom reference has already been made. Of him Horace Walpole writes bitterly:—"He was a man too much vaunted for talents "which he had proved he did not possess, and destitute of that wealth and interest which so often "supply the want of talents. By affecting personal attachment to the King, he had escaped in all the "late changes ; though his post would often have accommodated the administration, but the vanity of "his royal descent * having prompted him to ask the title of Duke of Clarence, and a refusal following, "he had flattered himself with obtaining it, as so many other titles had been wrenched from the "Crown by opposition. He absented himself on the first day of the session, and kept away his "relation, Earl Ferrers. The King, glad of an opportunity of getting rid of him, sent for the "golden key."

The Earl died during his mother's lifetime, in 1780, without issue, when the barony devolved upon his only sister, Elizabeth, Countess of Mona, and on her death descended to her son, the Marquis of Hastings, while the Earldom remained dormant. After 30 years it was successfully claimed by Capt. Hans Francis Hastings, R.N., who became eleventh Earl of Huntingdon (the author of "The Life and Times" says he was the twelfth Earl).

* The Earl was the direct heir of George, Duke of Clarence, whose daughter, Margaret, Countess of Salisbury, was mother of Henry Pole, Lord Montacute, whose eldest daughter and heiress married an Earl of Huntingdon.

to Bristol, says, "There seems to be a shaking among the dry bones at Bristol; "I trust *the scales will fall from their eyes shortly.*" The dry bones at Bristol had eyes, it seems. He paid some visits to Bath also when "*people of fashion* heard" him; "amongst them," he said, the "word seems to *run* and be glorified." But, he adds with some inconsistency, "my greatest grief at present is to see the Church "fallen from her first love, and iniquity *running down our streets*, and *very few* "*laying it to heart.*" Poor man! did he want "people of fashion" to "lay iniquity "to heart?" This is a specimen of the rubbish which the author of "The Life "and Times" quotes as if it were a kind of inspiration, and if such extravagances were permitted, it seems to have been one of the evils resulting from that imperfect supervision which characterized the organization. It is clear that men who might have been good carpenters or blacksmiths, if they had possessed industry, had only to assume superior sanctity, and they were at once dubbed "Reverend," and allowed to pollute things sacred with irreverent balderdash.

In 1766, after the Chapel was built, the "itinerants" are, happily, little seen and seldom heard. In the same year, Wesley being in Bristol, magnanimously [1] tendered his services to preach on each Sunday morning for a given period. Lady Huntingdon accepted his offer, because, as she put it, "the "morning was more suitable to her," the "great and the noble" whom she invited being able to attend; whilst the common people could partake later of the "crumbs that fell from the rich man's table." On this occasion, the first sermon preached by John Wesley, the Chapel was filled with distinguished members of the nobility. Amongst them was Horace Walpole, who describes the service and Wesley as follows :—

"They have (says he) boys and girls with charming voices that sing hymns in parts. The "chapel is very neat, with *true* Gothic windows. I was glad to see that luxury is creeping in upon "them before persecution. They have very neat mahogany stands for branches, and brackets of the "same in taste. At the upper end is a broad *hautpas* of four steps, advancing in the middle ; at each "end of the broadest part are two eagles with red cushions for the parson and clerk. Behind them "rise three more steps, in the midst of which is a third eagle for a pulpit. Scarlet arm chairs to all "three. On either hand a balcony for elect ladies. The rest of the congregation sits on forms. Be-"hind the pit, in a dark niche, is a plain table within rails ; so you see the throne is for the apostle. "Wesley is a clean elderly man, fresh coloured, his hair smoothly combed, but with a little *soupçon* of "curl at the ends. Wondrous clever, but as evidently an actor as Garrick. He spoke his sermon, "but so fast, and with so little accent, that I am sure he has often uttered it, for it was like a lesson. "There were parts and eloquence in it ; but towards the end he exalted his voice, and acted very "vulgar enthusiasm."

[1] We say "magnanimously," inasmuch as Charles Wesley, who had previously tendered his services, was refused the pulpit. Throughout this "Life and Times" we felt a loving sympathy with Charles Wesley, who was one of the few who showed perfect self-respect, combined with the attributes of a true Christian gentleman. The reason for rejecting Charles Wesley's assistance was purely because he would not teach the doctrine of Election.

This is cynical, but contains a good deal of truth. The shallowness, the hollowness of a system which depended upon mere impulsive emotions, and made its appeal exclusively to the nobles, as such, had no elements of vitality in it.[1] The personal influence of Lady Huntingdon was already beginning to fail at this time, and before her death, twenty years later, her personal authority had almost ceased. The scheme she formulated for the perpetuation of her *system*, if so unsystematic an organisation could be called a *system* at all, was resisted by Haweis,[2] her chaplain (who succeeded Whitefield and Townsend), and when she died, the net result, so far as Bath was concerned, was one chapel, which was not claimed as a gain by Nonconformists, and added nothing to the strength of the Church. Whitefield's reputation gained nothing by his association with this movement in Bath. It seems incongruous, and even humiliating, to find a man of his earnestness and sincerity, complacently boasting of the numbers of "the great and noble," because they were such, to whom he had administered the sacrament, and to read of his submissive docility, we might say subserviency, to his patroness. The Whitefield in Bath was not the Whitefield away from the influence of his imperiously pious director, whose rank and that of her great circle of noble friends seemed to overpower him.

[1] There was a great deal connected with it that was not without its amusing side. Lady Betty Cobbe and others were not above a joke, and they occasionally indulged in a little humour at the expense of some benighted Church, or some dull Christian to whom Calvinism did not present a Scriptural view of Christianity, and did not afford a very pleasant subject of contemplation, in the absence of that calm assumption of being in the ranks of the Elect, which Lady Betty always took for granted. This view of the case, we are told, is presumptuous; well, so it may be, but what about the right of private judgment?

Lady Betty Cobbe was a combination of Calvinistic piety and aristocratic waggery. She thought evidently that, in order to attain her ends, a little pious fraud was justifiable. There was a snug little corner in the chapel, curtained off to conceal the occupants, who, whether from shame or excessive modesty, preferred not being seen in the chapel. This corner was called *Nicodemus's Corner*. The author of *The Life and Times* says this corner was frequented by the Bishops. But Lady Betty only claims to have *smuggled* one Bishop into it—Dr. Barnard, the Bishop of Derry, who had formerly been Dean of Rochester, and it seems the poor old gentleman was in his second childhood. Lady Betty was a sort of head fuglewoman—a busy, merry, witty lady, who thought the limitation of God's mercies to a very select few the finest joke of the day. Lady Betty Cobbe was cousin to Lady Huntingdon, and her husband was a son of Dr. Charles Cobbe, Archbishop of Dublin.

[2] Haweis* died at his house, in Beaufort Buildings, in 1820. There was a very singular man during Haweis' connection with the Vineyards Chapel a *Rev. Dr. Sheppard*, who lived in *Chatham Row*. He had seceded from the Church of England, and preached occasionally in "Calvinistic pulpits." In "Bath Characters," he is described as *Doctor Skipper*, and the author puts into his mouth some very characteristic sayings. "Dr. Draweansir" (Dr. Daubeny), his antagonist, says to him—"Sir, *you're cracked*." "So much the better, Mr. Puff, *cracks let in light*, you know." He said his own Calvinistic *Church* was sound, and to be preferred to the "worm-eaten establishment," which "shuts the doors against all those who have not a *bishop*, as a master of the ceremonies, to "introduce them." The dialogue indeed is the finest in this amusing satire (see "Bath Characters, by Peter Paul Palette"). Sheppard was a most eccentric man. Some one said that his manner of preaching resembled "a windmill in convulsions." He was short in stature, spare in person, and dressed in the most fantastic style. He preached during Lady Huntingdon's life, and occasionally for many years after her death. He died in 1815.

* In "Bath Characters" he is called *Dr. Vineyards*.

BECKFORD HOUSE, Lansdown Crescent, was the residence of **WILLIAM BECKFORD, Esq.** William Beckford was the son of **Alderman Beckford.** Some men gain immortality by one means and some by another. Alderman Beckford insulted George III., served as Lord Mayor of London, was a toady of Lord Chatham, possessed sacks full of money, prated in bad English about liberty, denounced the tyranny of monarchs, but spared the tyranny of the slave-owner and the dealers in human flesh. To insult the King was a sure passport in Beckford's time to popular favour. Lord Albermarle, in his " Memoirs of the Marquis of Rockingham," speaks thus of Beckford :—

"William Beckford, a wealthy West Indian planter, was a noisy, vulgar "flatterer of Lord Chatham—and bombastic, as became the priest of such an "idol.[1] The satellite was content with the lustre he derived from the orb round "which he moved. To be the great man's mouth-piece eastward of *Temple Bar*, "appears to have been the height of his ambition. Beckford spoke a strong "cockney dialect, he had a great contempt for the rules of grammar, and was "very fond of quoting Latin."

"Mr. Burke's mispronunciation of the word *vectigal*,"[2] writes Cowper to Unwin, " brings to my remembrance a peculiar altercation that passed when I "was in the gallery, between Mr. Rigby and Alderman Beckford. The latter was "a very incorrect speaker, and the former, I imagine, not a very accurate scholar. "He ventured however upon a quotation from *Terence*, and delivered it thus—*Sine* "*Scere et Baccho friget Venus.* The Alderman interrupted him, was very severe "upon his mistake, and restored *Ceres* to her place in the sentence. Mr. Rigby "replied that he was obliged to his worthy friend for teaching him *Latin*, and "would take the first opportunity to return the favour by teaching him *English !*"[3]

"Under a semblance of good humour, Beckford concealed an overbearing "and tyrannical disposition. Obsequious to his political chieftain, he was "haughty and supercilious to everyone else. A spouter of liberty to the citizens "of London, he proved a hard task-master to his ill-used slaves in Jamaica."[4]

These portraits of Alderman Beckford are drawn by his political friends. His political opponents, perhaps, thought he was not worthy of their delineation.

---

[1] Walpole.

[2] Everyone remembers Mr. Burke's trip in the quantity of *vectigal*, but perhaps not so well another offence against prosody on the same evening. In a previous Latin quotation he had said *nimirum*, Lord North replied, that not to know the quantity of *nimirum* was very excusable, since only one man understood the true quantity.

"Septimius, Claudi, nimirum intelligit unus."
Hor., lib. i., Ep. 9, *v.* 1.

[3] Cowper's Works, edited by Southey, vol. 3, p. 317.

[4] Walpole's Memoirs of the Reign of George III.

He, being a popular politician, and affecting a warm sympathy with mobocracy and noisy demagogues, prided himself upon his illustrious descent from the Saxon Kings, and therefore claimed to be entitled to sepulture above ground. We do not know whether this distinction was accorded to the Alderman, but it is certain that his son's body lies *above* ground.[1]

William Beckford, of Bath, resembled his father in nothing, except in his irascible temper. The father liked and courted notoriety, even in its vulgar and most repelling form. He boasted of his amours, and prided himself upon his vices. The son was reserved, proud, haughty, and avoided society. He obtruded neither his virtues nor his vices upon the world. If he cared at all about public opinion, he was successful in concealing it ; and his love of magnificence and pageantry—if he did love them—gratified no one but himself. He hid himself from mankind, lived to himself and for himself, with the result that his life was one of mystery, and he died unregretted—his death excited only a short-lived curiosity—and added one more name to the list of selfish, departed misanthropes. Yet, withal, it is just to accord to Mr. Beckford a wonderful capacity for work, and an excellent knowledge of Bibliography. The sales of his books, during 1882, indicate unrivalled judgment in the collection of works of rarest merit. With all the aid he could have received from skilled and ingenious booksellers, there remains the fact that the directing mind, the accurate taste, and the fulness of knowledge which supervised and approved all, were his own. Price, condition, " perfect " or " imperfect," were questions never left to others ; and the Hamilton Library was a stupendous monument to the industry of this remarkable man. Since Lord Sunderland's Collection (dispersed about the same time), the Beckford Collection is the most remarkable that has been made, and especially if it be taken in conjunction with the Duke of Hamilton's, which was made simultaneously, and of which, at the time of the sale, it formed a part. It must be remembered, too, that the labours he bestowed upon his library were small, when compared with the time he must have devoted to building schemes, landscape gardening, bric-a-brac, art collecting, and other minor pursuits. The great work of his life had spent itself before he made Bath his residence. The choicest gems in literature and art were sent to Hamilton Palace before the sale at Fonthill,[2] and the extent therefore of his collections were not, could not be,

---

[1] Tunstall, in his Rambles, 1st edition, said the family claimed the privilege of being *buried above ground !*

[2] The best account of Fonthill is by Britton. Of the contents, without reference to the Library, which was transferred to Hamilton Palace, Hazlitt says in his sharp, cynical, but true critical style : "Fonthill Abbey, after being enveloped in impenetrable mystery for a length of " years, has been unexpectedly thrown open to the vulgar gaze, and has lost none of its reputation

fully known until the Hamilton sales in 1882. The amusement of his later years was to build the Tower on Lansdown, from which he could gaze upon the earlier folly of his manhood ;[1] and if that tower were a type of his career, so perhaps the diminished grandeur of his later palace, when his fortune was impaired by extravagance and depreciation in the value of Colonial property, might have shown him that even in this world there is something more to live for than selfish gratification and unmanly isolation. He had long ago perhaps discovered that

"Years steal
"Fire from the mind as vigour from the limb ;
"And life's-enchanted cup but sparkles near the brim."

The Tower Beckford built, in which to indulge his lonely fancy, and to meditate upon the past, now seems to look down with melancholy stateliness upon his

"for magnificence—though, perhaps, its visionary glory, its classic renown, have vanished from the "public mind for ever. It is, in a word, a desert of magnificence, a glittering waste of laborious "idleness, a cathedral turned into a toy-shop, an immense Museum of all that is most curious and "costly, and, at the same time, most worthless, in the productions of art and nature. Ships of "pearl and seas of amber are scarce a fable here—a nautilus's shell surmounted with a gilt triumph "of Neptune—tables of agate, cabinets of ebony, and precious stones, painted windows 'shedding "'a gaudy, crimson light,' satin borders, marble floors, and lumps of solid gold—Chinese pagodas "and Persian tapestry—all the splendour of Solomon's Temple is displayed to the view—in miniature "whatever is far-fetched and dear-bought, rich in the materials, or rare and difficult in the work-"manship—but scarce one genuine work of art, one solid proof of taste, one lofty relic of sentiment "or imagination !
"The difficult, the unattainable, the exclusive, are to be found here in profusion, in perfection; "all else is wanting, or is brought in merely as a foil or as a stop-gap. In this respect the collection "is as satisfactory as it is *unique*. The specimens exhibited are the best, the most highly finished, "the most costly and curious, of that kind of ostentatious magnificence which is calculated to gratify "the sense of property in the owner, and to excite the wondering curiosity of the stranger, who "is permitted to see or see (as a choice privilege and favour) even to touch baubles so dazzling and of "such exquisite nicety of execution ; and which, if broken or defaced, it would be next to impos-"sible to replace. The same character extends to the pictures, which are mere furniture-pictures, "remarkable chiefly for their antiquity or painful finishing, without beauty, without interest, and "with about the same pretensions to attract the eye or delight the fancy as a well-polished mahogany "table or a waxed oak floor. Not one great work by one great name, scarce one or two of the "worst specimens of the first masters, Lionardo's Laughing Boy, or a copy from Raphael, or "Correggio, as if to make the thing remote and finical—but heaps of the most elaborate pieces "of the worst of the Dutch masters, Breughel's Sea-horses with coats of mother-of-pearl, and "Rothenhamer's Elements turned into a Flower-piece. The Catalogue, in short, is guiltless of the "names of any of those works of art
"Which like a trumpet make the spirits dance ;
"and is sacred to those which rank no higher than veneering, and where the painter is on a precise "par with the carver and gilder.
"Mr. Beckford has undoubtedly shown himself an industrious *bijoutier*, a prodigious virtuoso, "an accomplished patron of unproductive labour, an enthusiastic collector of expensive trifles— "the only proof of taste (to our thinking) he has shown in this collection is *his getting rid of it.* "What splendour, what grace, what grandeur might he substitute in lieu of it ! What a hand-

[1] The Abbey of Fonthill, built by torchlight, and insecure from the first, passed into the possession of Col. Farquhar. Each morning as Beckford passed into the South Chamber of the Lansdown Tower, he directed his telescope to the distant one at Fonthill, once his own. On the morning after it fell it would have been curious to note the expression on that proud face, as he laid down the glass which no longer brought within view of his usual observation the familiar object which had now disappeared.

tomb. The pleasure-grounds so lovely, and yet so appropriate to the massive temple within them, now contain the fitting "companions of his solitude." The Fonthill collection, it must be mentioned, was the second, a former having been disposed of in 1801, after which he went abroad. On his return he built the Abbey, in which he made the collection we have referred to, the sale of which took place in 1822, when he made Bath his residence, in Lansdown Crescent. Beckford died in 1844. His body at first rested in the Abbey Cemetery, but in 1847 it was transferred to the grounds sur-

"writing might be spread out upon the walls! What a spirit of poetry and philosophy might
"breathe there! What a solemn gloom, what gay vistas of fancy, like chequered light and shade,
"might genius, guided by art, shed around! The author of Vathek is a scholar; the proprietor of
"Fonthill has travelled abroad, and has seen all the finest remains of antiquity and boasted speci-
"mens of modern art. Why not lay his hands on some of these? He had power to carry them
"away. One might have expected to see, at least, a few fine old pictures, marble copies of the
"celebrated statues, the Apollo, the Venus, the Dying Gladiator, the Antinous, antique vases with
"their elegant sculptures, or casts from them, coins, medals, bas-reliefs, something connected with
"the beautiful forms of external nature, or with what is great in the mind or memorable in the
"history of man,—Egyptian hieroglyphics, or Chaldee manuscripts on paper made of the reeds of
"the Nile, or mummies from the Pyramids! Not so; not a trace (or scarcely so) of any of these;—
"as little as may be of what is classical or imposing to the imagination from association or well-
"founded prejudice; hardly any article of any consequence that does not seem to be labelled to the
"following effect—*This is mine, and there is no one else in the whole world in whom it can inspire the
"least interest, or any feeling beyond a momentary surprise!* To show another your poverty is an act
"in itself ungracious, or null and void. It excites no pleasure from sympathy. Every one must
"have remarked the difference in his feelings on entering a venerable old cathedral, for instance,
"and a modern-built private mansion. The one seems to fill the mind and expand the form, while
"the other only produces a sense of listless vacuity, and disposes us to shrink into our own littleness.
    "If it were an apprehension of an invidious comparison between the proprietor and the
"author of any signal work of genius, which the former did not covet, one would think he must be
"at least equally mortified at sinking to a level in taste and pursuits with the maker of a Dutch toy.
"Mr. Beckford, however, has always had the credit of the highest taste in works of art as well as in
"*certâ*. As the showman in Goldsmith's comedy declares that 'his bear dances to none but the
"genteelest of tunes—'*Water parted from the Sea, The Minuet in Ariadne;*'*—so it was supposed
"that this celebrated collector's money went for none but the finest Claudes and the choicest speci-
"mens of some rare Italian master. The two Claudes are gone. It is as well they must have felt
"a little out of their place here - they are kept in countenance, where they are, by the very best
"company.
    "We once happened to have the pleasure of seeing Mr. Beckford in the Great Gallery of the
"Louvre—he was very plainly dressed in a loose great coat, and looked somewhat pale and thin—
"but what brought the circumstance to our minds was that we were told on this occasion one of
"those thumping matter-of-fact lies which are pretty common to other Frenchmen besides Gascons,
"*viz., That he had offered the First Consul no less a sum than two hundred thousand guineas for the purchase
"of the St. Peter Martyr.* Would that he had! and that Napoleon had taken him at his word! which
"we think not unlikely. With two hundred thousand guineas he might have taken some almost
"impregnable fortress. 'Magdeburg,' said Buonaparte, 'is worth a hundred queens:' and he would
"have thought such another stronghold worth at least one Saint.
    "The painted windows in the centre of the Abbey have a surprising effect the form of the
"building (which was raised by torch-light) is fantastical, to say the least—and the grounds, which
"are extensive and fine from situation, are laid out with the hand of a master. A quantity of coot,
"teal, and wild fowl sport in a crystal stream that winds along the park; and their dark brown
"coats, seen in the green shadows of the water, have a most picturesque effect. Upon the whole, if
"we were not much pleased by our excursion to Fonthill, we were very little disappointed; and the
"place altogether is consistent and characteristic."

* They, and other finer things, and the best portion of the Library, were sent to Hamilton Palace, and sold with the Collection in 1882.

rounding the Tower, which had then become the property of the Rector of Walcot in trust for the parish, and had been converted into a cemetery. The property having devolved upon his elder daughter, the Duchess of Hamilton, was sold by her grace to a publican, who proposed to make the Tower a beer-house, and the grounds public pleasure-gardens. The duchess, on a representation of the facts being made to her, re-purchased the property, and invested it in the Rector of Walcot for the time being, for the purpose described. On the tablet of Beckford's tomb is inscribed—

WILLIAM BECKFORD, ESQ.,
Late of Fonthill, Wilts,
DIED 2ND MAY, 1844,
AGED 84.

———" Eternal Power !
"Grant me, through obvious clouds, one transient gleam˜
" Of Thy bright essence in my dying hour ! "

Beckford was the author of " Biographical Memoirs of extraordinary Painters," 1780. and "An Arabian Tale (Vathek),"[1] from an unpublished MS., with Notes critical and explanatory (by Mr. Henley), 1786. In his 80th year, he wrote "Italy, with Sketches of Spain and Portugal, and Recollections of Alcobaça and Batalha," 2 vols., 1835.

1, LANSDOWN CRESCENT. JAMES HEYWOOD MARKLAND, F.R.S., D.C.L.

—From 1839 to 1864, the name of this estimable gentleman was associated with the city of his adoption. Mr. Markland was formerly a member of an eminent firm of solicitors in London. In 1821 he married Charlotte, sister of Sir Francis Freeling, Bart., by whom he had one daughter, who in 1853 married the Rev. Charles H. Conybeare, Rector of Itchen Stoke. Mr. Markland died in 1864, and Mrs. Markland in 1867. His residence was frequently designated "the Bishops' headquarters," because few came to Bath, either for business or rest, to whom he did not extend his hospitality, colonial bishops especially. Indeed, he seems to have had a very special love for bishops. No doubt Mr. Markland gave the preference to bishops with " Anglican " leanings, but an episcopal smile of any kind was irresistible. Well indeed that it was so, for in this great city, forming a part of the united See of Bath and Wells, there was, there is, no church dignitary to offer an occasional reception to an episcopal chief. So long as Mr. Markland lived, the public mind was never uneasy as to the fate of any ill-starred bishop or lesser dignitary

[1] "There thou, too, Vathek ! England's wealthiest son,
" Once form'd thy paradise, as not aware
" When wanton Wealth her mightiest deeds hath done,
" Meek Peace voluptuous lures was ever wont to shun."

Childe Harold.

who, by stress of circumstances, was obliged to put into the ecclesiastical port of Bath. The odour of sanctity clung to No. 1, Lansdown Crescent with tenacity.

Mr. Markland's hospitality was not confined to bishops, deans, and distinguished clerics. The young man preparing himself for the Church Mission work, or any special field of an exceptionally arduous nature, found in Mr. Markland a kind and encouraging friend and a most judicious adviser. His fine library was the delight of his bookish visitors, especially as he invariably left the key in each case, and made the room the most luxurious and attractive in his house. It must not be supposed that Mr. Markland limited his society to bishops, priests, and deacons; certainly not. He mixed freely with men of all shades of opinion, and though he seldom, if ever, came into collision with any, it was because he said very clearly by his *manner* that he claimed the right to hold his own opinions, and he distinctly disclaimed the right to interfere with others. So far as his limited fortune enabled him, he supported the institutions of the city;[1] he promoted and kept alive its intellectual life by his own example, and by associating freely and unreservedly with his contemporaries for that object. He was not a speaker, and, we take leave to say, not a correct, much less an able, writer. In the works he published, "*Essay on the Reverence due to Holy Places*," " Remarks on English Churches and on Sepulchral Memorials," he received important assistance from others; but in all things he was judicious, and, what is more, he was moderate, simple, and earnestly sincere. He edited an edition of Bishop Ken's Prayers for those who came to take the Bath Waters—a most useful manual, and he lent himself on all occasions with a heartiness and a cheerful willingness, which enabled him to do more good than many others who far excelled him in ability, and he has left a name which will long be held in honoured remembrance as one of the many " worthies " of whom Bath can boast.

HARTLEY HOUSE, Belvedere.—This house, now in the possession of

---

[1] It must be borne in mind that, if Mr. Markland's means did not enable him to gratify his disposition in promoting either local charity or those Church institutions with which he so strongly sympathised, so largely as he otherwise would have done, the measure of his power in the cause of Christian philanthropy and Church mission work, at home and abroad, was largely augmented by the munificence of others. We are about to make no indiscreet revelations. The fact we are about to state is, if a secret at all, one of those secrets which is known to many, and openly spoken about. A sum of £14,000 was placed at the disposal of Mr. Markland shortly after he settled in this city, to be used by him generally in the support of such Church purposes as he in his judgment might select. The ladies by whose liberality the institutions to which we have referred benefited were the three **MISS MITFORDS**, of Somerset Place. They were long inhabitants of this city, and although in the matter of this large sum they constituted Mr. Markland the almoner of their bounty, it in no respect interfered with their generous regard for every case of distress, public or private, and for the larger claims of our hospitals and public institutions. Those who knew them in private life admired the simple bearing of these three well-bred ladies -the most unselfish, cheerful, and devoted of Christians. They lived for others, and as God had bestowed abundantly they grudged nothing in His service.

MRS. C. RAMSDEN, also through Mr. Markland, founded the Missionary Sermons at Oxford and Cambridge.

Mr. Birth, a builder, was for many years the residence of **DAVID HARTLEY**. Mr. Monkland, in his *Literature and Literati of Bath*, says of him, he was "born "in 1705, was not only a physician, but a metaphysician, and was held in high "esteem as a philosophical writer; he was the author of an excellent and "much admired work, entitled 'Observations on Man.'" He built the house wherein he resided in Belvedere, and there he died (1757). "He had become "so enamoured of a nostrum, composed of soap and lime water, for *dysuria* "*calculosa*, with which complaint he himself was afflicted, that it is said he "swallowed no less than 200 lbs. weight of soap! But this, alas! by no means "proved the virtue of the specific, for which he had obtained the parliamentary "grant of £5000, for the female empiric *Mrs. Stephens!!* since he at length fell "a sacrifice to the disease."

"He was succeeded by his son, who became M.P. for Hull, and was "remarkable for his strenuous opposition to the American War, and also as being "one of the early promoters of the abolition of the slave trade." Hartley was a skilled financier, and a man who for his integrity and benevolence was highly esteemed, but as a speaker was dull and prosy. He was greatly opposed to the American War, and consequently to the policy and administration of Grenville; and in 1764 he wrote a celebrated pamphlet, entitled "The Budget," exposing the blunders and fallacies of Grenville's budget. In a note to Walpole's "Memoirs of the Reign of George III.," vol. 2, p. 7, the editor, Sir Denis Le Marchant, gives an interesting note in reference to this pamphlet, which we append :—

"The title is 'The Budget; inscribed to the man who thinks himself a minister.
" ' Emendare tuos quamvis Faustine libellos
" ' Non multæ poterunt, mea litura prodast.' "
(Either the author or the printer has made an error in this line. We think it should be—
" Non multæ poterunt, una litura potest.")
" It is a quarto of only twenty-two pages, slovenly written, and with little vivacity of expression.
" Mr. Hartley was a frequent writer of pamphlets on the side of the Opposition, chiefly on "the Revenue. He was attached both to Lord Rockingham and Mr. Pitt, and was the son of a "physician (who was also the most eminent metaphysician of his day). Mr. Hartley had the "honour of negotiating and signing the preliminaries of Peace with America in 1783, and of "moving the first resolution in the House of Commons against the Slave Trade. He was much "respected by all parties, but his speeches seldom found a willing audience. Tickell has parodied "him with the most ludicrous effect in the 'Anticipation;' and he is thus described by another "co-temporary --
" ' Peace to the rest, for Faction now,
" ' To shield her sons with poppied brow,
" ' Bids Hartley stand before me.
" ' Goddess, the potent charm I own;
" ' My breath is lost, my voice has flown,
" ' And dulness creeps all o'er me.'
New Foundling Hospital for Wit.

"He was a Fellow of Merton College, Oxford, until his death in 1813 at Bath, at a very advanced age. Flattering obituaries appear of him in the *Annual Register* and the *Gentleman's Magazine* of that year. A clergyman of his College, now deceased, described him to a friend of the Editor as 'an honest, high-principled man, but a dull talker, and a prosy speaker.'"

Hartley was eccentric in manner and dress.[1] In days when men wore cravats up to the crowns of their heads, as stiff as hair linings could make them, he donned a loose, large turn-down collar, fastened by a narrow black ribbon.

At No. 6, **EDGAR BUILDINGS**, lived **William Hoare, R.A.**, who was born in 1707, and at an early age, shewing great taste for the arts, was sent to Italy, where he studied for some years, first under Grisoni, and then under Francesco Imperiale. On his return to England, he settled in this city, where he died in 1792. Soon after the establishment of the Royal Academy, he was chosen one of its members. In the board-room of the Water Hospital is one of his pictures; it represents the first physician of the Hospital (Dr. Oliver), attended by the house apothecary (Mr. Pearce), consulting on the cases of three patients, who may be considered as personifying the maladies for the relief of which this noble institution is especially intended. In this board-room are other creations of Hoare's pencil, as also his own portrait, in crayons. His altar-pieces were in much repute; for that at the Octagon Chapel, "The lame man healed at the pool of Bethesda," he received £100, and was presented with a pew in the chapel.

His eldest son, **Prince Hoare**, was born in Bath, 1755; though best known as a dramatist, he was educated as a painter, and was a pupil of Raphael Mengs; he studied some time in Rome, and also visited other cities of Italy;[2] but just as he was rising into eminence his health failed, and he was obliged to relinquish the palette. He then gave his mind and his genius to authorship, wrote several works on the fine arts, and also a life of Granville Sharp; but he was more particularly distinguished as a dramatic writer. Some of his productions are still "stock pieces;" among them "The Haunted Tower," for which

---

[1] The Rev. Richard Warner, who knew him well, writes:—" David Hartley was singular in his dress and simple in his manners, and (perhaps) rather affected the quaint apparel of the puritans; *he never wore stockings!*" * * * "One day after dinner" (in the fellows' room of Merton College, Oxford, of which he was the second oldest fellow), "allusion was made to Hartley's *stocking-less* legs, and denounced as a dirty practice. 'I beg your pardon,' said Hartley, and throwing off his shoe, and spreading his naked limb upon the table, 'There, gentlemen, you see that there is not a speck of dust upon my foot.'"

[2] His autograph portrait hangs in the hall of painters in the Uffizii Palace, in Florence, and is inscribed "Princes Hoare." An anecdote is told of him in Murray, that on his first arrival at Florence he received an unexpected honour. Having written his name in the hotel book *Prince Hoare*, he was immediately saluted as "Il Principe Hoare," and *charged accordingly!*

Stephano Storace composed the music; and those amusing farces, "My Grandmother," "The Prize," etc., never forgetting that charming little musical piece, "No Song, No Supper," which must ever be in requisition when among the successive ornaments of the stage are to be found the whims of a Banister, the humour of a Suet, or the sweet warbling of a Storace.

After the death of Mr. Boswell, in 1799, Prince Hoare was elected Secretary for Foreign Correspondence to the Royal Academy. He died in 1835.

2, ALFRED STREET was the home of **SIR THOMAS LAWRENCE'S** boyhood. Thomas Lawrence, the father of our subject, was formerly Supervisor of Excise in Bristol, which office he resigned in June, 1769, and took the *White Lion Inn*. Thomas, his second son, was born in the parish of St. Philip, on the 4th of May previously. In 1772, the father left the White Lion, and took *The Bear*, at Devizes, and it was at this Inn[1] that the boy—a boy of most beautiful mien, full of expression and precocious intelligence—was brought up (and we may add educated), until he was ten years old; when his father left Devizes and came to live in Bath in 1782.[2] The family for two years lived on St. James's Parade, and then at 2, Alfred Street. Lawrence was by profession an attorney, and being a man of superior education and attainments, it seems more than probable that, inasmuch as this precocious son never went to any school after he was eight years old, that his father gave him *the* education which, by his own intelligence and innate superiority, enabled him to take his place in the society of which he became one of the brightest and most dignified ornaments. His mother was, moreover, of a good family, and a refined and sensible woman. Her father was the Rev. William Reed, and she exercised an admirable influence over her numerous children, especially Thomas, who was not only the pet of his parents, but also of his brothers and sisters. It has been generally thought that Thomas Lawrence was a

---

[1] It was the most celebrated Inn in the "old coaching days," on the Exeter and London road, except its namesake "The Bear," in Bath. Anstey refers to it:

"Miss Jenny made fun, as she always is wont,
"Of Prudence my sister and Tabitha Runt;
"And every moment she heard me complain,
"Declared I was vapoured, and laughed at my pain.
"What though at Devizes I fed pretty hearty,
"And made a good meal, like the rest of the party."

[2] Mr. Monkland in his *Literature and Literati of Bath*, says he kept a lodging-house, which is not strictly the case. A Mrs. Alcock, sister of Cumberland the dramatist, boarded with the family, and Lawrence's eldest son, Andrew, who was in Holy Orders, obtained the Lectureship of St. Michael's, with a stipend of £140 a year, out of which he paid his father £80. These sources of income, together with the young artist's earnings, constituted the bulk of the family means of living. The Rev. Andrew Lawrence became a Chaplain in the Navy, and in that capacity served at various periods with the most famous commanders of the day, including Nelson. He died at Haslar in 1820. The third son was William Read Lawrence, who attained to the rank of major, and died in 1818.

pupil of William Hoare, but if he received any instruction from that artist, it would have been only occasional, not systematic. From the time his father settled in this city, until 1788, when he left it, this wonderful youth, from 11 to 17, performed prodigies of labour. It is difficult to conceive a lad of 11 years old becoming a professional portrait painter, yet so it was. Hoare, himself, in painting a figure of Christ, took as his model a head and bust designed by Lawrence. But apart from the professional and technical instruction which he may have obtained in his art, he received the valuable assistance of Dr. William Falconer—a mentor of great intellectual gifts and attainments, without any prejudices of the schools to warp his judgment or to affect the disinterestedness of his counsel. One source of advantage also was his access to an admirable collection of the old masters belonging to the Honourable Mr. Hamilton (great uncle of the present Duke of Abercorn), who resided at Rock House,[1] and felt an immense interest in the youthful student, and to this must be attributed much of that excellence which showed itself in a later period of his career. The oval crayon drawings executed in Bath were done rapidly. He received four sitters a day, and at 12 and 13 years of age was (during professional hours) "as solemn as a "judge." One of the most beautiful of these drawings was that which he executed in 1783 of *Miss Shakspeare*. He saw her in the Theatre, and it is characteristic of the boy's appreciation of beauty and graceful expression, that the following day he drew her portrait from memory.[2] From an artistic point of view, however, the pencil drawing which he made about the same period of *Mrs. Siddons*, in her character of *Euphrasia* in *The Grecian Daughter*, when she stabs the tyrant, is more valuable. Lawrence witnessed the play in the Bath Theatre, and, although she "sat" to him afterwards, he had caught and carried in his "mind's eye" the impassioned expression of the great actress, which characterises the portrait. It was subsequently published and was largely purchased.

In 1788, when the artist was in his 18th year, his father went to reside for a brief period at Salisbury, and from thence to London, where the precocious youthful Bath professor developed into one of the most accomplished, dignified gentlemen of the time, and not the least able President of the Royal Academy.

5, ROYAL CRESCENT. CHRISTOPHER ANSTEY.—"The New Bath "Guide; or, Memoirs of the B-n-r-d Family," was the most successful satire published in an age which afforded too much scope for the satirist's pen. The

---

[1] The residence at a later period of the Hon. and Rev. W. J. Brodrick, Rector of Bath.

[2] This lady became the wife of J. Wiltshire, son of Walter, and mother of the late John Wiltshire, of Shockerwick Park. She was a woman of exquisite beauty and noble graces of character.

title, *New Bath Guide*, is now an anachronism; indeed it seems difficult now to see that at any time it could have had a special appropriateness. But be this as it may, the public were not slow to appreciate its wit and satirical force. In the present day, even, a reader, with the slightest sense of humour, who had never heard of the book, and who should know nothing of Bath society, its vices, follies, and many idiosyncracies, taking up the book by accident, would at once fasten upon it with avidity. It is such an amusing picture of the times and the people; such an exposure of the utter hollowness, deceit, lying, and debauchery which characterised a certain portion of society, that no one can doubt its reality. The clergy, the medical profession, the man and woman of "fashion," the adventurer, the gambler and fortune-hunter—all played a part.[1] The parson pandered to his fashionable flock; the empiric and the quack picked the pockets of his patient, who patiently submitted to it; the gambler swindled his victim, who thought it an honour; and the fortune-hunter and the fashionable idler ran away with some heiress, or pretended heiress, whose heart, if she had one, he broke by his cruelty or neglect.

Christopher Anstey was the son of the Rev. Christopher Anstey, D.D., of Brinkley, in the county of Cambridge, where he was born October 31st, 1724; educated at Bury St. Edmunds, whence he went to Eton, and was placed as an *oppidan*. After a creditable career at Eton, he obtained a scholarship at King's College, Cambridge, and took his B.A. degree; in 1745, he was admitted Fellow of his College. In consequence of some resistance to what he deemed an unfair and vexatious demand upon him to deliver the first oration, he was for a time refused his M.A. degree. In 1754, on the death of his mother, succeeding to the family estates, he resigned his fellowship, and in 1756 married Miss Calvert, daughter of Felix Calvert, Esq., of Albiny Hall, Hertfordshire, a lady of great accomplishments, who by her admirable qualities was "all in all" to a man of his keen intellect and humorous temperament. For fifty years, as Spenser says—

> "From that day forth, in peace and joyous bliss,
> They lived together long without debate;
> No private jarre, no spite of enemies,
> Could shake the safe assurance of their state."

We are unable to say, exactly, when Anstey first took up his residence in Bath,

---

[1] We have always maintained that at the period to which we refer, there were two phases of society as distinct from each other as the two hemispheres (see Appendix). No one discerned with clearer vision the evils of all the excitement, affectation of superior sanctity, and *familiar pretences of spiritual sympathy*, which was common amongst the revivalists of his day, than Anstey. The late Bishop of Exeter exposed it in a book entitled "Enthusiasm of Methodists and Papists compared." If any reader wishes to know what Anstey thought of its consequences, he will find it in Letters 14 and 15.

but we believe it was about 1764. He first occupied a house near St. James's Square, and a portion of that site was his garden. In 1770 he purchased the house in the Royal Crescent, and there he lived for 35 years. The *New Bath Guide* was written and published at Trumpington in 1766, and in the same year *James Potts*, at the *Swift's Head*, Dublin, also published an edition, but whether it was a piracy or not we cannot say. After the 2nd edition Dodsley[1] bought the copyright for £200, and made a very large profit by it. After publishing ten editions of the book, he restored the copyright in 1777 to Anstey. He continued to be the publisher for the author, we believe, until his death. The book, since that event, has had an immense sale. Many editions have been issued, and it has been embellished by the pencils of *Rowlandson* and *Cruickshank*, and many others of less eminence as artists. The large 4to. edition, with a memoir prefixed by the poet's son, John Anstey, contains all the author's works, with the exception of two, of which for obvious reasons he never admitted the authorship—*Dr. Bongout* and *The Priest Dissected*. Some have thought that this unwillingness to admit the authorship of Dr. Bongout was in consequence of its grossness and indelicacy. This is absurd, because there are passages in the *New Bath Guide*, as well as in some of the miscellaneous poems, far worse than any that are to be found in *Dr. Bongout*. The truth is, Anstey did not choose to allow that he was the author of a satire upon a well-known man then living; and as to the *Priest Dissected*, he found, after publishing it, that his victim, who was thought to be the author of a virulent attack upon him, was not the real *Simon Pure*.

Anstey was a man of simple manners, cheerful, hospitable, benevolent. In person he was remarkably handsome, and although he shrank from "the parade "and bustle of public business," he certainly took a warm interest in the various charitable institutions of the city, although we cannot find that he ever filled any official position in connection with either of them. Anstey had a family of thirteen children, for an account of some of whom, and of other branches of the family, see *Notes and Queries*, October 22nd, 1881, and June 14th, 1882 (*vide* Appendix). One of Anstey's daughters married Mr. Bosanquet, of Hardenhuish Park, near Chippenham, and there, during a visit in 1805, he died on August 3rd. His body rests in Walcot Church, a tablet being placed there to his memory, and a monument has also been raised to his honour in Poet's Corner, Westminster Abbey.

No other life of Anstey exists, except the graceful and well-written sketch

---

[1] The famous publisher. He had been a footman to the Hon. Mrs. Lowther, and was the author of a volume entitled "The Muse in Livery." He was an honourable man, an enterprising publisher, and regarded by authors of the highest eminence as worthy of their patronage and confidence.

which precedes the collected edition of his works published in 4to. in 1808, by **JOHN ANSTEY**,[1] his son, who was the author of "The Pleader's Guide," a most witty and amusing work. A writer in the *Gentleman's Magazine* in 1808, the year in which the book was published, makes a very apt comparison between the father and the son :—

"Their sentiments and souls seem congenial. The striking image of the "father (I do not mean in the engravings) presents itself in every successive page "of the editor, and as the eye seemingly in a portrait picture follows the person "looking at it, in every direction, round the room in which it is suspended. "Pindar, in his strains, speaks emphatically, and his words are : 'Who copy after "'the bright original left them by their ancestors, may take great satisfaction in "'often speaking of the best of progenitors, for they assume not the glory of other "'men's virtue for want of worth of their own, but uniting both in one, celebrate "'the authors of their descent and the models of their lines.' I am here paying a "small tribute to the author; his humour, his good humour, is constitutional, and "appears undeniably as we affirm in physiognomy, in the face of his compositions, "but without the 'broad grin.' And in the same piece, with 'laughter holding "'both his sides,' you must except, however, some specimens of the author's "writings, in which pathos excites other deep feelings, and proves the effects and "versatility of his genius. If I have not the pleasure soon of reading in your "valuable Miscellany some observations on the recent re-publication of Mr. "Anstey's Poetical Works, and of the editor's interesting account of his father's "life, I will endeavour to supply you with some further particulars and observations."

SIR SIDNEY SMITH.—During the boyhood of the future hero, his mother resided in *Catherine Place*, but the number of the house we cannot ascertain. Sidney was educated at the Bath Grammar School, and the head master, by whom so many distinguished men were educated, the **Rev. Nathaniel Morgan,** boasted that he had flogged the man who had flogged the French.[2] Smith must

---

[1] Father of John Thomas Anstey, Esq., of Lansdown Crescent, in this city.

[2] Mr. Monkland, an old Grammar-School boy, says :—
"As our anniversary school song used to record * :—
  "'For here, dauntless Sidney † famed heroes among,
  "'First dreamt of the laurels he gained at Toulon !'—
"Or, as the gifted Heber has more elegantly and poetically expressed his deeds at *Acre* :—
  "'What hero thus triumphant Gaul dismayed?
  "'What arm repelled the victor Renegade?
  "'Britannia's champion, bathed in hostile blood,
  "'High on the breach the dauntless seamen stood ;
  "'Admiring Asia saw the unequal fight—
  "'E'en the pale Crescent blessed the Christian's might !'"

  * Sir Sidney Smith.   † Written by William Meylor, editor of the *Bath Herald*.

have left the school when he was young, because, as his biographer, Sir John Barrow, informs us, he entered the Navy before he was 13 years of age.

At No. 2, ALFRED STREET,[1] formerly called "Alfred House," lived CATHERINE MACAULEY,[2] where she wrote the greater part of her History of England; her first volume was published in 1763, and the work continued to issue from the press in successive volumes, till, in 1783, it reached the eighth, all of which were *printed* by R. *Cruttwell;* the ninth was printed in London. This history takes in the period from the accession of James I. to the accession of the House of Brunswick.

Mrs. Macauley was very much the rage. Being a woman of great beauty, although not in her youth, she was the object of the idolatry of Rev. Dr. Wilson, (son of Bishop Wilson,) who made himself very ridiculous by his conduct to this lady. "Here they resided together, and so enthusiastic was the divine's admiration "of the authoress, that he actually placed her statue, *adorned as the Goddess of* "*Liberty, within the altar railing of the church of St. Stephen's Walbrook*, of which "parish he was rector";[3] but Thicknesse says she abdicated her *Princely Sopha* at *Alfred House*, deserted her "most excellent friend," Dr. Wilson, and married young Mr. Graham, brother to her aerial physician, a man about twenty-one years of age. "The statue did not remain long, as it was taken down again, by "the statuary who erected it, at the doctor's instigation; whether from motives of "revenge, on account of her marriage with Graham, or from fear, because the "vestry was about to cite him before the tribunals, it is hard to say. Be it as it "may, the Doctor, very soon after this transaction, sold the vault that he had "built with the intention of there depositing her remains."[4]

[1] The house afterwards occupied by the Lawrence family.

[2] Mrs. Macauley, or Macaulay, was the daughter of John Sawbridge, Esq., of Ollantigh. She was born in 1733, and being what is commonly called a "spoiled child," she grew up an ill-educated, wayward, headstrong young woman. With good natural intellect and acquisitive nature, she read a good deal in her own way, especially Roman History, and from this cause it is supposed she became strongly imbued with Republican opinions. In 1760 she married Dr. George Macaulay, a London physician. After his death she came to reside in Bath, and here she wrote her History. It is written in a rancorous spirit; shallow as it is intemperate, and one-sided. At first it was a novelty, and people bought it as a curiosity. The British public experienced a new sensation when they read this uncompromising Republicanism from a woman, who, at the same time, aspired to be a leader of fashion. Mrs. Macaulay replied to more than one of Burke's political pamphlets. Her works have shared the usual melancholy fate of such productions; those that have escaped the butterman, occupy the back parts of the upper shelves in fourth-rate book-shops. What is so amusing about Mrs. Macaulay is that, while affecting unbounded admiration for the rigid simplicity of Republicanism, she exacted as much homage as her coteries of slavish admirers were willing to pay her in the petty *regal court* which she set up. When at 50 she married the brawny young Scot, she was deserted by her friends, and gave unlimited scope to her enemies to blaspheme. Thicknesse was unmerciful upon her, and he knew so well from his large experience how to scarify a weak and foolish woman. She died at Binfield, Berks, Jan. 22, 1791.

[3] Monkland. [4] Ibid.

Perhaps the most foolish thing she did was to explain to Wilson why she married the Scotchman,[1] who, it appears, was the son of a leather cap-maker in the land o' cakes. It exposed her to much scorn and ridicule, and she soon left Bath (1778) for the residence of her youth, Leicester, and from thence to Binfield. Thicknesse's attack upon her is the cleverest bit of satire he ever wrote, but the most indecent. Being the advocate of quackery in his friend Tickell, he could not endure a rival, so he wrote an anticipatory epitaph on "Dr. Graham."[2] The man who wrote about his ailments in the "Valetudinarian's Bath Guide," and presented the reader with *fac-simile* diagrams of the nasty things which he said came from his inside, might have had a little mercy upon poor Catherine's nerves. Perhaps she had refused to take Tickell's *Ethereal Spirit*.

At **BELVEDERE HOUSE** lived the **REV. THOMAS BROADHURST**, a Unitarian Minister, a gifted and an accomplished man. As an author he wrote on "Female Education." He also published an elegant translation of "Funeral "Orations in praise of Military Men." In music he had much skill, and was devoted to the science.

This house is also associated with the name of **HARRIETT LEE** (who resided there), the author of *Canterbury Tales*. The house since the death of Mr. Broadhurst has been greatly altered and sub-divided into smaller "holdings."

TICKELL, the POET, it is well known, frequently visited Bath, but we cannot tell where he resided. Indeed, of that period, it is difficult, and often impossible, to obtain from any source—biography, local, public, or private records—anything more than general facts. There is reason to suppose from Guidott and Pierce that at the latter part of the 17th and the former part of the 18th centuries, visitors who came to Bath for a long course of the waters chiefly resided at the "lodgings," while the pleasure-seekers, or those who sought Bath society for change, naturally preferred the more cheerful quarters afforded by the *Inns*, of which no records, so far as we can discover, exist. Tickell was the Secretary and friend of **ADDISON**, who, much to the vexation of Steele, appointed him to the Under-Secretaryship of

---

[1] Of the elder brother, the notorious quack, "Dr. Graham," it may be remembered that his universal panacea was to plant his patients, *root and branch, in mud*—*i.e.*, to place them up to their chins in a hot and slab mass of earths and water! It was he, too, who used to exhibit the beautiful Emma Lyons - afterwards the celebrated Lady Hamilton—upon his curious piece of mechanism, *the celestial bed*, where she reclined as the *Goddess of Health and Beauty*, while the doctor lectured upon the charms of the one and the peculiar virtues of the other.

[2] " Here G———— lies. Mourn, reader, mourn the Man,
" Æthic, how vain! how short th' Electric Span!
" He who once went through Catherine's medium civil
" Is gone thro' Death's black medium to the devil."

State. In 1721, Tickell edited the first collected edition of Addison's Works in 4to. vols., to which he appended a masterly Preface and Poem. It is more than probable that Addison visited his friend here in 1708. In a very amusing paper in the *Spectator* of Sept. 25, 1811, purporting to be addressed to the editor, Addison describes a Whistling Match :—

"Sir,—Having lately seen your Discourse upon a Match of Grinning, I cannot forbear giving
"you an account of a Whistling Match, which, with many others, I was entertained with about three
"years since at the *Bath*. The prize was a guinea, to be conferred upon the ablest whistler, that is, on
"him who could whistle clearest, and go through his tune without laughing, which at the same time he
"was provoked to by the antic postures of a *Merry-Andrew*, who was to stand upon the stage and
"play his tricks in the eye of the performer. There were three competitors for the ring. The first
"was a plow-man of a very promising aspect ; his features were steady, and his muscles composed in
"so inflexible a stupidity, that upon his first appearance every one gave the guinea for lost. The pickled
"herring, however, found the way to shake him ; for upon his whistling a country jigg, this unlucky
"wag danced to it with such a variety of distortions and grimaces, that the country-man could not for-
"bear smiling upon him, and by that means spoiled his whistle, and lost the prize.
"The next that mounted the stage was an under-citizen of the *Bath*, a person remarkable
"among the inferior people of that place for his great wisdom and his broad band. He contracted
"his mouth with much gravity, and, that he might dispose his mind to be more serious than ordinary,
"began the tune of *The Children in the Wood*, and went through part of it with good success, when,
"on a sudden, the wit at his elbow, who had appeared wonderfully grave and attentive for some time,
"gave him a touch upon the left shoulder, and stared him in the face with so bewitching a grin, that
"the whistler relaxed his fibres into a kind of simper, and at length burst out into an open laugh.
"The third who entered the lists was a footman, who, in defiance of the *Merry-Andrew* and all his
"arts, whistled a Scotch tune and an Italian sonata, with so settled a countenance, that he bore away
"the prize, to the great admiration of some hundreds of persons, who, as well as myself, were present
"at this trial of skill. Now, sir, I humbly conceive, whatever you have determined of the grinners,
"the whistlers ought to be encouraged, not only as their art is practised without distortion, but as it
"improves country musick, promotes gravity, and teaches ordinary people to keep their countenances,
"if they see anything ridiculous in their betters ; besides that it seems an entertainment very particu-
"larly adapted to the *Bath*, as it is usual for a rider to whistle to his horse when he would make his
"waters pass."

Tickell died in Bath, April 23, 1740. The late Mr. Markland, President of the *Literary Club*, and the late Mr. Monkland (as the latter informed us), in vain tried to ascertain where he died and the place of his burial, but as to the latter there is every reason to believe it was the Abbey.

BEAULIEU HOUSE, Newbridge Hill. RICHARD TICKELL. Richard Tickell has been sometimes described as the nephew and sometimes as a "des- cendant" of Thomas Tickell. He was the grandson of the latter, and possessed no little of his ancestor's genius ; he was poet, pamphleteer, essayist, and satirist, and a contributor to "The Rolliad ;" but he was something more than these —he was the discoverer of that wonderful elixir, *Ethereal Anodyne Spirit*, which, puffed by Thicknesse with persistent effrontery in his books and daily conversation, if it did the patient no good, helped much to supply the *vacuum* which, like Nature, Thicknesse's pocket abhorred. Richard Tickell was the author of "The Project" and "Wreath of Fashion," but the work by which he was best known was "Anticipation,"[1] in which he gave cleverly simulated speeches of the most prominent parliamentary men of the day, together with admirable characteristic touches of their manners and peculiarities.[2] He built Beaulieu House. Tickell married Mary Linley,[3] sister of Mrs. Sheridan, so that he was closely associated with the city of his adoption. By that lady he had three daughters, one of whom was the mother of a gentleman whose connection with Bath was not less conspicuous than that of his grandfather—the Right Hon. John Arthur Roebuck. Mrs. Tickell died in Bristol, and her body rests by the side of her sister, Mrs. Sheridan, who died in 1792, in Wells Cathedral. Tickell married as his second wife a widow lady—Mrs. Ley—a lady described as of much beauty and amiability. He is said to have been a toper, and, like his brother-in-law, could stand up under a couple of bottles. He was for some years a Commissioner of the Stamp Office. After his second marriage, he lived at Hampton Court Palace, in the apartments assigned to him, and from one of the parapets, on which he delighted to read, he fell, and was killed in 1793.

Nos. 1 and 35, ST. JAMES'S SQUARE, 3, RIVERS STREET; WALTER SAVAGE LANDOR.

"So over violent or over civil,
"That every man with him was God or Devil."

It is related that at a dinner-party, on which occasion Charles Lamb was present, a gentleman sitting next to him gravely observed that he "thought Shakspere was a clever man," upon which Lamb arose and begged permission

---

[1] Some of his effusions will be found in Locker's "Lyra Elegantium," and Walpole refers to him in his Letters.

[2] Moore, in his Diary, tells us that Mrs. Sheridan sang once after her marriage, on the occasion of Lord North's installation at Oxford; and as there were degrees conferred *honoris causâ*, Lord North said to Sheridan that he (Sheridan) ought to have one *uxoris causâ*. Tickell was not satisfied that Sheridan had done what he might to bring him forward. He describes Tickell's anxiety on the first night of Parliament's meeting after the publication of his pamphlet, "Anticipation." The laughable effect on the house of Col. Barré's speech, he being the only one (having just arrived from the country) ignorant of the pamphlet, and falling exactly into the same peculiarities which the pamphlet quizzed, particularly that of quoting French words and then translating them. At every new instance of this kind in his speech there was a roar of laughter from the house, which Barré could not understand. A friend went off to Tickell (who in his fidgets had gone off to bed in a coffee-house in Covent Garden) to tell him of the successful effect of his pamphlet. Lord North, for this clever pamphlet, rewarded Tickell with the commissionership alluded to in the text.

[3] Gainsborough painted her portrait, as well as that of Mrs. Sheridan, both of which are in the Dulwich Gallery.

to feel the gentleman's head! We should expect, if we told our readers that Walter Savage Landor was a "clever man,"—a man of genius, that they would regard the remark in much the same light as Charles Lamb regarded the critical observation on Shakespere. The life, character, and genius of Landor have been described by Forster, Lord Houghton, Sidney Colvin, Mrs. Barrett Browning, and incidentally by his friends, and by various correspondents [1] in the *Atlantic Monthly Magazine*, 1866, and in *All the Year Round*, 1869. In an article in the latter, Dickens, as Mr. Ward explains in his "Memoir of Dickens" (*Men of Letters*), supplements his sketch of Landor in *Bleak House*, under the character of *Laurence Boythorn*—"Landor with his intellectual greatness left out." But the most interesting notice of Landor, so far as the period to which it refers is concerned, is that in *Fraser's Magazine* for July, 1870, written by his *protégé*, Mrs. E. Lynn-Linton, because it abounds with so many characteristic touches of the man, distinct from his intellectual genius as a poet and a writer. She was, she is, and very naturally so, an enthusiastic admirer of Landor, and a stout defender of his fame and character. We have to speak of Landor as a citizen of Bath and as a dweller amongst us for 21 years. Some time after Landor's return from Italy, in 1837 he came to Bath, and after a few weeks, took apartments at No. 1, and in 1846 he removed to No. 35, St. James's Square, and there he continued to reside until 1852, whence he removed to 3, Rivers Street. We suspect that, apart from the natural and, if we may judge from a passage in his *Imaginary Conversations*,[2] the architectural beauties of Bath, which he so enthusiastically praised, he was happy—happy as such a man could be—in the city of his adoption, because he could choose his friends where he pleased, without fear of fussy intrusions from ill-bred people, actuated by a vulgar desire to see the "lion in "his den." He might have led the life of a hermit if he had so determined, without apprehensions of undue curiosity from the citizens of Bath. We know that before Landor had chosen Bath as his residence, he had passed through those vicissitudes, so well related by his friend, John Forster, and others, which were not calculated to improve his temper, or to diminish his natural susceptibility with regard to acts of impertinence or discourtesy. Yet he bears testimony

---

[1] Leigh Hunt's "Lord Byron and his Contemporaries"; Lady Blessington's "Idler in Italy" and "Life and Correspondence"; Emerson's English Tracts, etc. etc.

[2] "In London with St. Paul's and St. Stephen's before us, in Bath with Queen's Square, the "Crescent, and the Circus (which lost nothing in Rome or in the world is equal to), we build cottages "like castles and palaces like cottages; and where the edifice is plain and simple, the window is a "hole in the wall, looking like an eye without eyebrow or lashes, or else is situated in the midst of an "arch, as if a ruin had been hatched up to receive it." *Note to Imaginary Conversations,—Pericles and Sophocles.*

to the fact that he never once had to resent an insult or to complain of a want of due respect during his long residence in the city of his adoption. This is the more remarkable, because those who knew Landor in Bath will have a lively recollection of the appearance and habits of the man. It was impossible for a child even to see and to watch him and listen to his "*crescendo* roars," mixed with those of his faithful dog, *Pomero*, without wanting to take part in the fray. We have seen him on many occasions on the High Common give the word of command to *Pomero* to go through some favourite antics to please the admiring juveniles looking on. But it was for juveniles only. He took no notice whatever of others about him, who could not fail to be struck with the grandeur, and, in his earlier days amongst us, the exquisite beauty of his countenance. He was a man, indeed, whom it was impossible to see without feeling a strong desire to watch with curiosity and interest. But somehow he escaped from that scrutiny, and it seems the Bathonians had, by a sort of instinct, got to know that "he did not like it," and left him and *Pomero* to enjoy themselves as they were wont. Landor, as is well known, passed many of his earlier and happier days in Bath, and made many lifelong friendships here. In 1805 Landor's younger brother "found him in Bath with the reputation of very great wealth, and the certainty, "at his mother's death, of still greater. A fine carriage, three horses, two men-"servants, books, plate, china, pictures, in everything a profuse and wasteful "outlay, all confirmed the grandeur." On this occasion he lived in the South Parade and Pulteney Street alternately. After his marriage he also visited Bath, and with reference to these visits we give a characteristic letter from Southey to Landor (in 1812), and the reply of the latter. Southey goes back to the days of his childhood, and it is curious to see how vividly the impressions of that period still haunted his mind. "*The Cottage*" to which he refers in Bathwick, we think, must be *The Villa*, which, at that time, was surrounded by pretty grounds and public gardens.

SOUTHEY TO LANDOR.

"Will this find you in the Vale of Ewyas, or have you taken wing for Bath, which, in spite of "thirty years' labour toward spoiling it, still remains the pleasantest city in the kingdom? I "remember it when it ended at the Crescent, and there was not a house on the Bathwick side of "the river. The longest walk in which I was ever indulged was to a cottage — *the* cottage we called "it, in a little orchard, a sweet sequestered spot at that time – my *ne plus ultra* then, beyond which "all was *terra incognita*. No doubt it is now overgrown with streets. But the only alteration "which I cannot forgive is the abominable one of converting the South Parade into one side of a "square, and thus destroying the finest thing, perhaps the only thing, of its kind in the world. I "have often walked upon that terrace by moonlight, after the play, my head full of the heroics "which I had been imbibing — and perhaps I am at this day the better for those moonlight walks."

LANDOR TO SOUTHEY.

"You remind me of Bath! if not a delightful, a most easy place. I cannot bear brick "houses and wet pavements. A city without them is a city fit for men before the Fall. But, alas, "they fell before they built. The South Parade was always my residence in winter. Towards "spring I removed into Pulteney Street—or rather towards summer, for there were formerly as "many nightingales in the garden, and along the river opposite the South Parade, as ever there were "in the bowers of Schiraz. The situation is unparalleled in beauty, and is surely the warmest in "England. I could get a walk into the country without crossing a street, which I hate. These "advantages often kept me in Bath until the middle of June, and I always returned in the "beginning of November. I wonder that your grave meditations were not disturbed there; for "as sure as ever there was moonlight, a train—not *qualis per juga Cynthi exercet Diana choros*— "was ready to invite you. I always hated plays and playhouses, and in the nine first years I was "only once at the Bath Theatre; but if I had a very large fortune I would have one of my own, "and give a company a thousand pounds to act once a week in the summer, for me and four or five "more. I would have only the best actors and the best audiences, and I would have no comedies, "except Molière's, for the ladies."

About 1807 he acquired the Llanthony[1] estate, and went to reside on it after his marriage. The estate, Landor said, "is a noble estate; "it produces everything but herbage, corn, and money." From this time until 1837, Bath knew only what all the world knew of him. His life, his troubles, his family quarrels, and return from Italy, are only more interesting to us, because the immediate result was that Bath became his chosen abode, the home of his adoption. At this period (1837) his estates were yielding him upwards of three thousand pounds a-year, of which mortgages and insurances absorbed one thousand four hundred a-year. Out of the one thousand six hundred left, he provided for his eldest son at Fiesole, Mrs. Landor, and the younger children, besides setting aside a fund to accumulate for their future benefit. This left him two hundred per annum to live upon, but finding this wholly inadequate, he drew an additional two hundred from the reserved fund, making four hundred per annum, which represented his income in Bath. Nevertheless, scanty as was this allowance which he made for himself, he occasionally received and entertained his Bath friends, and, as we know, his literary friends from a distance, but his own habits were frugal in the extreme. When

---

[1] The first Abbey of Llanthony stands in a wild and secluded valley among the hills of the Black Mountains of Wales, and Giraldus Cambrensis, the great scholar and tutor to King John, describes its situation "as truly calculated for religion, and more adapted to canonical discipline than "all the monasteries of the British Isles." Notwithstanding this, the monks of Llanthony were continually ill-treated and pillaged by the Welsh, so that in the year of grace 1136 a second Monastery was erected at Gloucester, and now Master Dene is prior.* Llanthony is famous for its crypt, where many noble corpses lie buried, but is even more dismal than that of the Abbey of Gloucester, for there is a perfect labyrinth of stone pillars and dismal arches, with corners filled with grinning skulls, while a fearful echo reverberates at every sound, making night hideous. *Medieval Chase.*

* Dene was made Prior of the Gloucester and Welsh Establishments in 1460.

Lady Blessington, Count d'Orsay, and other friends[1] visited Prince Louis Napoleon during his stay in Bath, in 1846, Landor entertained them at his lodgings, 35, St. James's Square, at one of those cosy little dinners which were so charming and so elegant. The Prince frequently visited Landor, and, during his few months' residence in Bath, never gave a dinner-party at which Landor was not present—" the guest of the evening." The Prince indeed exercised a fascinating influence over Landor, as indeed he did over everybody with whom he associated, but he seemed to have deceived no one so thoroughly, perhaps for the reason that less bold men than Landor abstained from topics relating to the Prince's political future.[2] The visits of Dickens[3] and Forster are events told

---

[1] Carlyle visited Landor in Bath in 1850, and in a letter to Forster two years after, Landor said, "you may discover Carlyle to be quite as much a hero as Cromwell." And Carlyle writing of Landor, some years after, expresses his delight with his Bath friend :—" On which evening, till near noon of "next day, I was Walter Savage Landor's guest, much taken with the giantesque, explosive, but "essentially chivalrous and almost heroic old man."

[2] Napoleon III. he first thought the incarnation of the Republican spirit ; then his opinions changed to one of intense personal animosity. "He has the fewest virtues and the faintest resem-"blance to them of any man that has risen by his own efforts to power," Landor said, and after the *coup d'etat* of December, poured forth the full vials of his wrath upon his quondam friend. He affected to approve tyrannicide, and offered a pension to anyone who would murder a despot ; and with reference to Napoleon he said, "Why did we not kill him when we had him here?" Everybody knew that this was Landor's rhodomontade. We should have been curious to see Landor's countenance and to have heard his words, if any scoundrel had presented himself as the agent ready to execute so diabolical a commission! Like his friend, Sir W. Napier, he spoke unadvisedly with his lips. The latter used most violent language in Bath in connection with the Reform Bill, but we know what he thought of the proposal made to him to lead a Brummagem army to force it upon the government. Landor was a combination of contradictory qualities, fiery and gentle impulses. We were once the medium of a communication to him respecting a Florentine Italian gentleman who, from misfortune, was in Bath without means. The result was that Landor provided a large portion of the expense to send him back to Florence. We had the satisfaction of knowing afterwards that there was no deception.

[3] There is scarcely a modern reference made to Bath by Journalists, that is not founded upon Pickwick, when amusement and fun are the object, and upon Dickens' depreciatory description of Bath when ridicule and contempt are intended. Landor praised what Dickens abused, after the latter had conceived that violent prejudice against Bath and the Bathonians, for reasons neither creditable to his judgment or candour. In 1869, writing to Forster from Bath, Dickens says :—"Landor's ghost goes "along the silent streets here before me... The place looks to me like a Cemetery, which the dead "have succeeded in rising and taking. Having built streets of their old gravestones, they wander "about scantly trying to 'look alive.' A dead failure!" Nor is this extract the only evidence of the *animus* Dickens displayed towards a city whose worst offence against him was a generous hospitality, a due appreciation of his genius, and a decided inability to applaud him and his colleagues of the "Guild of Literature" in the performance of the play of *Not so Bad as we Seem*, under conditions which absolutely precluded the audience from hearing more than a confused sound, and from seeing anything more than certain gentlemen and ladies going through a dumb show. We remember well the expression of blank disappointment on the countenances of those present on the occasion, not because they were listless or indifferent, nor because the actors failed, but simply that from within the *proscenium* set up by Dickens within the room,[*] not one distinct syllable could be heard. The arrangement was due entirely to the headstrong perversity of Dickens, who never forgave the Bathonians the offence of being too enlightened and too independent to offer incense at the shrine of a dumb idol. Dickens never forgave the "insult." He showed it by every means in his power ; by word, by deed, by slights, by sneers, and by misrepresentations. His resentment was unjust ; nay, it was *little*, and to the last degree unbecoming ; but there are spots on the sun !

[*] Large Room at the Assembly Rooms. Charles Knight, one of the Guild present, told us that he and others remonstrated with Dickens, in vain, on the arrangement, the acoustic failure of which was inevitable.

by themselves, but perhaps the most memorable is the visit paid by them and Maclise in 1840, as given by Forster :—

"A day or two after the date of the last letter quoted, Dickens and his wife, with
"Maclise and myself, visited Landor in Bath, and it was during three happy days we passed
"together there that the fancy which was shortly to take the form of *Little Nell*, first occurred to
"its author. I have mentioned the fact in my Life of Landor; and to the passage I here add the
"comment made by Dickens when he read it. It was at a celebration of his birthday in the first of
"his Bath lodgings, 35, St. James's Square, that the fancy which took the form of Little Nell, in
"the Curiosity Shop, first dawned on the genius of its creator. No character in prose fiction was a
"greater favourite with Landor. He thought that, upon her, Juliet might for a moment turn her
"eyes from Romeo, and that Desdemona might have taken her hair-breadth escapes to heart, so
"interesting and pathetic did she seem to him; and when, some years later, the circumstance I
"have named was recalled to him, he broke into one of those whimsical bursts of comical extrava-
"gance out of which arose the fancy of *Boythorn*. With tremendous emphasis he confirmed the
"fact, and added that he had never in his life regretted anything so much as his having failed to
"carry out an intention he had formed respecting it; for he meant to have purchased the house,
"35, St. James's Square, and then and there to have burnt it to the ground, to the end that no
"meaner association should ever desecrate the birth-place of Nell.* Then he would pause a little,
"become conscious of our sense of his absurdity, and break into a thundering peal of laughter."

Nothing could be more strikingly characteristic of Landor than Mr. Sidney Colvin's language:—

"Wherever Landor went he made the same impression, which was that of a king and a lion
"among men. In appearance he had gained greatly with age. As sturdy and as florid as ever, he
"was now in addition beautifully venerable. His bold and keen grey eyes retained all their power,
"his teeth remained perfectly strong and white, but his forehead had become bald and singularly
"imposing, high-vaulted, broad and full beneath its thick white fringe of backward flowing hair.
"Every man's face, as has been truly said, is in great part his own making; and the characters
"which time had imprinted on Landor's were not those of his transient bursts of fury, but those of
"his habitual moods of lofty thought and tender feeling. All the lines of his countenance were
"large, and, except when the fit was upon him, full of benignity, his smile especially being of an
"inexpressible sweetness. His movements were correspondingly massive, but at the same time
"clumsy; not, of course, with the clumsiness of ill-breeding, but rather with that of aimlessness
"and inefficiency. The physical signs of the unpractical man were indeed all of them written upon
"Landor. He had short arms, with constrained movements of the elbows, and even when his fists
"were clenched in wrath, there was a noticeable relaxation about the thumbs, a thing never yet
"seen to accompany tenacity of practical will or tact in practical dealings. He would put his
"spectacles up over his forehead, and after oversetting everything in the wildest search for them,
"submit himself with desperate resignation to their loss. In travelling he would give himself
"worlds of trouble to remember the key of his portmanteau, but utterly forget the portmanteau
"itself; and when he discovered that he had lost it, he would launch out into an appalling picture
"of the treachery and depravity of the railway officials concerned, and of their fathers and grand-
"fathers to the remotest generation. Next, after a moment's silence, the humourous view of the
"case would present itself to him, and he would begin to laugh, quietly at first, and then in louder
"and ever louder volleys, until the room shook again, and the commotion seemed as if it would

---

* This is characteristic of that heedless exaggeration peculiar to Landor. He forgot that it was not enough that the house should have been his own to justify him in burning it down. It would have been a punishable offence, as endangering the public safety.

"never stop. These tempests of hilarity seemed to some of Landor's friends almost as formidable
"as the tempests of anger to which he continued to be subject at the suspicion of a contradiction
"or a slight. But both were worth undergoing for the sake of such noble and winning company as
"was that of Landor in his ordinary moods. Then not only was his talk incomparably rich and full,
"it was delivered with such a courtly charm of manner and address, such a rotundity, mellow-
"ness, and old-world grace of utterance as were irresistible. His voice, especially in reading aloud,
"was as sympathetic as it was powerful; 'fibrous in all its tones, whether gentle or fierce,' says
"Lord Houghton; deep, rich, and like the noblest music, 'with a small, inartificial quiver, striking
"'to the heart,' adds another witness,* who by-and-by attached herself to the grand old man with a
"filial devotion, and who has left us the most life-like as well as the most affectionate portrait of
"him during these years. His pronunciation of certain words was that traditional in many old
"English families: 'yallor' and 'laylock' for yellow and lilac, 'goold,' 'Room,' and 'woonderful,'
"for gold, Rome, and wonderful."

The closing period of Landor's connection with Bath is well described by
Sidney Colvin. The circumstances by which he was driven from the city in
which he had dwelt so long are too painful to be revived, but we do not believe
that the lady upon whom Landor cast so much abuse deserved it, any more than
we believe in the transcendent virtues of others of whom he is said to have been
the "champion." Forster seems to have thought the group fairly summed up in
the expression, *Par nobile fratrum.*

"From about the beginning of the next year, 1857, there seemed to be coming over him a
"change for the worse. His letters bespoke both physical decay and mental disturbance. Worse
"followed; it was found that he had allowed himself to be dragged headlong into a miserable and
"compromising quarrel between two ladies at Bath. One of these was the wife of a clergyman, the
"other a young girl, her bosom friend until the quarrel arose; both had been very intimate with
"Landor during the last few years. To the younger he, with his royal and inveterate love of
"giving, had lately made over a small legacy in money, which had been left him as a token of
"friendship by Kenyon. In the course of the quarrel the older lady, who had shortly before
"accepted help from the younger out of Landor's gift, took exception to the nature of her
"intimacy with the giver. Landor on his part utterly lost control of himself. Regarding himself
"as the champion of innocent youth against an abominable combination of fraud and calumny, in
"the frenzy of his indignant imagination he remembered or invented all kinds of previous mal-
"practices against the foe. He betook himself to his old insane weapons, and both in print and
"writing launched invectives against her in an ultra-Roman taste. He wrote odious letters to her
"husband. Legal steps being set on foot to restrain him, his unfailing friend Forster came down to
"see what could be done. By his persuasions, joined to those of Landor's own lawyers, the enraged
"old man was with difficulty induced to sign an apology, coupled with an undertaking not to repeat
"his offence. But Mr. Forster had felt, at the time when this engagement was made, that Landor
"could hardly be trusted to remember or observe it. Age, illness, and indignation had rendered
"him for the time being uncontrollable and irresponsible. For the first time in more than twenty
"years he proceeded to act in defiance of Mr. Forster's advice in a matter of publication. Having
"recovered from the hostile party in the dispute a number of scraps in verse, the least considered
"and least valuable that he had thrown off during recent years, he entrusted them to an Edinburgh
"house to be sent to press, under the plea that copies of them were abroad, and would be made

* Mrs. E. Lynn-Linton.

"public by others if not by himself. The volume appeared early in 1850, under the title--*Dry
"Sticks, fagoted by W. S. Landor;* 'by the late W. S. Landor,' the old man had at first insisted that
"the title should run. The book was made up of the recovered scraps and epigrams in question ;
"with a few others in Latin ; besides a reprint, after an 'occultation,' as Landor puts it, 'of sixty
"'years,' of the *Poems from the Arabic and Persian;* and a number of complimentary pieces
"addressed by various writers to himself. Unhappily the old man had not been able to restrain
"himself from adding also, in defiance of his signed engagement, one or two of his worst lampoons
"against his enemy. The enemy seems to have been nothing loth to take advantage of the fault,
"and a suit for damages was immediately set on foot. Before it came on Landor had a stroke,
"which left him insensible for forty-eight hours, and for some weeks afterwards he hung between
"life and death. His extraordinary strength, however, carried him through, and he came to
"himself better both in body and mind after his illness. The trial was in the meantime coming on
"at the August assize. Practically there could be no defence ; the attacks were on the face of
"them libellous, and Landor's friends advised him to go abroad, in order if possible to protect him-
"self against the consequences of the inevitable verdict ; first selling his personal property and
"pictures, and making a formal transfer of all his real property to his oldest son. This was accord-
"ingly done, and just before the trial came on the forlorn old man set out to leave his native land
"once more."

Besides the libels published which formed the subject of the action, we have seen others consisting of letters and verses, which, in grossness and indelicacy, are almost sickening. It would be impossible to believe that Landor could have conceived anything so coarse and so prurient, except on the hypothesis that senility and violent passion had so depreciated his moral and mental sense, as to render him scarcely responsible for his actions. We shrink from giving any opinion upon the merits of the quarrel itself, but we know that amongst other charges he levelled against the lady with whom his quarrel chiefly lay, one was that she had assumed the distinction of " Honourable," *to which she was not entitled,* as a prefix to her name, and yet a month before the quarrel he entered a bookseller's shop and requested "a copy of the Poet Landor's works to be sent to " the *Honourable* Mrs. — — —." It is certain that rage, *infatuation,* disappointment, and some real cause for resentment, had upset the balance of his mind, and made shipwreck of his judgment—never too calm in his best days.

A GROUP OF POETS.

COWPER, SHENSTONE, BOWLES, MOORE, CRABBE, HAYNES BAYLY.

—Cowper appears to have been in Bath only once, and on that occasion he composed " Verses Written at Bath on finding the Heel of a Shoe." If he were in Bath at any other earlier or later period, the fact would not have escaped the writer of the "Life and Times of Selina, Countess of Huntingdon," more especially as the Poet's Life and Poetry were so influenced by the founders of Methodism and their teaching. "Cowper, the greatest English Poet of the closing years of the 18th "century, devoted his graceful and tender genius mainly to its service,"[1] and would have had a prominent place in those Memoirs in connection with Bath, if he had joined the band of enthusiasts in this city. **Shenstone** repeatedly visited his friend Graves, at Claverton, between the year 1744 and his death in 1763, and on those occasions he usually spent a few weeks at the *Boarding-House* of *Mrs. Hodgkinson* in the *Orange Grove*. The house, which was a handsome structure, extends into Orange Grove Court, but has fallen into a shabby condition, and is partly obscured by the house built up in front of it. Of **William Lisle Bowles, Rector of Bremhill,** near Devizes, Canon of Salisbury and St. Paul's, Mr. Monkland writes as follows:—"Like his brother poet, Shenstone, he "must have considered that he found 'the warmest welcome at an "'Inn;' since, in his frequent visits to Bath, from youth to age, he "always made the house in which we are now assembled [2] his head-quarters; "or he might have said—

"Freedom I love and form I hate—
"So chouse my lodgings at an Inn."

"At all events, so it was; and although a Tavern does not carry with it the idea "of being a temple of Apollo or the seat of the Muses, I doubt not that in some "of its chambers—perchance, this very one—he penned many a pensive sonnet, "and in some, I dare say, composed a merry song.[3] He was passionately addicted "to music,[4] as well as poetry; and often did the voices of the gleemen at the "Harmonic Society call, and the Orphean strains from Rauzzini's[5] Concert-"room draw him from his retired parsonage at Bremhill, where more recondite "studies occupied him, as his *Hermes Brittanicus*, and other learned and "antiquarian works prove. His first publication, entitled—" Fourteen Sonnets,"

[1] Lecky's Eighteenth Century, vol. 3, p. 615.

[2] The York House. This is not correct. He frequently visited his relations, Mrs. and Miss Bowles, at *No.* 13, *Seymour Street*, and on many occasions he stayed at **The Castle**, Mrs. Temple, to whose memory we offer a tribute of loving respect, was a great favourite of the poet, who always treated her with chivalrous courtesy, as indeed did every true gentleman. The poet was, in his later years, very "absent," and it was no uncommon thing for him to forget to eat the dinner prepared for him in the coffee-room. On returning to converse with the old lady, who was informed of the fact, she would say in her inimitable way, "When you have dined, Mr. Bowles." Mr. S. C. Hall, in his "Retrospect of a Long Life," tells a story of him: on passing through a turnpike-gate, Bowles put down twopence to pay the toll for the horse which he imagined he was riding.

[3] In the "Life of Moore," by Lord John Russell, the translator of "Anacreon," states, that on one occasion he found the rev. poet "in the bar of the *White Hart*, dictating to a waiter (who "acted as amanuensis for him) his ideas of the true sublime in poetry."

[4] Even his sheep-bells were tuned in thirds and fifths.

[5] A very famous musician in Bath, a friend and colleague of Herschell, and the early instructor of Braham. He is buried in the Abbey. A notice of him will appear in the SECOND SERIES.

"issued from our local press, and was printed by the father of the late Richard "Cruttwell. Byron, who, in his satirical moods, lashed right and left, has, in "' English Bards and Scotch Reviewers,' fallen foul of poor Bowles, for his "edition of Pope's Works, and accompanying critique —

> "If Pope, whose fame and genius from the first,
> "Have foiled the best of critics, needs the worst,
> "Do thou essay," etc.

"He nevertheless gives him most *substantial* credit for his Sonnets, the founda-
"tion probably on which his fame will rest, for he writes, 'Stick to your Sonnets,
"' man, *at least they sell!*'"

During an illness he resided at **5, South Parade,** and on a restless night he could hear the fall of the waters of the Avon which runs near, on which he wrote the well-known verses, beginning

> "When I lie musing on my bed alone,
> "And listen to the wintry waterfall;
> "And many moments that are past and gone,
> "Moments of sunshine and of joy recall."

Bowles died at Salisbury, April 7th, 1850.

MOORE'S residence, **Sloperton Cottage,** and the Rectory of Bremhill, were not far distant from each other, and the two poets often met at Bowood, the seat of the Marquis of Lansdowne. Moore's visits to Bath, from 1820 until his mind became overshadowed, were very frequent, and on all occasions, except when on a private visit, he made the *White Hart* his home; we say his home, for the reason that the little man was so happy and vivacious in the old-fashioned Inn. His account of the opening of the Royal Literary Institution we give in his own charmingly egotistical but lively language:—

"The Lansdownes off to Bath after breakfast, and I (after singing a little for the girls) fol-
"lowed them with Col. Houlton. The grand opening to-day of the Literary Institution at Bath.
"Attended the inaugural lecture by Sir G. Gibbs at two. Walked about a little afterwards, and to
"the dinner at six; Lord Lansdowne in the chair. Two Bishops present; and about 108 persons
"altogether. Bowles and Crabbe of the number. Lord L. alluded to us in his first speech, as
"among the literary ornaments, if not of Bath itself, of its precincts; and in describing our respective
"characteristics, said, beginning with me, 'the one, a specimen of the most glowing, animated, and
"impassioned style,' &c.; this word 'impassioned' spoken out very strongly in the very ear of the
"Bishop of Bath and Wells, who sat next him. On the healths of the three poets being given, though
"much called for, I did not rise, but motioned to Crabbe, who got up and said a few words. When
"it came to my turn to rise, such a burst of enthusiasm received me as I could not but feel proud
"of. Spoke for some time, and with much success. Concluded by some tributes to Crabbe and
"Bowles, and said of the latter, that 'his poetry was the first fountain at which I had drunk the pure
"freshness of the English language, and learned (however little I might have profited by my learning)
"of what variety of sweetness the music of English verse is capable. From admiration of the poet,
"I had been at length promoted into friendship with the man, and I felt it particularly incumbent

"upon me, from some late allusions, to say, that I had found the life and the poetry of my friend to
"be but echoes to each other; the same sweetness and good feeling pervades and modulates both.
"Those who call my friend a wasp, would not, if they knew him better, make such a mistake in
"natural history. They would find that he is a *bee*, of the species called the *apes neatina*, and that,
"however he may have a sting ready on the defensive, when attacked, his native element is that
"garden of social life which he adorns, and the proper business and delight of his life are sunshine
"and flowers.' In talking of the 'springs of health with which nature had gifted the fair city of
"Bath,' and of her physicians, I said, 'it was not necessary to go back to the relationship between
"Apollo and Esculapius to show the close consanguinity that exists between literature and the
"healing art; between that art which purifies and strengthens the body, and those pursuits that
"refine and invigorate the intellect. Long,' I added, 'may they both continue to bless you with
"their beneficent effects! Long may health and the Muses walk your beautiful hills together, and
"mutually mingle their respective influences, till your springs themselves shall grow springs of
"inspiration, and it may be said,
"'Flavus Apollo
"'Pocula Castaliâ plena ministrat aquâ.'
"Quite overwhelmed with praises, I left the room, Elwin[1] and I, accompanied by Bayly, and a
"sensible Irishman, E., introduced me to Ellis;[2] went to the play together. Home to Elwin's house,
"where I slept.
"22nd. Bowles highly gratified with what I said of him. Asked by every one to give a
"correct copy of it for the newspapers, but shall not, for it would break the charm which all lies in
"manner, the occasion, &c. &c. Duncan of Oxford said to me, 'I have had the sweet oratory
"ringing in my ears all night. Bowles gave me a copy of his 'Roscoe pamphlet,' with an inscription
"in it, *inter Poëtas suaves suavissimo*, &c. &c. Left Bath with Bowles, having bought some grapes
"for Bessy's patient, Miss Starkey. Bowles dropt me at Buckhill, from which I walked home,
"carrying the basket of grapes. Found all pretty well.
"23rd to 25th. Received a Bath paper, giving an account of the dinner, and luckily rather
"describing than attempting to *give* my speech. Had a letter from Cruttwell asking me to send
"him a correct report of it, but too late to do so.
"26th. Took my dear Anastasia to school.[3] Dined at Bayly's, in order to go to the Dramatic
"Ball in the evening: nothing could be more brilliantly got up than the latter. An amateur play
"first, and the fancy ball afterwards; an allusion to me in the epilogue spoken by Bayly—'Erin's
"'matchless son,' etc., which brought plaudits and stares on me. Came away with Elwin before
"two, and supped and slept at his house.
"9th. Took Bessy to Bath to see Liston. Had received an invitation from the Houltons to
"come over, Bessy and I, to them the following Saturday (12th), to stay till Monday, and go to the
"Subscription Ball at Bath; but the two frisks rather too much. The Phippses already at Bath.
"Dined at Elwin's; company, Mr. and Miss Bayly, Miss Pinney and Tom Bayly. Went to the play
"afterwards, and laughed a good deal at Liston in 'Solomon Grundy' and 'Peter Finn.' Slept at
"Elwin's."

The late **W. Everitt**, an old and highly-esteemed Bath citizen, told us a story of himself and Moore, which is amusing. In former days, Everitt sang a good song, and was always ready to gratify his friends. On one occasion, just

---

[1] Hastings Elwin.
[2] Joint author of the "Life of Lord Bacon."
[3] Miss Fournier's, Lansdown Crescent. Misprinted in Diary Furness.

after Moore's Melodies were published, he and other Bath friends were going to London by the Salisbury coach. The day was lovely, and on crossing Salisbury Plain a friend said, " Everitt, give us a song," to which he responded by singing one of Moore's melodies; then another, and when about to begin the third, a head was observed to protrude from the window of the coach, and the owner of the head cried out, " I say, sir, who the d—l are you, singing all my best songs?" A great laugh followed, and as Everitt used to say, with high glee, " I knew he "was inside, and that I should have him!" Of course, it was Moore himself.

Rev. G. Crabbe, Vicar of Trowbridge from 1814 to 1830. It will be seen that it was not unusual for Crabbe, Bowles, Moore, and Bayly to be in Bath together and guests at the same table. Crabbe always "put up" at *The Castle*, or, as it was then called, *The Castle and Ball*. He frequently slept there, and although reserved, he was gentle and courteous, and, like Bowles, invariably sought an interview with the venerable old queen, **Mrs. Temple**, with whom to exchange compliments.

Haynes Bayly was born Oct. 13th, 1797, at Mount Beacon House, the residence of his father, Nathaniel Bayly, a solicitor, and a gentleman of good family. He married, July 11, 1826, Miss Hayes, a lady of great accomplishments, who, after the death of her husband, edited an edition of his works, to which she prefaced a sketch of his life. Originally intended for the law, to which he took an invincible dislike, he cultivated a taste for literature. Being a man of good presence and excellent manners, he was sought by "society," which he amused by his ballads and charmed by his art and his genial conversation. He resided, after his marriage, in *Catherine Place*, but delicate health compelled him to seek a more genial clime abroad, where he died, in 1839.

BATHWICK may be said to have become an integral part of the city of Bath about a century ago. The area comprehends about 675 acres, and was formerly accessible from the city only by the Ferries from Boatstall Lane, the East Gate (which was really nothing more than a *postern*), and that opposite the site of South Parade. We are not historians, and do not, therefore, propose to tell our readers to whom the Manor belonged immediately after the Creation, as some will expect. Of course, at one time, it belonged to one of those fighting Bishops who came over in swarms with William. The holy man to whom William granted "Wiche" was Geoffrey, Bishop of Coutance, and as a reward, not for saving souls, but for skill in training soldiers to destroy life. William gave the saintly Geoffrey 280 Manors. It is probable that this disinterested Christian gentleman, with a view to save his own soul, bequeathed the Manor to the Benedictine Nunnery of Wherwell, in Hampshire; at any rate, after his death, it formed a part of the Wherwell possessions. Wherwell, it may be remembered, was founded in 986 by Queen Elfrida, the heroine who murdered her first husband, Ethelwolfe, and her son-in-law, King Edward. Historians say that this pious act was to expiate the guilt of these murders. Bathwick and Wolley, in 1293, then called Wick Abbas and Wolley Abbas, being united conventual estates, were valued at £12 5s. Between this period and the reign of Edward II., some victorious ecclesiastic, having most likely to be rewarded for some heroic services to himself or some long-suffering sovereign, it was found expedient to plunder Elfrida's Nunnery of Wherwell, for at this period a re-grant of one messuage and 40 acres of land in Bathwick was made to the said Nunnery, and subsequently a further re-grant of 20 acres was made. At the dissolution of Conventual and other Religious Houses, Bathwick reverted to the Crown, and we know that the Prince, Henry VIII.—whose virtues, continence, and saintly moderation and wisdom, are duly set forth by Mr. Froude in his history—did not leave the church which he reformed one penny of that income from Bathwick,[1] which had formerly belonged to the see of Bath and Wells for the use of the former in its reformed character. This and every other source of income was alienated with a remorseless disregard for either the spiritual or temporal interests of the see of Bath; the church was left to decay; the city to desolation; and the people to heathenism; until the church was sold in the market as old materials,[2] like an old barn or a disused prison, and only saved eventually by the public spirit and the pious resolve of a private individual. In the reign of Mary I. (we refrain from using epithets), the Manor, with its liberties and advowson, was granted to Sir Edmund Neville, by whose family it was held, until it came into the possession of Capel, Earl of Essex, whose descendant in 1726 sold it to Pulteney, afterwards **SIR WILLIAM PULTENEY**, and then **EARL OF BATH**. At this period there was a small irregular street, consisting of a few cottages and the church, dedicated to S. Mary. There is one house still standing — **the Crown Inn**,— and the street ran northward in a line from the inn; the church

---

[1] A portion of the Manor had at some time been granted to the See of Bath. See Warner's Appendix, page 75.

[2] By Letters Patent from King Henry, dated 1543, the Abbey, with all its privileges and property, was sold to Humphry Colles, who soon after sold it to Colthurst, whose son, Edmund, gave the Abbey—then become ruinous, and stript of its lead, glass, and bells, and everything else that could be sold for money, together with the ground upon the east, west, and north sides of it, to the Mayor and citizens of Bath. The Abbey House,* with the part called the Priors' Park, was sold to Fulke Morley, from whom it descended to the Duke of Kingston, who sold it to Ralph Allen.

* See Peirce.

and churchyard, at the end of the street, occupied the site of the present road opposite to that leading to Henrietta Park. Towards the close of the century there were about 250 inhabitants, and 50 houses which were not depicted on the maps, in many of which nothing but the old mill and the old church are to be seen. The latter was 64 feet in length, and 17 wide. As Pulteney found Bathwick, so he left it. This eminent man lived at *The Bear Inn* during his occasional residence in Bath; he became president of the General Hospital, took an active part in its erection and endowment, and chose his title from Bath. His name is associated in many public matters with that of Lord Chesterfield and less distinguished men, but yet he seems less known in our annals than they. He was a friend of Lady Huntingdon, and although he was not in the habit of denying himself any indulgence, was a man of inveterate dislikes; and, though by no means of exalted public principles or inflexible virtue, he was ticketed as one of the elect! Pulteney was turbulent, irascible, eloquent, and a persistent writer of pamphlets. He aimed at epigram, which Pope ridiculed—

"How sweet an Ovid, Murray was our boast!
How many Martials were in Pulteney lost!"

Pulteney married Miss Gumley, on whom Pope wrote the poem of *The Looking Glass*:—

"With scornful mien and various toss of air,
Fantastic, vain, and insolently fair,
Grandeur intoxicates her giddy brain;
She looks ambition, and she moves disdain.
Far other carriage graced her virgin life,
But charming Gumley's lost in Pulteney's wife.
Not greater arrogance in him we find,
And this conjunction swells at least her mind:
O could the sire, renowned in glass, produce
One faithful mirror for his daughter's use!
Wherein she might her haughty errors trace,
And by reflection learn to mend her face:
The wonted sweetness to her form restore,
Be what she was, and charm mankind once more!"

The history of this lady is still the subject of controversy. We think it is of little importance, *per se*, what Lady Bath's father was. E. Linley was a lady of humble birth, but she was the grandmother of three ladies of title—a Duchess, a Countess, and a Baronet's wife. Miss Gumley's history, however, is a mystery, or at any rate mysterious, and we give it as *Notes and Queries* give it to their readers:—

"I had hoped in the fourth volume of Pope's works, just published, to have seen in reference

"to his verses on Mrs. Pulteney, entitled *The Looking Glass*, a note on the line,—
"'But charming Gumley's lost in Pulteney's wife,'
"and not merely the old tale that Miss Gumley was the daughter of 'John Gumley, the proprietor
"of a china manufactory at Isleworth, who had a shop in Norfolk street.' When I lived at Isle-
"worth, some years since, I always understood that Gumley House was built by John Gumley, Esq.,
"who made a large fortune by army contracts and South Sea speculation; but I never heard any-
"thing about a china factory. Nor is there any mention of one in Aungier's *History of Isleworth*.
"It is said that John Gumley had two sons and a daughter, the latter, Miss Anna Maria
"Gumley, the 'charming Gumley' of Pope's line, first printed, I believe, in the *Court Poems* in 1717.
"She is described by Cooke (*Life of Bolingbroke*, 1836, vol. i. p. 11) as 'the most beautiful courtesan
"of her day,' who presided at St. John's revels; but he does not render it at all clear at what period
"this was the case. The next statement is that of her marriage with W. Pulteney, jun. This is
"given in the *Historical Register*, Appendix. December, 1714, p. 30, under date December 18:—
"'About this time William Pulteney, Esq., Secretary at War, was marry'd to Mrs..........Gumley.
"daughter of John Gumley, of Isleworth, in the county of Middlesex, Esq.' At this time Mr.
"Pulteney sat for Heydon, in Yorkshire, and probably suggested to his wealthy father-in-law to
"enter Parliament, for John Gumley was returned for Steyning, in Sussex, in 1722. Two years
"later he was appointed, on the death of Mr. Huxley, Commissary and Muster Master-General of
"the Army. This caused a new election, and though opposed by Mr. Harrison, he was re-elected
"for Steyning. At the general election, in 1727, his name does not appear as a candidate; but
"John Gumley, jun.—I presume his eldest son—was returned for Bramber, in Sussex. He seems
"to have been shortly after unseated on petition, the House, March 4, 1728, ordering his name to
"be replaced by that of James Hoste. In 1746 Col. Samuel Gumley was elected for his brother-in-
"law's old borough of Heydon, but was unseated on petition, and his name replaced by that of Luke
"Robinson, to the great disgust of Lord Bath and to the great delight of Horace Walpole. Of these
"two younger Gumleys the records seem to be very scanty. Probably the father died about 1730,
"and they, or at all events the colonel, came into large estates. The colonel tried to get into Par-
"liament and failed; Walpole also mentions that he fought a duel with General Braddock.
"John Gumley subscribed to Pope's *Odyssey* in 1725; he died, I presume, about 1730, and I
"believe his sons died *s.p.* Eventually his daughter became his sole heir, and it is around her that
"the chief interest centres in relation to Bolingbroke, Pulteney, and Pope. There is the scandalous
"story about her, generally known as the writing-desk legend, and the oft quoted statement that
"she was a notorious courtesan; but if all that is said against her is true, Pope's line,—
"'Far other carriage grac'd her virgin life,'
"seems hardly applicable to her; the words are not appropriate to one who at that very time had
"forfeited all claim to be considered virtuous. Pope's lines do not seem fair if applied to a young
"woman of no character, who, having married a respectable man, tried to recover her social rank.
"I therefore venture to think that the 'far other carriage' refers to an earlier period in Miss Gum-
"ley's life than the time when she 'aided St. John,' and when she still really was a beautiful virgin.
"One would prefer to think that Pope was contrasting the imperious pride of the married woman
"with the guileless innocence of a merry young virgin. Be this as it may, it does not appear that
"Pope acknowledged these lines as his own during his life-time, or even that they were published
"as his by Warburton.

"It would be of interest to know a little more about the Gumley family. What was the
"early history of John Gumley; what was his business; if he had a factory, where was it situated;
"and where did he die? Swift mentions him, I think, only once, as investing in South Sea stock
"with Alderman Barber, but whilst he states that the alderman gained largely, he says nothing
"about Mr. Gumley. The widow, Mrs. Gumley, died Jan. 25, 1751, aged seventy-seven, and left

"considerable property to her only son, Col. Gumley. The daughter, 'charming Gumley,' died
"Countess of Bath, Sept. 14, 1758."
   "John Gumley—I have with more than one contemporary allusion to John Gumley's
"trade as a glass and china seller, but cannot, unfortunately, lay my hand at the moment on any
"reference save one to Steele's paper in the *Spectator* for Oct. 14, 1712:—
   "'So though we are at this day beholden to the late witty and inventive Duke of Buckingham for the
"'whole Trade and Manufacture of Glass, yet I suppose there is no one will aver that were his Grace yet living,
"'they would not rather deal with my diligent Friend and Neighbour Mr. Gumley for any Goods to be prepared
"'and delivered on such a Day than he would with that illustrious Mechanic above mentioned.'
"I know not on what authority Malcolm says, 'John Gumley rented all the upper part of this
"'building, in 1714, as a warehouse for pier and other glasses, framed and unframed.'"

By this lady Pulteney had one son and one daughter, and the story connected with his will is curious, but no doubt authentic. Accompanied by Lord Barnard, the youthful heir to the then Earl of Darlington, the Earl of Bath went to his solicitor to make his will. After Lady Bath, and his son and daughter, to whom he bequeathed everything, his more distant relatives came on in due succession according to their degrees of relationship. The solicitor suggested putting in some other person in "remainder" for the Somersetshire property. The Earl thought it needless, but being pressed by the legal adviser, said, "Well, put in "Harry"—the young Lord Barnard. The son and daughter and the Countess died; the brother, General Harry Pulteney, succeeded and died. He was succeeded by his and the late Earl's cousin, Miss Pulteney, who married Mr. Johnstone, afterwards Sir W. Johnstone Pulteney.[1] One daughter was the issue of this marriage; she married Sir James Murray, who assumed the name of Pulteney. This lady was created Baroness and then Countess of Bath,[2] and dying childless, in 1808, and all other relations named in the Will having died also, the son of that "Harry," the Earl of Darlington (afterwards Duke of Cleveland), father of the present Duke, became the heir to the Somersetshire property. The Earl of Bath left a fortune of upwards of a million sterling, which, with a trifling exception, he bequeathed to his brother, General Pulteney, who had served at *Fontenoy* and Dettingen. It was a great surprise to the gossips of the day, because for some reason (no doubt a good one with such a saint as the Earl) he "hated" his brother with true fraternal hatred.

[1] His younger brother, George, was the famous Governor Johnstone, one of the Commissioners who were sent to adjust the differences between the British Government and the revolted American colonies.

[2] It was reported about 1778, and the report was generally believed, that Charles James Fox was going to marry this lady who, after the death of her mother, inherited the entailed as well as the unentailed estates of the Earl of Bath as well as the bulk of his large fortune. In a letter at this time to George Selwyn from James Hare he observed, alluding to the black hair and swarthy complexion of Fox, and the pale face and red locks of the lady, "Well, if the marriage takes place, "their children will inevitably be duns, with black tails and manes"!

Pulteney, in 1731, quarrelled with the famous Lord Hervey,[1] son of the Earl of Bristol, in consequence of an attack upon him in "*The Craftsman.*"

"Lord Hervey sent a message to Mr. Pulteney, desiring to know whether he wrote the late "pamphlet called '*The Reply*' to that of '*Seditioa and Defamation displayed ;*' in answer to which "Pulteney said he would not satisfy Lord Hervey till he knew whether his Lordship was the author "of the '*Dedication*' to the latter. Accordingly, Lord Hervey sent him word that he was not; and "Mr. Fox, who carried this message, asked Mr. Pulteney what answer he would give about '*The* "*Reply ;*' to which Mr. Pulteney said, that since Lord Hervey did not write the '*Dedication*' he "was satisfied. But Fox insisting upon some other answer with relation to '*The Reply,*' Pulteney "then said that he might tell Lord Hervey that whether he (Pulteney) was the author of '*The Reply*' "or not, he was ready to justify and stand by the truth of any part of it at what time and wherever "Lord Hervey pleased. This last message your Lordship will easily imagine was the occasion of the "duel ; and, accordingly, on Monday last the 25th, at between three and four o'clock, they met in "the Upper St. James's Park,* behind Arlington Street, with their two seconds, who were Mr. Fox "and Sir J. Rushout. The two combatants were each of them slightly wounded, but Mr. Pulteney "had once so much the advantage of Lord Hervey, that he would have infallibly run my Lord "through the body if his foot had not slipped, and then the seconds took an occasion to part them. "Upon which Mr. Pulteney embraced Lord Hervey, and expressed a great deal of concern at the "accident of their quarrel, promising at the same time that he would never personally attack him "again, either with his mouth or his pen. Lord Hervey made him a bow, without giving him any "sort of answer, and (to use the common expression) thus they parted."—*Letter from Mr. Pelham to Lord Waldegrave.*

* Now the Green Park.

It was not until the Estate had fallen into the possession of Mr. Johnstone, afterwards Sir William Johnstone Pulteney, that it was used for building purposes. By an Act of Parliament the Bridge across the Avon was begun about 1776, and in 1789 Argyle Street appears on the map ; then in rapid succession Laura Place, Johnstone Street, and Pulteney Street, and finally, Sydney Place. Before the close of the century Bathwick was a favorite resort of many of the best families who visited Bath ; and the historic associations, if not so time-honoured as many others recorded, are interesting and not without their special value. The parish, from a quiet rural retreat, soon became one of the first importance, and although it was not within the *liberties* of the City Charter, it was efficiently and well governed by local commissioners, until, in 1835, it was incorporated with the city and enfranchised by the Municipal Corporations Act. The architect's plan, though never fully carried out, is, almost of necessity more complete, and realizes a more perfect design than any other city or town in the kingdom, from the fact that the configuration of the site, and the absence of old buildings and conflicting interests,

1 Lord Hervey was a man so delicate that he subsisted chiefly on ass's milk. He had the misfortune to incur Pope's displeasure, who thus satirises him under the name of *Sporus* in his *Epistle to Arbuthnot*— "What ! that thing of silk?
Sporus ! That mere white curd of ass's milk."
The Herveys were a race possessed of singular and, in the case of the nobleman here mentioned, of rare characteristics. We think it was Horace Walpole who said, "God made men, women, and "Herveys." Dr. Johnson had a strong love for the Hervey family ; he said, "call a dog 'Hervey,' "and I should love him."

left the architect (Baldwin) free to exercise his taste and judgment as his genius directed. The sudden expansion of this suburb was met by corresponding efforts to meet the ecclesiastical and religious needs of such a large accession of population. The old church was doomed, but was not pulled down till the present church was built in 1820.

The Independents built Argyle Chapel, which was opened in 1792; and at a much later period—viz., in 1862—St. John's Church was built, and later still a new ecclesiastical district was "carved out" of the original ecclesiastical parish. St. John's is now a distinct vicarage, with full ecclesiastical privileges.

Laura Chapel was built in 1796, and takes its name from *Laura, Countess of Bath.*

[We have been permitted to use the private Journal of the late Lady Jervis, who was a niece of Earl St. Vincent, and assumed the name of Jervis in compliance with his will. She first married Mr. Osborne Markham, son of Archbishop Markham, and secondly Sir William Cockburn, Bart. Another portion of the Journal will be given in the **SECOND SERIES OF HISTORIC HOUSES.**]

"**8, ARGYLE STREET.**—Lady St. Vincent came to Bath to drink the " Waters, the Earl being then at the Admiralty. There was a ball on the occa- " sion of the victory at Copenhagen, which my aunt and grandmother attended. " They had white muslin gowns, and wreaths of laurel in green foil across their " breasts. They went together to offer their congratulations to **Lady Nelson,** " whom they found stretched on her bed in an agony of distress, *all* but herself " having heard from the hero. She was very handsome when I recollect her " many years afterwards. She was much attached to the wife of Captain Nesbit, " who, from a kind of companion to herself, ended in becoming her daughter-in- " law. He was a strange, uncouth-looking mortal.

"The **DUCHESS OF YORK** came to drink the Waters in Bath. She had " in her suite a young lady who used to be called her protégé, **Madlle. Pauline.** " When she walked out, Lady A. Culling Smith and Col. (afterwards Sir Herbert) " was in attendance, and she was surrounded by a multitude of dogs of various " species. Her hair, which was a light brown, fell over the back of her neck. " Once the **DUKE OF YORK** came while she was in Bath. I believe that their " Royal Highnesses much noticed the **Rev. Dr. Randolph**[1] He had suffered

[1] Incumbent of Laura Chapel. He was a fine, courtly, handsome man, whose person the clerical dress of the period set off to much advantage. There was a slight, unconscious pomposity about him in the pulpit. In reading the Psalm in which David protests his humility, the doctor

"much undeserved odium about some letters which had been entrusted to him
"by the Princess of Wales to her mother, as he was going to the court of
"Brunswick. Just, however, as he was on the point of starting, he was stopped
"by intelligence of Mrs. Randolph being seized with dangerous illness. He
"forthwith repaired to Carlton House for information as to the mode of returning
"the letters to the Princess of Wales. He was told to enclose them to the
"lady in waiting—Lady Jersey; *she* delivered them to the Prince, who, not
"understanding German, carried them to the Queen! The sequel may be
"imagined, as the letters were indited in the fullest confidence of a child to her
"parent, and epithets were not spared. The charge of treachery was not merited
"by Dr. Randolph, who believed (perchance in ignorance of courts) that a letter
"was sacred. To return to the Duchess of York; she sojourned at **21, Pulteney
"Street**,[1] and my sister and I used to watch the dogs as they jumped out of a
"caravan, in which I suppose that they took air and exercise. We were sent,
"after the whooping-cough and measles, to recruit at a house on Claverton
"Down, kept by some people of the name of Marchant; they had a white
"Pomeranian dog, called *Bingo*, to whom the Duchess of York took a fancy,
"and purchased.

"The servant of our aunt, Lady Cavan, came to see us, and was full of
"the glories of my uncle,[2] who had lately returned from the Egyptian campaign,
"and she told us that our cousins, Honora and Alicia, had been taught to play
"on the cymbals. At this time my sister had a tiny China rose-tree, in a pot,
"given to her. I believe that they were then quite a novelty.

"The Misses Gubbins and Bedingfield were then the reigning beauties
"in Bath.

"Mr. Levi, a wealthy Israelite, who lodged in the parlours of No. 8,
"Argyle Street, possessed a collection of valuable engravings, which he sent up
"for the amusement of my sister and self when we had the measles.

"One afternoon my grandmother met Dr. Randolph in Laura Place, and
"he told her of the rupture of the peace, and that he had received a letter from
"a friend concluding with—

"'Sir George Rumbold is just come on shore;
"'I have not time to say any more.'

"protested too much." Looking round the chapel, he used to declare, with the proudest gestures
and in impenitential tones, "Lord, I am not high-minded, I have no proud looks."

[1] The house in which the eminent physician, Sir William Watson, afterwards lived.

[2] Earl of Cavan.

"We went in the summer to Middle Hill, near Bath, and we used to be much amused with watching the drill of some clowns, who had enrolled themselves as Volunteers. Their uncouth appearance was irresistible, and in the mornings following we used to pick up abundance of knives, which they had dropped. Soon after our return to Bath a corps of Yeomanry Cavalry attended Divine service at Laura Chapel, when Dr. Randolph preached an impressive sermon on I. Samuel xvii. A body of them were shown into the recess, in which we used to sit. Apropos of the recesses, some of those who had sittings in them were the famous Mrs. Piozzi and the Archbishop of Tuam, with his extremely beautiful daughter, afterwards Lady Beresford. Mrs. Piozzi was short and active, and wore a plaister of rouge on each cheek. She used to call my sister and me 'pattern girls,' because we were so attentive at church. The Archbishop was tall and very handsome, and the attention paid to him by his daughter was charming. One Sunday Mr. Thomas Hope was in the same recess at Laura Chapel. After the service some one said to him, 'I am afraid that 'Miss Beresford has spoiled your devotions.' Soon after they were married.

"In my notices of 1802, I have omitted to state that in recovering from the whooping-cough, my sister and I were out to take the air in a sedan, on the South Parade, which was peculiarly warm and sheltered. I overheard a discussion as to the formation of a Canal to traverse the gardens on each side of the Avon, which occupied the space to the foot of Widcombe Hill. I have lived to see the Kennet and Avon Canal, and the Great Western Railway, successively make their appearance on the disputed territory. Gardens stretched to the spot where St. Mary's Church now stands, and the road up Bathwick Hill was rough and lonely, a rivulet trickling down the side.[1] Round Sydney Gardens was a ride frequented by gentlemen of a certain age, who used to discuss the news of the day, while a knot of politicians would meet at Bull's Library.

"At Kirkby, where my grandmother went on a visit to Lord and Lady Wentworth, my sister and I fell in with a young companion, Mr. Fitzernest, an illegitimate son of the Duke of Cumberland. He was much deformed, in consequence, he told us, of having been overturned in an open carriage, which was driven by H.R.H., and the wheel going over his back. He was at that time staying at Winkley, in order to be under the care of Mr. Cheshyre, the celebrated orthropedite; I believe that his system, if not exploded, is now

[1] Which found its way into an open ditch running through the site of Bathwick Street.

"seldom adopted. A leather strap passed under the chin, and was attached to
"an iron, which, arching over the head, was screwed at the summit to
"another down the back, to relieve the spine from the weight of the head, but
"this was to the injury of the face, the cheeks being forced upwards, by the
"pressure of the strap. Mr. Fitzernest afterwards was entered at Exeter College,
"Oxford, but did not distinguish himself in the pursuit of academical honours.
"After my marriage with Mr. Osborne Markham, he called on me in London,
"and I believe died soon afterwards. From a boy his manners were excellent;
"in countenance he much resembled Queen Charlotte.

"I think that it was in the spring of this year (1805) that the **PRINCE OF
"WALES** passed a few hours with **Lord Thurlow**, who was then staying at **53,
"Pulteney Street**. On the opposite side, No. **27**, resided **Mrs. Smythe**, the
"mother of **MRS. FITZHERBERT**, but I fancy no notice was taken of this fact,
"of which, perchance, the Prince was not cognizant. She was a beautiful old lady,
"and was very gracious to my sister and myself when we were taken to see her
"by our friend Madame Cinq Mars, to whom Mrs. Smythe was especially kind.
"We were permitted to go upstairs, where we were enchanted by some magnifi-
"cent mirrors in the drawing-room, which had been presented by the Prince to
"Mrs. Smythe. They were sold after death, and were purchased by Mrs. Hare.

"Viscount St. Vincent was an intimate friend of Mr. Walter Smythe, who
"introduced him to Mrs. Fitzherbert. He greatly disapproved of her marriage
"to the Heir-Apparent, which he said lowered an old Catholic family. Mrs.
"Smythe told Madame Cinq Mars that every precaution had been adopted to
"substantiate the marriage in a religious point of view. At the time of Lord St.
"Vincent's introduction, she was living in Sydney Place, and he was often at her
"parties when the Prince of Wales was present, and a circle was formed for
"H.R.H. and Mrs. Fitzherbert. After their first separation, Queen Charlotte
"earnestly besought the latter to live with her son, as she feared that he might
"commit some act of desperation. In the latter years of her life Mrs. Fitz-
"herbert resided at a large house in the Steyne, at Brighton. She was highly
"respected by the Royal Family."

58, PULTENEY STREET was long the residence of **FLETCHER
PARTIS**, a distinguished philanthropist, founder of the College bearing his
name. The provisions of his will were to have been carried out after the death
of his widow; but she, with true appreciation of her husband's beneficent
intentions, anticipated his design by carrying it out, in its integrity, during her
lifetime, in 1826. The College occupies a lovely site on the edge of Newbridge
Hill.

Historic Houses in Bath and their Associations. 141

It has been a debatable point as to the house in which **WILLIAM PITT**[1] lived when he came to Bath in 1802. On the one hand, it has been contended that **15, Johnstone Street** is the house, from the fact that there are stone cupboards which in all probability were especially constructed for the safer custody of Pitt's despatches. As Pitt was *not in office* he would have required no such accommodation. On the one hand the late **Mr. George Phelan**, a gentleman possessed of a good memory, used to say, some fifteen years ago, that as a boy, he was in the habit of watching at the corner of the street to see the great man come out of the house for his daily exercise or on his way to the Pump room. On the other hand, we have a distinct statement made by Lord Stanhope that Pitt " took "a house in Pulteney Street." In the life of Wilberforce there is a passage in one of his letters in which he speaks in feeling terms of the solicitude he experienced on passing that house, **26, Pulteney Street**, in which, the night before, he had met Pitt. It is difficult to decide. It is not improbable that, Johnstone Street being closely contiguous to Pulteney Street, some confusion of terms may have occurred, and it may be that Wilberforce met Pitt at the house of a common friend at **26, Pulteney Street.** We incline to the belief that the house 15, Johnstone Street was *the* house, more especially as we feel so much confidence in the evidence of the person referred to, though we confess that as a rule we do not like evidence of mere memory. The late Mr. Goodridge, we have it on the

---

[1] ON MR. PITT'S ARRIVAL AT BATH.
Bath Chronicle, November 4th, 1802.

"SAFE in her port, with flying streamers gay,
"As late the Royal ship *Britannia* lay.
"Her crew on shore, their leisure hours employ'd,
"And what they gain'd in wars in peace enjoy'd.
"Sudden ! a dreadful hurricane arose ;
"From every point the wind with fury blows,
"The cable's strained, the anchor soon gave way,
"By *force* the peaceful vessel's driv'n to sea :
"On billows mountain high she now is tost ;
"Now in the dreadful gulph to fight is lost.
"Then, all aghast ! they pump, they pray, they swear ;
"Each ' heart of oak ' now sickening in despair,
"All but their pilot PITT—he undismay'd,
"Fixed at the helm, with coolness gives his aid ;
"His royal charge with skill consummate guides,
"Which o'er the dreadful storm triumphant rides,
"Pursues her course ; till now the joyful crew
"Of distant land the welcome prospect view.
"But PITT fatigu'd, all difficulties o'er,
"Lets others steer the vessel to the shore.
"His health impair'd, from public life withdraws,
"Blest with his country's wishes and applause.
"At BATH recruits his strength, and finds repose,
"While every British heart with pleasure glows."

assurance of his son, **Mr. J. F. Goodridge,** frequently alluded to the fact that he also was one of many others who assembled at the opposite corner of the street to see Pitt emerge, with his faithful attendant[1] and body servant, from 15, Johnstone Street.

He confined his society to his political friends, some of whom were already in Bath—Lord Camden, Lord Carington, etc. And others came shortly afterwards—Lord Malmesbury, Lord Mulgrave, Wilberforce, Canning, and Rose. Other politicians came also to confer with him.

MR. PITT TO MR. ROSE.

"Bath, Nov. 7, 1802.
"DEAR ROSE,—

"I had been meaning to write to you to tell what I know you will be glad to hear, that I am
"much the better for my visit hither . . , and you would make me very happy if you can let
"me have the satisfaction of seeing you while I am here. There are many points too long for a
"letter which I shall be very glad, if we meet, to talk over with you. I mean to go on Thursday
"to my mother's, but shall return here in time for my afternoon's draught of the waters on Satur-
"day, and from thence shall continue here till the business of the Session calls me to town . . .
"Perhaps even the circumstances may be such as to make me doubt about going at all before
"Christmas. . . "Ever sincerely yours,
"W. PITT."

On the 13th Mr. Rose did accordingly arrive at Bath, and had some political conversation that same evening when quite alone with Mr. Pitt.

MR. CANNING TO MR. ROSE.

"Conduit Street, Monday, Dec. 6, 1802.
"MY DEAR SIR,—

"I have this moment received your letter of yesterday, and as you talk of leaving Bath on
"Wednesday, lose not a moment in answering it. . . I entreat you to let me have your last
"words from Bath. I cannot but be concerned that you are leaving him.
"Ever, my dear Sir,
"Most sincerely yours, G. C."

Pitt left Bath[2] on the 9th December for Cuffnells.[3] In 1805, he came to visit his friend, the **EARL OF HARROWBY,** who was then residing at **11, Laura Place,** the house built for Hugh, **DUKE OF NORTHUMBERLAND,** and for a time occupied by his son, Hugh, second Duke, of present creation.

[1] After Pitt's death the old man received a Government Pension, and retiring to Bath, died on Beacon Hill about 1847.

[2] Charles James Fox was twice in Bath, for the use of the Waters; the last time in 1780. On both occasions he was one of a gay party at *The Bear*.

[3] Mr. Rose's seat.

At **No. 55, Pulteney Street** lived a lively, garrulous, amiable, kindly natured gentleman, **DR. WILKINSON**, commonly known as **Dr. Caraboo**. He was the author of a treatise on the Bath Waters, published in 1831, at which time the author resided at **Kingston House** (*i.e.*, the recent Free Public Library). The doctor "went into" everything; nothing was above or beneath his grasp; it was amazing to hear him theorize upon every new invention, and dogmatize upon every conceivable topic. In 1817 the doctor was in high glee, having met with a distinguished specimen of humanity, who, like "Mesty" in Midshipman Easy, with the difference of sex, was "princess in own country." The story is substantially as follows :—

"A very interesting looking female knocked at the door of a well-known charitable lady in "the vicinity of Clifton; her language was unintelligible, but, by action and expressive gesture, "she made known that she came from a far distant land, had been shipwrecked, and wandered "about in a state of destitution, till she became the pitiable object she then appeared. Mrs. W. "most humanely took her in, revived, and cherished her; but although she made her wishes under- "stood by signs, and implied by her manner and stately carriage, that, in her own country, she was "a PRINCESS, yet none of the family or neighbours could understand a word of the language she "spoke with much volubility. Several *savants*, from the neighbouring city, were applied to, who "went and saw this mysterious female, but not a syllable could they trace to any tongue they had "ever heard before. She was requested to write some sentences, which she did, and signed them, "as they understood her to say, 'CARABOO;' these were transmitted to London and to the "Universities, when sundry conjectures were ventured on, and learned opinions issued from "professors' chairs, but the character was such as could not be discovered even in Fry's Panto- "graphia, and no conclusion could be arrived at. It does not appear that any one, at this time "harboured an idea of imposture. At this juncture, our Bath philosopher and linguist went to pay "his homage to the Princess Caraboo; he had sundry interviews; he noted down all she said, and "attempted forming a key, by which he was enabled to proceed, much to his own satisfaction, "feeling convinced that he should yet master her language; so confident, indeed, was he, that he "wrote a pamphlet on the subject, but just as he was flattering himself that his labors would be "rewarded, the bubble burst! The cheat was detected, and it proved that this interesting and "mysterious Princess Caraboo, was neither more nor less than an Abigail out of place, who, with a "superior wit and genius, and a cunning, surpassing even that of the class to which she belonged, "had succeeded for weeks in passing off this *hoax* upon the humane, the learned, and the wise!!

"'A narrative of a singular imposition,' has appeared, by which it appears that the overseer "of the parish of Almondsbury called at Knoll Park, to inform the worthy possessors that a young "female had entered a cottage in the village, and had made signs that she wished for a night's "lodging, but not speaking a language which its inhabitants or the overseer understood, the officer "thought it right to refer to Mr. W., a magistrate, for his advice. Thus it was that she was first "introduced under this hospitable roof with apparent reluctance on her part and where she "remained for ten weeks. When asked to write her name, she declined, but, pointing to herself, "cried *Caraboo! Caraboo!* and, according to the notes made by a gentleman conversant with the "East, and well acquainted with the customs of China, it appeared by the signs she made, and "certain Eastern words he extracted from her, that *she was a Princess of Javasu;* that she had been "seized by pirates, and in the course of time, and after many adventures, had arrived on the coast "of England, and, in consequence of the ill-treatment she had received, jumped overboard, and "swam to shore! The description of her person is as follows:—Her head small, her eyes and hair "black; forehead low; nose short; complexion that of a brunette; her cheeks faintly tinged with "red; mouth rather wide; teeth white; lips large and full, the under lip a little projecting, and :" her chin small and round; her height five feet two inches; her age appeared about twenty-five. "There are two portraits of her in this pamphlet, the one from a drawing by E. Bird, R.A., and "the other by Mr. Brandwhite. They are neither of them very prepossessing in appearance. The "cheat was detected in consequence of some of Dr. Wilkinson's letters appearing in the Bristol "papers, when Mrs. Neale, of Lewen's Mead, with whom Mary Wilcox, alias Caraboo, had lodged, "recognised her by the description therein given of her person, etc., and solved the mystery. The "artful manner in which the imposition was carried on was worthy of Salmanazor, Johanna "Southcote, or the fasting woman of Tetbury!!"

WILLIAM JAY, Minister of **ARGYLE CHAPEL**.[1]—Ordained to the ministry on January 30, 1791, he continued his ministrations for 62 years. He resigned January 30, 1853, and died at his house, **4, Percy Place**, the same year. It is a proof of Mr. Jay's rare qualities that for so long a period he maintained his influence over a large congregation, unimpaired almost to the last. He was a man of fine courage, great ability, and possessed preaching power of a high order. These were attributes which enabled him to win and hold that ascendency over his people, which he used with a moderation and wisdom that marked the character of the man. Mr. Jay devoted himself exclusively to his ministerial duties,[2] turning neither to the right nor to the left after other pursuits. In relation to the Church, to politics, and the exciting questions of the day, during his long and honoured life, his conduct was characterized by great caution, candour, and sound judgment; and he always acted towards those with whom he differed in opinion, on the principle that there are generally two, if not more,

[1] CONGREGATIONAL CHURCH NOW MEETING IN ARGYLE CHAPEL.
Rev. William Henry Dyer succeeded him in 1853, and remained pastor until his resignation in 1874. He died September, 1878. The present minister, Rev. Henry Tarrant, was elected in 1875.

BAPTIST CHAPEL, MANVERS STREET.
First minister, Mr. Parsons, elected in 1752 as minister, although he had preached in connection with the meeting for 6 years previously; he died Feb. 28, 1790. Rev. John Paul Porter was ordained in August, 1791; he died Oct. 10, 1832. 1837.—Rev. William Peachey became minister; he resigned in 1838. 1839.—Rev. David Wassell was appointed minister. Rev. John Davis became assistant-minister, and on Mr. Wassell's death sole pastor. On his resignation he was succeeded by the present minister, Rev. James Baillee.

YORK STREET BAPTIST CHURCH, commenced Jan. 7, 1828.
Rev. Philip Cater became the minister Sept. 28, 1831; resigned March 21, 1841. Rev. John Mortimer Stephens was minister from Sept. 8, 1841, till his resignation, March, 1847. Rev. William A. Gillson was pastor from June, 1848, till his removal to Saffron Malden, June 24, 1853. Rev. Robert White, from Appledon, was minister from Sept. 29, 1854, to January 26, 1857. Rev. Philip Cater returned to Bath and was the last pastor of the church, from July 5, 1857, till his retirement, Dec. 25, 1858. On March 3, 1859, the last meeting was held and the church dispersed.

[2] Mr. Jay was a voluminous writer, his works being generally of a devotional character.

sides to every question. Mr. Wilberforce no doubt was attracted towards Mr. Jay by this breadth of character and eclectic taste. It may be thought that Mr. Jay clung with too much tenacity to the position he had so long filled. It was natural that a man of so much energy and intellectual vitality should be unwilling to admit the decaying powers and enfeebled physical ability which had become painfully apparent to others, and that he should resist the proposed assistance proffered by his congregation. He did not object to an assistant, but a co-pastor was to him highly distasteful. "If," he said, "two ride on horseback, "one must ride behind." The reply to which was very simple, namely, that as to a co-pastor or assistant there could never arise a dispute as to which place Mr. Jay was to occupy. The end was that during the closing years of his ministry, he had the aid of a coadjutor of singular eminence, in the person of **ROBERT ALFRED VAUGHAN**, a man of great accomplishments. Mr. Vaughan came to Bath in 1848, and removed to Birmingham in October, 1850, where he remained until 1855. He died in 1857, too soon for the church of which he was one of the brightest and most gifted ministers; and for literature, on which he left the impress of his power and learning in various Essays, and in that remarkable work, "Hours with the Mystics." His sermons were full of exquisite thoughts, showing deep reading and immense diligence. We believe that Mr. Jay, before he died, was brought by reflection and by what he discerned around him, to believe that something more than praying and preaching were indispensible in a pastor; that a knowledge of his people, of their thoughts, and habits, and personal lives was needful, and that it was desirable to meet and see them in their homes as well as in his chapel. This he did not do, and the fault was not all his own. He had grown up with a system which did not insist so much upon pastoral care and general regard for the flock, as upon pulpit exhortations and long prayers.

REV. THOMAS TUPPEN had been a preacher in Lady Huntingdon's Connection, through Whitefield, at Portsea. Tuppen, with several others, seceded from that Connection, and he came to Bath in 1785, and established the Independent Congregation. At first the number attending his ministrations was about twenty-five persons. This number rapidly increased, until the congregation, in 1789, was powerful and wealthy enough to build Argyle Chapel, which was opened October 4, 1790. Tuppen never preached in it, so that practically Jay was the first minister of the Chapel, though not of the congregation. Tuppen was a man of whom not much is known, but he appears to have been a man of great earnestness, though not possessing any great intellectual distinction.

Tolerant of others who differed with him, he was characterized by great independence of character, and there was nothing of the charlatan about him—a quality which many men of his day assumed as indicating originality; or as "evidences of "spiritual grace;" or as a cover for slender ability and knavish designs. Tuppen, from the time he came to the city, was in a declining state of health, and this may account for the fact that less is known of him than his character and good qualities otherwise well deserve.

REV. EDWARD MANGIN was born in Dublin, July 14, 1772, or on St. Swithin's Day (15th). He was the eldest son of Lieut.-Col. Samuel Henry Mangin, of the 12th Royal Irish Dragoons. His mother's maiden name was Susanna Corneille. The Corneilles were from Normandy, and the Mangins from Metz, in Lorraine—both refugee families, who fled to England at the time of the Revocation of the Edict of Nantes. Mangin was educated at Balliol College, Oxford, where he was the contemporary and friend of Southey.[1] He was for a short time a Chaplain in the Royal Navy, Prebendary of Rath, and Rector of Rath and Dysart, in the Diocese of Killaloe. Perhaps few men were so long before the Bath public as the gentleman whose name heads this notice. He came to Bath in the year of the Union, and we believe that he then took the house, **No. 10, Johnstone Street**, which he continued to occupy until the year of his death, which occurred on October 17th, 1852. His retentive memory, vast knowledge, extensive reading, and copious flow of sonorous English, rendered him one of the most interesting as well as the best of talkers. He was a frequent contributor to the *Bath Herald*, in the early part of the century, many of his collected essays having been published in 1805, under the title of "Parlour Window;" another little work he published, entitled "A Voice from "the Holy Land;" and a very remarkable little volume called "Letters of a "Centurion," now very scarce, besides many Letters and Dramatic Essays.[2] He also published a little work on Mrs. Piozzi, *Piozziana*. Hunter says of him : "Mr. Mangin was no common man, nor is he to be estimated "solely by his printed writings. He was one of those quick to discern the "earlier manifestations of genius, and assiduous in his endeavours to bring it "out of obscurity. Few that have written so much have written with so little

[1] In "Forster's Life of Goldsmith," reference is made in the Preface to Mangin's acute criticism on the poet, of whom he was a great admirer.

[2] Mangin strongly condemned the conduct of the Corporation in selling the Church Patronage of the City to the Simeon Trustees. About the time this was accomplished he met a friend, who enquired the result of the negociations. "Sir," said Mangin, "Virtue has arrived at the highest possible pitch to which Vice can attain!"

"acrimony." He had a noble countenance, and it is said that the colossal head in the Park, by Osborn,[1] is modelled after Mr. Mangin's fine head. If this be not so, then the similarity is a remarkable coincidence. With many peculiarities, Mangin was a man of great kindness of heart, of winning manners, and high-bred courtesy. The fascination of his conversation was irresistible, and only those who have listened to it, as we have, could appreciate it. Mr. Mangin was in fact a singularly gifted man. We have been oftentimes enchanted by his anecdotes and stories, and by his reminiscences of the past during his own times. He was not a "society" man, but in the public resorts all men of intellectual eminence were pleased to exchange a word with one so well known as Mr. Mangin. As a draftsman he was skilful, and the facile mode in which he depicted objects on wood by a heated poker, or other instrument, was very remarkable. These objects reminded one very much of some of the rude pre-Raphaelite drawings. He edited an edition of Richardson's Works, published in 1810. The text of this edition is adapted for an *edition de luxe* of the novelist's works, now in course of publication, by Mr. Sotheran, of Piccadilly, London.

THE SYDNEY GARDENS were laid out in 1795 by the late **Masters Harcourt.** These gardens, in situation, arrangement, and disposition, are very superior to their two predecessors. The house, which forms a handsome and appropriate termination to Pulteney Street, was built to afford the necessary accommodation to the gardens during fetes and galas, which at one time were fashionable and popular. The house has experienced many vicissitudes. It has been an hotel, then an hydropathic establishment, then an hotel again, then the Bath Proprietary College—the predecessor of the present Bath College. At the time these gardens were laid out, summer was the *Bath season*, and snug little

---

[1] Osborn was a working mason, but a man of great native genius, as the colossal figure in the Park attests. Many years before the death of Mr. Mangin, he described to us the manner of Osborn's death, and a few days later he brought us a written account of it, which we quote *verbatim et literatim*. At the top of the paper a drawing is given showing the precise form and final development of the swelling. "Case of Mr. John Osborn, Sculptor, Bath, June 10, 1839. About the month of "January, 1838, he complained to me of having a slight swelling on the left side of his neck, unac-"companied by pain. The enlargement increased almost daily, and topical bleeding, embrocations, "etc., were tried ineffectually. At the date of this memorandum the patient had kept his bed about "three weeks, and was, when I saw him, slowly dying of hunger and suffocation, the swelling being "inward as well as external, and consisting apparently of hard solid flesh. Many eminent surgeons "had seen the man, and agreed in thinking that any attempt to operate with the knife would be fatal, "by dividing the involved arteries. The right side of the throat was considerably swollen, and the "patient suffered acute pain in the left temple; he was 43 or 44 years old, and was of a scrofulous "habit, but had been always temperate. He died June 26, 1839." We quote this in full because it is not a little remarkable that the circumstances related seemed to have so deeply impressed Mangin's mind. Whether it was so or not, and whether he felt any presentiment as to his own death, we cannot say; but certain it is he died from similar swellings. He once or twice referred to Osborn's case, observing, "It is now a question with me of a few weeks."

breakfast parties were given in the alcoves which extended from each side of the house. These parties in fact superseded the coteries, which until then used to meet in the Pump Room and talk away the reputations of their neighbours and their *friends*. The gardens were Vauxhall on a large scale, admission, except to the Galas, being a privilege similar to that of gaining the *entrée* to the "Zoo," in Regent's Park, on a Sunday. As an hotel in recent times the house has been visited by many distinguished personages. In 1846, **PRINCE NAPOLEON**, after his escape from Ham, resided in it for many months, and during that period he acquired a certain kind of popularity. His habits were dignified, but he affected none of that reserve and mysteriousness which have commonly been imputed to him. Several of his friends, including Lady Blessington, Count D'Orsay, and Prince Jerome Napoleon, and others, visited him at this time. We remember on one occasion, we were strolling in the gardens, near a large double swing, set up between two parallel quick set hedges; one of the daughters of the lessee (Mr. Barnard Watson) was in the swing, which "wobbling" violently threw her out. The Prince, being on the upper side, at once sprang through the hedge, caught her up, and finding her not hurt, gently chided her for her temerity, and then led her into the house to her father. Twenty years after, when as Emperor he was again an exile, he brought his son to Bath and took him down to show him where he (the Emperor) had lived in times when he dreamed of future greatness—

"Which was not all a dream."

We cannot foretell the fate of the house, but we trust to see it applied to some purpose in accordance with the changing habits and dispositions of the age; but the gardens, so lovely, and yet so capable of improvement, we hope they may continue to be

"A joy for ever."

BATHWICK VILLA.[1]—This house, at the entrance of Villa Fields, which take their name from it, lay a little to the north-east of Sydney Gardens. It was formerly—*i.e.*, from the middle of the last century to about 1790—surrounded by subscription pleasure-gardens. In the front there were balconies, in which were several "private boxes;" ladies in full dress, and gentlemen with bob-wigs, swords, and the full dress of the period, occupied them. The amusements were of the usual kind—fireworks, gymnastics, conjuring, and the like. In "Chambers' Journal" for August 20, 1853, there is a very amusing story founded upon some

---

[1] Southey in a letter to Landor, about 1807, refers to his visit to this Villa, but he makes the mistake of calling it *The Cottage*. In the time of Southey's childhood the Villa could be seen from his aunt's house in Walcot Street.

traditions connected with the house. After the Gardens were closed, the "Villa" was occupied by the eccentric Dr. John Trusler. Spring Gardens[1] were established a little later, on the bank of the river, opposite the Monks' Mill. It was in a grotto in these gardens that Sheridan wrote the verses to the lovely Miss Linley, beginning :—

"Then tell me, thou grotto of moss-covered stone."

JANE AUSTEN, when she first arrived in Bath, was 26 years of age, and resided with her family at **4, Sydney Place,** from the spring of 1801 until 1805, when she removed to **1, Gay Street,** and then, after a brief residence in **Green Park Buildings,** she removed to Castle Square, Southampton, from whence, in 1809, she, with her mother and sister, removed to what her biographer called the *second* and last home, **Chawton,** which must be considered the place most closely connected with her career as an authoress. It is the place, where "in the maturity of "her mind, she either wrote or re-arranged, and prepared for publication, the books "by which she has become known to the world."[2] Whilst this is so beyond all doubt, it was in Bath where her studies were pursued, and where she formed those ideas of character to which she gave form and life in her books. Miss Austin's life in Bath was simple, and as she was "unknown to fame" at that period, "Society" knew and sought her not. She seems to have been chiefly

---

[1] The "Public Breakfast," as described by Anstey in "The New Bath Guide," is the raciest scene in the book. The breakfast was given by Lord Ragamuffin.

"He said it would greatly our pleasure promote,
"If we all for Spring Gardens set out in a boat.
"I never as yet could his reason explain,
"Why we all sallied forth in the wind and the rain, etc.
          *   *   *   *
"You've read all their names in the news, I suppose,
"But, for fear you have not, take the list as it goes :
    "There was Lady Greaswusler,
    "And Madam Van-Twister,
    "Her Ladyship's sister ;
    "Lord Cram and Lord Vulter,
    "Sir Brandish O'Culter,
    "With Marshal Carouzer,
    "And old Lady Mouser ;
"And the great Hanoverian, Baron Pansmowzer
"The Peer, comes to grief on the return of the party,
"In handing old Lady Bumfidget and daughter,
"This obsequious Lord tumbled into the water ;
"But a nymph of the flood brought him safe to the boat,
"And I left all the ladies cleaning his coat."

[2] Mr. Bentley has just issued an *edition de luxe* of her works in 6 vols., large 8vo., and also an edition in 6 vols., small 8vo. These are the only complete modern editions of her works. The publication of these editions at the present time is a proof of the enduring reputation of the authoress, as well as of the enterprise of the publisher.

occupied in correspondence, and in those studies which made her the first female novelist of her age. *Northanger Abbey* sets forth more distinctively the "scenes and characters" of Bath Society—*i.e.*, the best side of it, which she saw and so well describes; though she refers again and again in her other works to those phases of life and action which she had seen in Bath, and on which she dilates with such charming interest.

"Her literary activity falls into two distinct sections. She began 'Pride and Prejudice' in October, 1796, at the age of 20, and finished it in August, 1797.[*] 'Sense and Sensibility' was begun November, 1797. 'Northanger Abbey' was composed in 1798. Then came a pause. During the nine years passed at Bath and Southampton, extending from her 26th to her 35th year, we do not know that she wrote anything except the short but striking history of 'Lady Susan,' a novel in letters, though it is probable that the fragment which Mr. Austen-Leigh entitles 'The Watsons,' was begun in these nine years. She published nothing till 1811; but from that date onwards, novel followed novel with great rapidity. 'Sense and Sensibility,' after undergoing revision, was published in 1811; 'Pride and Prejudice' in 1813; 'Mansfield Park' followed in 1814; 'Emma' at the end of 1815; and 'Persuasion' came out with 'Northanger Abbey,' after her death in 1818.

"This silence may be explained by the discouragement which Miss Austen's first attempts to put her work in print. A proposal made by her father to Mr. Cadell for the publication of a novel "comprising three volumes—about the length of Miss Burney's 'Evelina'"—('Pride and Prejudice') was declined by return of post. The fate of 'Northanger Abbey' was still more humiliating. It was sold in 1803 to a publisher in Bath † for ten pounds, but 'it found so little favour in his eyes that he chose to abide by his first loss rather than risk further expense by publishing such a work.' The 'Thorps,' 'Tilneys,' and 'Catherine Morland' for ten pounds, and dear at the price! Afterwards, when four novels had been published, Jane wished to recover the copyright.

"One of her brothers undertook the negotiation. He found the purchaser very willing to receive back his money, and to resign all claim to the copyright. When the bargain was concluded, and the money paid, but not till then, the negotiator had the satisfaction of informing him that the work thus lightly esteemed was by the author of 'Pride and Prejudice.'"—Article in *Temple Bar*.

---

[*] It is clear from this statement that the authoress must have been a frequent visitor to Bath, these books having been written previous to her residence in the city.

† The publisher, we believe, was Bull.

APPENDIX.

[The author in the following Note corrects the errors into which, by an oversight, he had fallen on page 27.]

At No. 11, NORTH PARADE.—In this house, in 1771, **VISCOUNT CLARE**, afterwards **EARL NUGENT**,[1] sojourned, some years previous to that last visit of Burke's, which we have described (page 28). The Earl was a genial, kind-hearted nobleman. He was the friend of Johnson and of Johnson's beloved friend, **OLIVER GOLDSMITH**. Lord Clare, on this as on former occasions, invited Goldsmith to visit him in Bath. In the same year, and at the same time, **THE DUKE AND DUCHESS OF NORTHUMBERLAND**[2] were at **No. 10, NORTH PARADE.** This was the first Duke of

---

[1] Robert Nugent, of Carlanstown, only surviving son of Michael Nugent, 5th in descent from Sir Thomas Nugent, who was a younger brother of Richard Nugent, 8th Lord Delvin (the 10th Lord was created Earl of Westmeath 1627), was created Viscount Clare and Baron Nugent 1766 and Earl Nugent 1776. He married, 1730, Lady Emilia Plunkett, 2nd daughter of the Earl of Fingall, by whom he had one son, Col. Nugent, who died in 1771. His second wife was Anne, daughter of Secretary Craggs, and widow of Robert Knight, of Gosfield (Gosfield became the Earl's property for his life), which lady died without issue. The Earl married as his third wife, Elizabeth, relict of Augustus, 4th Earl of Berkeley, by whom he had issue one daughter, Mary Elizabeth, born 1758, married April 12, George, Marquis of Buckingham. She was created Baroness Nugent, with remainder to her second son, Lord George Grenville-Nugent Temple. The Earl died without male issue Aug. 13, 1788, and the title of Earl Nugent devolved, according to the limitation of the patent, to his son-in-law, George, 1st Marquis of Buckingham. The Marchioness died in March, 1813, and was succeeded, agreeably to the limitation of the patent, by the said Lord George in the Irish Barony of Nugent. He was an author of some repute, best known by his "Memorials of John Hampden," on which Lord Macaulay's exquisite essay was written. Lord Nugent, who was well known in Bath, died in 1850.

It was during the Earl's residence in Bath that Gainsborough painted that fine, full-length portrait of him which was formerly at Stowe, and purchased at the Stowe sale by Field-Marshal Sir G. Nugent, Bart. The Earl was a man of wit, good humour, and ability. He loved ease and luxury, was a patron of learning, but will be best remembered as the friend of Goldsmith. It was to the Earl as Viscount Clare that Goldsmith's poem was addressed. About the year 1771, Lord Clare sent Goldsmith to his lodgings in the Temple from his seat, Gosfield Park, a haunch of venison. Those who are familiar with Goldsmith's poems will be equally familiar with the famous lines in which he acknowledged the compliment :—

"Thanks, my lord, for your venison, for finer or fatter
Never rang'd in a forest, or smok'd in a platter," etc.

Those who do not know them should turn to Forster's Life of Goldsmith, book 4, c. ix., in which will be found the best literary account of the lines and almost a complete key to the characters and allusions, without which the poem loses much of its interest.

[2] In a little book, entitled "Memorable Houses," it is mentioned that the Dukes of Northumberland occupied a house in Westgate Street from 1683 to 1720. During that period there was no *Percy*, Duke or Earl of Northumberland. The error was pardonable, because Mr. H. V. Lansdown, in his paper delivered before the Archæological Institute in Bath, in 1858, fell into a similar error, and the author of "Memorable Houses" seems to have adopted it and enlarged upon it. We can find no evidence to connect the Percy family with the house in question (see Article, "Grapes Tavern.")

the present creation. He was Sir Hugh Smithson, who (after his marriage with Lady Elizabeth Seymour, daughter of the Duchess of Somerset, who was the sole heir of the Percys) assumed the name of Percy, and was created Duke of Northumberland in 1766. In Forster's "Life of Goldsmith," the following incident is related :—

"Goldsmith continued with Lord Clare during the opening months of "1771. They were together at Gosfield and at Bath; and it was in the latter "city the amusing incident occurred, Æt. 43, 1771, which Bishop Percy has "related, as told to him by the Duchess of Northumberland. The Duke and "Duchess occupied a house on one of the Parades, next door to Lord Clare's, "and were surprised one day, when about to sit down to breakfast, to see "Goldsmith enter the breakfast-room as from the street, and, without notice of "them, or the conversation they continued, fling himself unconcernedly 'in a "'manner the most free and easy,' on a sofa. After a few minutes, 'as he was "'then perfectly known to them both, they enquired of him the Bath news of "'the day; and imagining there was some mistake, endeavoured by easy and "'cheerful conversation to prevent his being too much embarrassed, till, "'breakfast being served up, they invited him to stay and partake of it'; but "upon this, the invitation calling him back from the dreamland he had been "visiting, he declared, with profuse apologies, that he had thought he was in his "friend Lord Clare's house, and in irrevocable confusion hastily withdrew. "'But not,' adds the Bishop, 'till they had kindly made him promise to dine "'with them.'" The Duke purchased **11, Laura Place**, when it was in course of erection, and it was the occasional residence of the second Duke until his death.

THE DUKE AND DUCHESS OF KINGSTON.—KINGSTON HOUSE,

occupying the site s.w. of the Abbey in Kingston Buildings, was built by Evelyn, Duke of Kingston, about the middle of the last century. The Kingston Arms are sculptured on the Pediment. It was intended as an occasional residence for the Duke when he visited his Bath estate, but it does not appear that he occupied it more than once, and then for a day or two only, after he married Miss Chudleigh. The Duke was an amiable, unassuming man, liberal, open-handed, beneficent, *weak*. It is probable that if he had never contracted the marriage with this woman his name would by this time have been forgotten. The history of Elizabeth Chudleigh, daughter of Colonel Chudleigh, is romantic and remarkable. There is nothing to show that she was naturally ill disposed. Her greatest misfortune was her beauty and her exposure to unusual temptations in an age of lax morality. Her father was poor, at his death leaving his daughter about £200 per annum. Through the friendship of Sir W. Pulteney (afterwards Earl of Bath), Colonel Chudleigh obtained for his daughter the post of Maid of Honour to the Princess of Wales, mother of George III. Her natural talents and attractions, and the charms of her manner and conversation, soon surrounded her with a host of distinguished and enthusiastic admirers. One of the most conspicuous of these was the Duke of Hamilton,[1] who made her an offer of his hand, and was accepted. Circumstances, however, prevented their immediate union; the parties agreed to hold themselves as engaged, and the Duke went upon a Continental tour, during which he corresponded with Miss Chudleigh. In the meantime, Capt. Augustus John Hervey, R.N., second son of Lord Hervey,[2] became enamoured of her, and it is said his suit was favoured by Miss Chudleigh's aunt, Mrs. Hanmer. The result was that the Duke was supplanted by Capt. Hervey, and the parties were privately married at Lainston, near Winchester. This ill-advised step proved the foundation of all her subsequent perplexities, and developed most of the terrible faults of her character. Captain Hervey, fearing his father's anger, concealed the marriage, and his wife had to endure all the inconveniences of her dubious position. One son was the result of the marriage, who soon quitted the world as he had entered it—in secrecy and obscurity. It seems clear that she married in haste and repented at leisure, and the result was that a feeling of aversion on her part towards her husband followed. Captain Hervey, whose jealousy was violently excited by the attentions paid to his wife, as Miss Chudleigh, threatened to proclaim their marriage to the public, whilst she became only more determined to find some pretext for its legal dissolution. With this view, she is said to have gained access to the register in which her marriage was recorded, and destroyed the evidence of it by tearing out the leaf. The officiating clergyman was dead. Not long afterwards her husband succeeded, by the death of his brother, to the Earldom of Bristol, upon which she contrived, by bribing the officiating clerk, to get the leaf re-inserted in the register from which she had previously torn it. At

[1] This is the Duke of Hamilton who married the widowed Duchess of Argyll, who was one of the beautiful sisters Gunning. She was the wife of two and the mother of four dukes. The Duke of Hamilton was killed by Lord Mohun in a duel.

[2] Lord Hervey was called to the Upper House during his father's lifetime, June, 1733, and died August 15, 1743, never having attained to the Earldom. He married in 1720 the beautiful Miss Lepell, by whom he had a numerous family, of whom Augustus John was the second son, and succeeded his brother George William, as third Earl of Bristol, March 20, 1775.

this time she was informed that Captain Hervey was about to marry a Miss Moysey of Bath, and she received from him a message expressing his willingness to consent to a divorce. which she for a time refused, saying "I can either be "Countess of Bristol or Duchess of Kingston." There is no doubt that an illicit connection had long subsisted between the Duke and the lady, and by this time Lord Bristol himself strongly desired a divorce to enable him to marry the lady referred to, and he therefore readily concurred in a process of *jactitation* of marriage in the Ecclesiastical Courts, which by an adroit suppression of evidence terminated in a decree of nullification. The path being thus, in their opinion, cleared, the Duke and the Countess were married at his house in Arlington Street, on the 8th of March, 1769. From this time the worst features of her character rapidly developed. She was gluttonous, too fond of wine, and in temper a virago ; her outbursts of passion were frequent and violent, and though she maintained her ascendancy over the Duke, there is no doubt his calm temper and gentle disposition were oftentimes very much disturbed by her overbearing manner and the coarseness of her language. A few days after the ceremony of marriage was performed, the Duke and the Duchess visited Bath and occupied the house[1] built near the site of the Roman Baths, after the excavations of 1755, but they remained nine days only. During this brief residence the Duchess engaged two chairmen for a fortnight, and as she resolved to leave before the time expired, she objected to pay for the whole period. The Mayor (Chapman), who at that time had full jurisdiction, ordered payment of the full amount. The Duke, on two occasions when he came alone, engaged apartments at the **THREE TUNS**. In 1773 the Duke and Duchess visited Bath for the last time. First the Duchess took lodgings at what then was a famous resort of fashionable people, viz., *Mrs. Hodgkinson's* in the *Orange Grove*.[2] This house is in the corner next to the Athenæum, and extends into *Orange Grove Court*. It is almost hidden by the house in front of it, but it has traces of former grandeur. After a dispute with Mrs. Hodgkinson the Duchess removed, with the Duke, into the Baths House, and in a few days to **No. 5, SOUTH PARADE**, where the Duke died. The Duke bequeathed to her a very large income, which for three years she "enjoyed" in her own peculiar fashion. The Duke's nephew, Sir Charles Meadows, Bart., who for some reason had been excluded from the succession, resolved to dispute

[1] The house which was used as the provisional Free Public Library. It was then called **The Baths House**. It has in recent times been called "**Kingston House**."

[2] After refusing to pay Mrs. Hodgkinson for a month's lodgings, the Duchess gave her a piece of plate worth ten times the amount. She seems to have acted upon her own motto, "*Aut vincit, aut perit.*"

the validity of his uncle's will. Through information received from a Mrs. Cradock, who had been one of the witnesses to the marriage of Miss Chudleigh with Captain Hervey,[1] Meadows indicted the Duchess for bigamy.[2] At this time she was abroad, but returned to prevent an outlawry. The trial began on April 15, 1776, before the House of Lords in Westminster Hall, and it resulted in her

[1] In 1773 Captain Hervey petitioned the King, through the Queen, on account apparently of some displeasure manifested by the former towards him because of this marriage. He says, (the papers) "contain a melancholy account of such a series of outrageous wrongs, as no human creature "ever suffered before, since man was made, and to quicken my sense of them, and their horrid "consequence, I owe them to an ungrateful, vile, and *vicious* woman," etc.

[2] Of the trial itself, Hannah More gives the following graphic description :—
"Garrick would have me take his ticket to go to the trial of the Duchess of Kingston ; a "sight of which, for beauty and magnificence, exceeded anything which those who were never "present at a coronation, or a trial by peers, can have the least notion. Mrs. Garrick and I were in "full dress by seven. You will imagine the bustle of five thousand people getting into one hall ! "yet, in all this hurry, we walked in tranquilly. When they were all seated, and the king-at-arms "had commanded silence on pain of imprisonment (which, however, was very ill observed), the "gentleman of the black rod was commanded to bring in his prisoner. Elizabeth, calling her- "self Dowager-Duchess of Kingston, walked in, led by Black Rod and Mr. La Roche, curtseying "profoundly to her judges. The peers made her a slight bow. The prisoner was dressed in deep "mourning ; a black hood on her head ; her hair modestly dressed and powdered ; a black silk "sacque, with crape trimmings ; black gauze, deep ruffles, and black gloves. The counsel spoke "about an hour and a quarter each. Dunning's manner is insufferably bad, coughing and spitting "at every three words, but his sense and his expression pointed to the last degree : he made her "Grace shed bitter tears. The fair victim had four virgins, in white, behind the bar. She imitated "her great predecessor, Mrs. Rudd, and affected to write very often, though I plainly perceived she "only wrote, as they do their love-epistles on the stage, without forming a letter. The Duchess "has but small remains of that beauty of which kings and princes were once so enamoured. She "looked much like Mrs. Pritchard. She is large and ill-shaped ; there is nothing white but her "face, and had it not been for that, she would have looked like a bail of bombazeen. There was a "great deal of ceremony, a great deal of splendour, and a great deal of nonsense ; they adjourned "upon the most foolish pretences imaginable and did *nothing* with such an air of business as was "truly ridiculous. I forgot to tell you the Duchess was taken ill, but performed it badly." The writer adds in a subsequent Letter :—"I have the great satisfaction of telling you, that "Elizabeth, calling herself Duchess-dowager of Kingston, was, this very afternoon, *undignified* and *unduchessed*, and very narrowly escaped being burned in the hand. If you have been half so much "interested against this unprincipled, artful, licentious woman as I have you will be rejoiced at it "as I am. Lord Camden breakfasted with us. He is very angry that she was not burned in the "hand. He says, as he was once a professed lover of hers, he thought it would have looked ill- "natured and ungallant for him to propose it ; but that he should have acceded to it most heartily. "Though he believes he should have recommended a cold iron." The Duchess claimed the benefit of the peerage, under the statute of the first of Edward VI., and was accordingly discharged without punishment.

[*Letter by Mr. J. H. Round, of Brighton, to "Notes and Queries," respecting the Bradford property, belonging to the Kingston family.*]

Kingston House, Bradford-on-Avon, was the property of the Pierrepont family, derived from the Hall family. "Rachel, Lady Kingston. While recently consulting Peter le Neve's *Memoranda* "*in Heraldry*, as edited by Mr. J. G. Nichols, I noted the following passage under the year 1711:
"'Evelyn, Lord Marquis of Dorchester, his son Will" Pierpoint, esq., commonly called Lord "'Kingston, to marry [   ] dr. and heir of John Hall, esq., a private act of Parliament past "'this Sessions to settle the Marquis' estate and John Hall's on William.'
"To this the editor appends a note, quoting, as against this statement, the marriage of Lord "Kingston with Rachel Baynton, as given in Collins's *Peerage*, and gravely adds :—
"'This marriage must consequently have taken place very soon after the arrangement men- "'tioned in the text had been set aside.'
"The 'arrangement,' however, never was 'set aside,' and the true explanation of the seeming

conviction. Before a writ *Ne exeat regno* could be issued she escaped to Calais, and never returned to England. Her conviction was followed by an attempt on the part of the Duke's heirs to set aside his will, which proved unsuccessful. She lived a reckless, dissipated life in France, bought property, got into litigation, lost an important suit, which threw her into a fury, resulting in the rupture of a blood-vessel, which caused her death. **FOOTE**, the dramatist, wrote a farce upon the Duchess,—*A Trip to Calais*, in which she figures as "Lady Kitty Crocodile." It was an infamous proceeding, the object of which was to extort money, but the play was interdicted by the Lord Chamberlain.

[*From Doran's "Court Fools."*]

"Lord Ligonier, the husband of one of Alfieri's worthless idols, was English Ambassador at the court of Madrid during a portion of the reign of Charles III., which lasted from 1759 to 1788. After Lord Ligonier's introduction to the King, he was conducted to the apartments of the Heir to the Crown, the Prince of the Asturias. The latter was, subsequently, that Charles IV. who was his own Queen's especial fool throughout the term of their married lives. As Lord Ligonier approached the Prince's chamber, he saw issuing therefrom a number of grandees, each wearing, with proud gravity, a fantastic fool's cap. On inquiring the meaning of such a pageant, he was informed that his Royal Highness possessed the fancy of distinguishing his most cherished friends as his 'fools.' The Prince, too, was often pleased to confer this mark of his favour on celebrated foreigners. Lord Ligonier was alarmed.

"'I represent,' he said, 'a great sovereign; and am myself a foreigner not altogether unknown. I must add, that my gracious master would be seriously offended, if the Prince of the Asturias were to think proper to cover the representative of the King of England with this decoration. You had better go in, sir,' he said to his introducer, 'and say as much to his Royal Highness.'

"The reluctant official undertook the mission; but he presently returned, with the intimation that the Prince could not give up an old-established custom. Upon which, Lord Ligonier turned on his heel, declaring that he would not visit a Prince who thus exposed an Ambassador to insult. The court officials were thrown into a state of amusing terror by this declaration; they maintained, that if the Ambassador retired, it would be a flagrant insult on the Prince. Ultimately, and after many messages and countermessages had passed between the Prince in his room and the English Envoy in the antechamber, announcement was made that the Prince of the Asturias would not attempt to clap the fool's-cap on the head of Lord Ligonier. His lordship consequently entered the apartment, but not without being more than usually vigilant against surprise. He found the sage Prince with his back to the hearth and with his hands behind him.

"discrepancy will be found in my note on this subject where it is shown that this 'heiress' of John Hall, through whom the Pierreponts and their descendants inherited his extensive estates, was in truth his daughter, but by the wife of Thomas Baynton his nephew by marriage. The two statements are thus reconcilable, the one referring to Lady Kingston's true, and the other to her putative, father. The curious history of the Private Act alluded to by Le Neve will also be found in the above note."

"The Prince remained in that position and invited the Ambassador to approach. The English lord "obeyed; but as he advanced, he perceived that the Prince held a paper object, and the Ambas-"sador stopped short to converse with his Royal Highness at a very respectful distance. At the "conclusion of the interview, he had to bow low; but, as a sailor might say, his weather eye was "open, and he watched the Prince narrowly. The latter was resolved upon effecting his object and "as narrowly watched the Ambassador. The bow was almost at its lowest, when the Prince, seizing "the most favourable opportunity, suddenly brought the fool's-cap from behind him, and endea-"voured to fix it on the head of Lord Ligonier; but the old soldier who, by one glorious action at "Laffeldt, had disconcerted all the projects of Marshal Saxe, was not to be foiled by a foolish "prince. As soon as his eye caught sight of the cap his hand was upon it, and almost as soon it "lay crumpled up beneath his feet. His sudden action nearly threw the Prince out of his equili-"brium; and leaving that illustrious fool's-cap maker to recover himself as he best might, the old "warrior quitted the apartment with a smile of scorn upon his lip."

[*Anstey's* "*Bath Guide.*"]

"The *Monthly Review* for June, 1776, has the following remarks, not much in the style or "phraseology of modern criticism, on the 'New Bath Guide':—'There is a species of humour in "'these *droll* Epistles, which has the greater force, as it seems to proceed from a simple and "'unembellished character, the hopeful offspring of a considerable family in the north. There are "'a thousand strains of humour in these high-wrought Epistles, some of which do not occur to "'you at the first reading. The author frequently heightens and enriches his humour by parodies "'and imitations.'

"The Rev. Dr. Roberts, provost of Eton, in an Epistle on the English Poets, thus speaks of "the 'New Bath Guide':—

——— "'While old Bladud's sceptre guards
"'His medicinal stream, shall Simkin raise
"'Loud peals of merriment.'

"Warner, the historian of Bath, in his *Literary Recollections*, has, like Mr. Campbell, "erred in placing too much reliance on memory. A reference to dates and common biographies "shews us that Smollett's 'Humphrey Clinker' was subsequent to the 'New Bath Guide'; and a "slight perusal of both works is sufficient to prove the superior dramatic powers of the latter author "for poignant satire and delineation of character. When we recollect, also, that Anstey's 'Election "'Ball,' 'Epistle to Sir Charles Bampfylde,' and other poems, were formerly popular at Bath, and "are re-printed in the collected edition of his works, every reader will be surprised at Mr. Warner's "statement in his 'Literary Recollections,' which, like his other writings, abound with eloquent "and interesting passages. They contain, likewise, many pleasing biographical sketches of eminent "persons who resided at Bath between the years 1794 and 1820. Speaking of Mr. Anstey, he says: "'It is somewhat singular that the author of a work so witty, so satirical, and novel, as the 'New "'Bath Guide,' should have left behind him merely this solitary monument of his lively fancy and "'peculiar genius; but no other publication, save this, as I am aware, has been attributed to him. "'The 'New Bath Guide' might have been considered as a perfectly *original* work, had not its "'subject been obviously suggested by the 'Humphrey Clinker' of the inimitable *Smollett* who was "'for some time resident at Bath, and probably an intimate acquaintance, as well as a favourite "'author, of Mr. Anstey." We have referred to this unaccountable error of Warner's in another part of this work.

Appendix.

[Well of Saint Winifred.]

"Winifred House, Bath; Nov. 17, 1882.

"DEAR MR. PEACH,—

"A friend of mine sitting with me not half-an-hour ago pointed out to me, in the work you are now writing, 'The Historic Houses of Bath,' mention made there of S. Winifred's Well (page 5). A footnote speaks of it as situate in Winifred's Dale. Curiously enough, since she left, I have been perusing an abstract of the title-deeds of this place, and read the following:—

"'All that said Close of Ground, called the Barn-piece, by the now abstracted Indenture, described as, All that Close of Pasture-Ground, called the Barn-piece, *wherein was a well called Winifred's Well*, with the Barn thereon standing, containing 5 acres more or less.'

"The heading of the Abstract of Title is as follows:—

"'Abstract of Title to a Freehold Close called the Barn-piece in the Parish of Walcot, Somerset, and to a Mansion-House and Premises thereon erected, called Winifred House.'

"I think this shows pretty plainly that the well exists within the boundaries of this place. In fact, in the middle of the paddock on the east side of my house, may be seen the man-hole which leads to the well. And, further on the back of one of the folios of the Abstract, is the extract from the Proceedings of the Quarter Sessions, held at Bridgwater on 17th July, 1805, showing that by order of the Justices a public footway across the Barn-piece was stopped, accompanied by a plan figuring the footway and the position of the well.

"I know you value accuracy, and to contribute towards the accuracy of the work you are engaged on (which I think is the duty of anyone possessed of certain knowledge), I venture to communicate these (perhaps unimportant) facts.

"Believe me, faithfully yours,

"P. E. GEORGE."

Mr. George's letter substantially confirms the description given. The identification of the spot adds an interesting fact; as it has always been supposed that no trace of the Well existed. We thankfully accept Mr. George's letter.

[See page 14, Introduction, Footnote.]

POPULATION OF BATH.

Year.	Population.	Year.	Population.
1801	34,160	1851	54,248
1811	38,434	1861	52,525
1821	46,588	1871	52,579
1831	50,800	1881	54,000
1841	53,200		

The stagnation is more apparent than real, large numbers of the labouring population during the past twenty years having emigrated, whilst a new Bath has grown up in the suburbs, the residents of which do not count in the city returns.

ERRATA.

Pages 27 and 28, although allowed to remain *in situ*, as originally printed, contain erroneous matter, which is practically superseded and corrected by the Article in the Appendix.

Page 34, the name of "Lawrence" should be spelt "Laurance."

,, 35, line 9, for "russe" read "rus."

,, 39, in Footnote 2, for "Bouchier" read "Bourchier."

,, 44, line 12, for "deny" read "assert."

,, 50, for 1602 read 1693, birth of Ralph Allen.

,, 51, for "Lawrence" read "Laurance."

The Article on the Duke and Duchess of Kingston will be found in the Appendix, which must be taken as a substitute for that on page 54.

Page 60, John Wood the Younger was not the Architect of Camden Crescent; the Architect was Eveleigh.

Page XVII., Introduction, line 11, for "persued" read "pursued."

[*Well of Saint Winifred.*]

INDEX.

GENERAL SUBJECTS.

	PAGE.
Adair, Dr. Mackittrick	85, 86
Addison, Joseph	118
Adequate Peace, the	75, 80
Albemarle, Lord	104
Allen, Major R. S.	ix.
Allen, Philip	ix.
Allen, Ralph	iv., ix., xii., 23, 38, 50, 67, 69
Amusements of Bath Gentry	xv.
André, Major	87
Anecdotes—Booth, Mrs., of Cheshire	6
,, Cobbe, Lady Betty	103
,, Everitt, W., and the Poet Moore	130
,, Gainsborough	151
,, Goldsmith	27
,, Hartley, David	111
,, Ligonier, Lord	156
,, Macaulay, Catherine	117
,, Queen Elizabeth	4
,, Queen of James II.	5
,, Quin, the Actor	32
,, Randolph, Rev. Dr.	137
,, Sheppard, Rev. Dr.	103
,, Temple, Mrs., of the Castle Hotel	128
,, Wesley and Nash	99
,, Wolfe, General	54
Anne, Queen of Denmark	4
Anstey, Christopher	xvi., 19, 113, 149, 157
Appendix	151
Archives of Paris	iii.
Atherston	xvii.
Austen, Jane	xvi., 149
Baldwin, Thos., City Architect	ix., x., xii., [14, 23
Barker, Benjamin	xvii.
Barker, Thomas	xvii.
Bath, its Modern Growth	xi.
Bath, Earl of	x., 132
Ditto, Will of	135
Bath, Earls of	39
Bath, Marquis of	14, 17
Bathurst, Lord	34
Bave, the Physician	vi., 34
Bayly, Haynes	xvii., 127
Beckford, William	104
,, Alderman of London	104
Bedford, Duchess of	7
,, Duke of	xiii., 7, 93
Bellanus's Tree	ii.
Bellot, Thomas	ii.
Benedictine Mission, the	25
Bibliography of Bath	xiv.

	PAGE.
Bimburio, the Seven Sisters	ii.
Borlase, Rev. J. W.	9
Boswell	62
Bowles, William Lisle	127
Brewer, John	26
Britton, John	19
Broadhurst, Rev. Thos.	118
Brodrick, Hon. and Rev. W. J.	34
Brookman, of the White Hart	20
Bull, the Bath Publisher	xv., 150
Burke, the Statesman	xiii.
Burney, Miss	xvii.
Burrington, the Village of	ix.
Butler, Bishop	40
Cambridge, Duke of	11
Camden, Earl	63, 65
,, Marquis	14
Canning, George	14
Caraboo, Princess	143
Caricature of the Corporation of Bath	79
Carr, Bishop	36
Castlereagh, Lord	xiv.
Carte, the Jacobite Rector	iv., 22, 36
Chandos, Duke of	xiv., 53
Chapman, the Family of	vi., 22
Charles the Xth., King of France	x.
Charter of Queen Elizabeth	58
Chatham, Earl of	67
Chatterly, Mrs.	42
Chesterfield, Earl of	29, 133
Clare Lord, (see Nugent)	
Clarence, Duchess of	16
,, Duke of	x., 13, 14
Classic Ground of Bath	xiii.
Cleveland, Duchess of	xv.
Cleveland, Duke of	x.
Clive, Lord	93
Connaught, Duke and Duchess of	17
Cooper, Sir Hutton	16
Cork and Burlington, Earl of	34
Cork and Orrery, Earl of	34
Cowper, the Poet	127
Crabbe, Rev. G.	127
Cranch, W., the Artist	xvii.
Crook, Rev. C.	iv., 15
Cunard, Sir Samuel, Bart.	ix.
Darlington, Earl of	x.
Davis, J. F., M.D.	16
Davis, C. E., F.S.A.	xviii.

	PAGE
Delany, Mrs.	46
Dickens', Chas., Description of Bath	124
Disbrowe. Colonel, M.P.	14, 15
Dismell, The Right Hon. B.	xvi.
Dover, John, of the Lamb Hotel	xvii., 20
Duel in the Orange Grove	44
Duel between W. Pulteney and Lord Hervey	136
Duffield, the Artist	xvii.
Dyer, Rev. William Henry	144
Earle, Rev. Professor	ix.
Edgeworth, R. L., and his Daughter	32
Edridge, John	17
Eminent Residents of Bath	xvi.
Errata	158
Essex, Earl of	x.
Execution of Major André	89
Execution of John Butler, at Bath	26
Falconer, Dr. William	85
Fielding, the Novelist	xii., xvi.
Fitzherbert, Mrs.	140
Fleming and his Daughter	57
Foote, the Dramatist	156
Fraser, Sir Alexander	24
Frederick, the Publisher	xv.
Gainsborough, Thomas	xvii., 89
Gay, the founder of Gay Street	61
Grosst, Rev. John, M.A.	53
Glanville, Rev. Joseph	36
Gloucester, Duke of	11
Godwin, John	35
Godwin, J. C.	xviii.
Goldsmith, Oliver	vii., viii., 27, 44, 151, 152
Goldsmith's Life of Nash	vii.
Gordon Riots	26
Greaves, Dr.	vi.
Green, Emanuel	3
Grenville, Sir Bevil	39, 47
Guidott, Dr.	vi., xiv., 35
Grinley, the Family of	133
Harcourt, Masters	147
Hardwick, the Artist	xvii.
Hardwicke, Lord Chancellor	8, 55
Hardy, the Three Brothers	xvii.
Harington John, of Kelston	6
Harington, Sir John	iv., 4
Harington, Dr.	90
Harris, Mrs. J. D.	xvii.
Harrowby, Earl of	142
Hartley, David	110
Hazard, the Publisher	xv.
Henley, Robert, Earl of Northington	63
Herschel, Caroline	48
Herschel, Sir William	xvi., 47
Hervey, Lord, Memoirs of	9
Hewlett, the Artist	xvii.
Hippisley, the Manager of the Public Rooms	xi.
Hoare, William, R.A.	111

	PAGE
Hoare, Prince	111
Hoblyn, the Misses	57
Howth, Earl of	34
Hungerford, Sir E.	4
Hunter, Rev. Joseph	xv., 81
Huntingdon, Selina, Countess of	94
Introductory Chapter	i.—xviii.
Jacobite Conspiracy	38
Jay, Rev. William	144
Jervis, Lady, Private Journal of	137
Jervis, Mrs. Henley	ii., iii., xviii., 26
Johnson, Dr.	iv.
Johnstone, Sir William, M.P.	x.
Jones, Inigo	xii.
Kemble, Rev. C.	36
Ken, Bishop	xv.
Kent, Duchess of	16
King of Bath	viii., 7, 8
King James I.	4
King Charles I., his Queen, and Prince of Wales	5
King Charles II.	5
King James II.	5
Kingston, Duchess of, Trial of	152
Kingston, Duke of	54, 152
Kitson, John, Mayor	13
Landor, Walter Savage	xvii., 11, 120
Lansdown, Lord	39
Lansdown, H. V.	39
Laurance, the Family of	34, 77
Lawrence, Sir Thomas	xvii., 112
Leo, Harriett	118
Leake, the Publisher	xv.
Legge, Right Hon. H. B.	70
Legacies to William Pitt	68, 69
Leigh, Colonel	11
Leighton, Sir F.	xvii.
LETTERS:—Ralph Allen	76, 77
Rev. P. E. George	158
Mrs. Henley Jervis	iii.
Lord Ligonier	71
G. Matcham	31
Earl of Nottingham	6
Hutton Perkins	8
William Pitt	71—77, 142
Between Southey and Landor	122, 123
Life at Prior Park	xii.
Ligonier, Sir John	65, 67
Linley, Thomas, and his daughter	30, 55
,, Eliza Anne (Mrs. Sheridan)	30, 55
Llanover, Lady	47
Long, Mr., R.A.	xvii.
Louis XVIII. of France	x.
Lukin, Mr.	20
Lunn, Sally	23
Lytton the Novelist	xvi.

Index.

	PAGE.
Macaulay, Lord...	v., vi.
Macaulay, Catherine	117
MacKittrick, Dr.	85
Madox, Willes ...	xvii.
Mail-Coach, The First	xvii.
Malmesbury, Lord	xiv.
Mangin, Rev. Edward	146
Manvers, Earl	54
Maplet, Dr.	vi.
Marlborough, Duchess of	94
Marlborough, Lord and Lady	6
Mary Beatrice of Modena	5, 6
Matcham, G.	31
Melfort, Lord ..	6
Memoir of Major André	87
,, Gainsborough	89
,, Countess of Huntingdon	94
,, J. H. Markland	108
,, Thicknesse Family	82
Mitford, The Misses	109
Monkland's Book	82
Moore, Thomas ..	127, 129
Morgan, Rev. Nathaniel ...	116
Morris, J. W., Esq.	xviii.
Moysey, Dr. Abel	41
,, Miss	154
Murray, Sir James, Bart.	x.
Murch, Jerom, esq.	xii., xviii.
Napoleon III. ...	x.
,, Prince Louis ...	124, 128
Nash, Beau ... v., vi., vii., viii., ix., xvi., 43
Naylor, Father Placid	iii.
Nelson, Admiral Lord	30
Nelson, Lady	137
Nelson, Rev. Edmund	31
New Bath Guide	xvi., 114
Northington, Earl of	63
Northumberland, Duke of	142, 151
Nottingham, Earl of	6
Nugent, Dr. Christopher	29
,, Earl	151
,, Lord	27
O'Bryen, Lord James	16
Old Coaching Days	xvii.
,, Lodging-houses	v.
,, Physicians and Doctors	vi.
Palmer, John	ix., 12, 20
Parry, Dr.	34
Partis Fletcher ...	140
Peirce, Dr. ... vi., xiv., 4, 5, 6, 24
Phelan, George ...	141
Phillott, The Three Brothers	19
Pickwick, Eleazer	20
Piozzi, Mrs.	xvii., 61, 139
Pitt, William ... x., xii., xiii., 67, 141
Poem of the "Looking-Glass"	133
Poets, A Group of	127
Pope, a	xii., 9

	PAGE.
Population of Bath	xiv., 158
Portsmouth, Duchess of ...	xv.
Pratt, Hon. John Jeffreys	66
Prince Consort, The	17
,, George of Denmark	6
,, Leopold ...	15
,, of Orange	8
,, of Wales (afterwards Charles II.)	5
,, (afterwards George IV.)	11, 140
,, and Princess of Wales (1738)	9
Princess Amelia ...	xii., 7
,, Anne ...	6
,, Charlotte	
,, Elizabeth	13, 14
Princesses Mary and Caroline (1740)	10
Princess Victoria	16
Provence, Count de	11
Prynne, William	vi.
Pulteney, Frances	x.
,, Henrietta Laura	x.
,, General Harry	x.
,, John	x.
,, Sir William	x., 132
Queen Anne	iv.
,, Anne Hyde	
,, Charlotte...	x., 13, 14
,, Catherine of Braganza	
,, Elizabeth...	iv., 3
,, Mary of Modena ...	5, 6
,, James	31
Ramsden, Mrs. C.	109
Randolph, Rev. Dr.	137
Rauzzini	xvi., 50
Reade ...	xvii.
Richardson's Marriage	xv.
Roebuck, John Arthur	120
Ronchi...	5
Rose, the Statesman	xiv.
Rosenberg, Miss	xvii.
,, Mr. G.	xvii.
Royal Visits to Bath	3
Russell, Mr. C. P.	v., xviii., 21
St. Vincent, Lady	137
Sandwich, Earl of	35
Satires and Satirists	xvi.
Scott, Sir Walter	32
Sebright, Sir John, Bart.	65
Shenstone, the Poet	127
Sheppard, Rev. Dr.	104
Sheridan, Richard Brinsley	xiii., xv., 55
Sheridan, Tom ...	55
Sherlock	xii.
Sherston, William	iv., 3, 4, 58
Smith, Sir Sidney	116
,, Rev. Sidney	104
Smollett, Tobias	xvi.
Southey, Robert	33
Squire Western ...	xii.

	PAGE.
Steele	98
Stockmar, Baron de	15
Strahan, John	40
Strickland, Miss...	iv.
Sussex, Duke of...	11
Syer, Mr.	xvii.
Temple, Mrs., of the Castle Hotel	128, 131
Thicknesse, Philip	79, 80, 118
Thurlow, Lord	140
Thynne, Lord John	47
Tickell, Thomas, the Poet	118
„ Richard	119
Titley, W.	xviii.
Townsend, Rev. Joseph	103
Tugwell, G. H., esq.	13
Tuppen, Rev. Thos.	145
Tyler, Miss	33
Vaughan, Rev. R. A.	145
Wade, Marshal	22, 23, 38, 50, 63
Walpole, Horace	43, 102
„ Sir Robert	x.
Warburton, Bishop	xii., 78
Warner the Historian	4, 6, 9, 23, 37
Wassell, Rev. D.	144

	PAGE.
Watson, Sir William	49, 138
Watts, Mr.	xviii.
Webb, the Town Clerk	8
Webster (Nash's predecessor)	vii., xv.
Wedgwood, Josiah	42
Wesley, John and Charles	95, 96, 97, 98, 99, 100, 101, 102
Weymouth, Viscount	47
Whistling Match, A	119
Whitefield	95, 96, 97, 98, 99, 100, 101, 102, 103
Wilberforce	xi., xiii., 28, 145
Wilkinson, Dr.	143
Willan, Mr. J. N., M.A.	xviii.
Willcox, Mr.	xviii.
Williams, Rev. F. Anselm	5
Wiltshire, Lessee of Rooms	vii., viii., 45
Wiltshire, Walter, Friend of Gainsborough	92
Wolfe, General	54
Wood, John, the elder and younger	ii., v., vi., ix., xiii., xiv., xv., 60
Woolburytype, by Perren	xviii.
Wordsworth, the Poet	xiii., 34
Windham, Rt. Hon. W.	28, 29
York, Duke and Duchess of	10, 57
„ „ (Edward Augustus)	10, 137
York, Charles	55, 56

HISTORIC HOUSES, PUBLIC BUILDINGS, STREETS, Etc.

Abbey, the Bath	35, 36
„ Cemetery	36
„ Churchyard, No. 14	38, 39
„ House	4
Ainslie's Belvedere, No. 8	89
Alfred Street, No. 2	112, 117
Allen's, Ralph, Town House	i.
Ambury Mead	27
Argyle Chapel	114
Argyle Street, No. 8	137
Assembly Rooms	15, 21
Axford Buildings	79
Barton Farm	59
Barton House	iv., 58
Barton Lane	46
Bathwick Old Church	x.
„ The Estate of	ix., 131
„ Villa	148
Bear Inn	19, 62, 65, 133
Bear Street	ii.
Beaulieu House, Newbridge Hill	119
Beckford House, Lansdown Crescent	104
Beckford's Tower	16, 106

Bell Tree House	ii., iii., 25, 26, 27
Bell Tree Lane	ii.
Bellot's Hospital	ii.
Belvedere House	118
Bowling Green, The	xv., xvi.
Burnhamthorpe Rectory	51
Camden Place, or Crescent	23, 60, 65
Castle Hotel	128, 131
Chandos Buildings	xiv.
„ House	xiv., 53
Chapel Court	44
Chapel, Laura	137
Chapman's House	40
Cheap Street	38
Church Lane	xii.
Circus	xiii., xvii., 50
„ No. 7	xii., 67
„ No. 11	93
„ No. 15	xiii., 93
„ No. 23	87
„ No. 24	89
„ House	29
City Gates, The	i.

Index.

	PAGE.		PAGE.
City Walls, The...	... xiv.	New King Street, Nos. 7 & 19	... 49
Cloth Factories of Walcot	.. 62	North Parade ...	ii., 10
Clubs ...	... xv.	,, No. 9	... 34
Cross Bath	... 6	,, No. 10	... 151
Cross Keys Inn ...	... 34	,, No. 11	... 27, 28, 151
Crown Inn, Bathwick	... 132		
		Obelisk, The (Orange Grove)	... 9
Edgar Buildings, No. 4 ...	... 94	Orange Grove ...	8, 9, 34, 35, 44
,, ,, No. 6 ...	... 111	,, No. 7	... 57
		,, Nos. 14 & 15	... 35
Fonthill Abbey ...	... 105	Orchard Street Theatre ...	12, 32
Freemasons' Hall	... 11		
		Parades, The ...	... xiii.
Galloway's Buildings	23, 47	Pear Tree Lane...	... 26
Garrick's Head Inn	45, 46, 47	Pelican Inn (Walcot Street)	... 62
Gay Street	xiii., 60	Percy Place, No. 4	... 144
,, No. 1	... 149	Pierrepont Street	29, 32
,, No. 8	... 61	,, No. 2	... 30
,, No. 41	... 60	,, No. 5	... 30
General Hospital	... iv.	Prior Park ...	ix., xii., 16, 51, 79
Grand Pump-room Hotel	20, 37	Pulteney Bridge	... x.
Grapes Tavern, (Westgate Street)	... 38	Pulteney Street, No. 21 ...	49, 188
Green Park Buildings	... 149	,, ,, No. 26 ...	... 141
Grenville Monument	... 39	,, ,, No. 34 ..	... 11
Greyhound Inn...	... 21	,, ,, No. 53 ...	... 140
Guildhall	ix., 21	,, ,, No. 55 ...	... 143
		,, ,, No. 58 ...	... 140
Hampton Down	... ii.	Pump Room ...	... ix.
Harrison's Walks	.. 8		
Hartley House (Belvedere)	... 109	Queen Square ...	xiii., 34, 60
Henrietta Street, No. 20	... 30		
Henry Street, No. 6	... 53	Raby Place, No. 13	... 30
Hermitage, The	80, 85	Rectory House (Abbey) ...	... iii.
Hetling House ...	v., 4, 10	Rectory House (St. James')	... ii.
		Rivers Street ..	... 49
Inns of other Days	... 19	,, No. 3 ..	.. 120
		Rock House ...	... 113
John Street, No. 7	... 57	Roman Catholic Mission House	... ii.
Johnstone Street, No. 10	... 116	Rose Inn (Avon Street) ...	... 62
,, No. 15	... 141	Rosewell's House	xiv., 39, 40
		Royal Crescent ...	16, 60
Kingsmead	... xiv.	,, No 5 ...	... 113
Kingsmead Square	... 39	,, No. 9 ...	.. 80
Kingsmead Street, No. 13	... 41	Royal Lansdown School ..	... 17
Kingston House	143, 152	,, Literary Institution	... 35
		,, United Hospital ..	ii., iii.
Lamb Inn, The ...	xvii., 20	Royal Victoria Park	... 17
Lansdown Crescent, No. 1	... 108		
Laura Place, No. 11	28, 142, 152	S. Catharine's ...	... iv.
Leake's Library	... 55	S. James's Rampier	... 34
Lilliput Alley ...	28, 38, 51	S James's Square, Nos. 1 & 35	120, 125
Lock's Lane	... 19	S. John's Court	15, 44, 47
Lodge, The (Bathampton)	... 80	,, Gate	... 57
Londonderry, or Rosewell's House	39, 40	,, Hospital	... 46
Lower Rooms, The	... 35	S. Katherine's Hospital ...	... ii.
		S. Michael's Church	.. 60
Manvers Street Baptist Chapel	... 114	S. Winifred's Well	5, 153
Masonic Hall ..	... 12	Sham Castle	... ii.
Mount Beacon House	... 131	Sloperton Cottage (near Bremhill)	... 129
		South Parade, No. 5	120, 151
Nassau House ...	8, 34	,, No. 6	... 32

Index.

	PAGE.
Spring Gardens...	xvi.
Stall's Church and Churchyard	37
Stall's Vicarage House	37
Summerhill	34
Swainswick	58
Sydney Gardens	xvi., 16, 147
Sydney Place, No. 4	149
,, Nos. 93 & 103	13
Three Cups Inn (Northgate Street)	62
,, (Walcot Street)	62
Three Tuns Inn...	xvii., 20, 154
Trim Street, No. 5	54
Turley House	28
Twerton	xii.

	PAGE.
Wade's Alley	37
Walcot Terrace, No. 6	80
West Gate	xiv., 3, 4, 7, 39
Westgate Buildings	xiv., 42
Weymouth House	47
White Hart Inn	xvii., 20, 62, 129
White Lion Inn	xvii., 26
Widcomb of Camalodunum	xiii.
Widcombe House	xii.
Winifred's Dale (Sion Hill)	5
Wood Street, No. 1	55
York House	xvii., 11, 12, 15, 16
York Street Baptist Church	144

www.ingramcontent.com/pod-product-compliance
Lightning Source LLC
Chambersburg PA
CBHW032129160426
43197CB00008B/571